# THOMAS HARDY

# Modern Critical Views

*These and other titles in preparation*

*Modern Critical Views*

# THOMAS HARDY

*Edited and with an introduction by*
## Harold Bloom
Sterling Professor of the Humanities
Yale University

CHELSEA HOUSE PUBLISHERS ◊ 1987
New York ◊ New Haven ◊ Philadelphia

© 1987 by Chelsea House Publishers, a division
of Chelsea House Educational Communications, Inc.
133 Christopher Street, New York, NY 10014
345 Whitney Avenue, New Haven, CT 06511
5014 West Chester Pike, Edgemont, PA 19028

Introduction © 1987 by Harold Bloom

Printed and bound in the United States of America

∞ The paper used in this publication meets the minimum
requirements of the American National Standard for Permanence
of Paper for Printed Library Materials, Z39.48–1984.

Library of Congress Cataloging-in-Publication Data
Thomas Hardy.
    (Modern critical views)
    Bibliography: p.
    Includes index.
    Summary: A collection of critical essays on
Hardy, his novels, and poems with a chronology of
events in the author's life.
    1. Hardy, Thomas, 1840–1928—Criticism and interpreta-
tion.  [1. Hardy, Thomas, 1840–1928—Criticism and
interpretation.  2. English literature—History and
criticism]  I. Bloom, Harold.  II. Series.
PR4754.T46   1986     823'.8      86–14789
ISBN 0–87754–645–2 (alk. paper)

# Contents

# Editor's Note

This book gathers together a representative selection of the best criticism devoted to the novels and poems of Thomas Hardy. The criticism is reprinted here in the chronological order of its original publication. I am grateful to Jennifer Wagner for her devoted assistance in editing this volume.

My introduction, after considering the relation of Hardy both to Schopenhauer and to Shelley, centers itself upon *The Return of the Native, The Mayor of Casterbridge, Tess of the D'Urbervilles, Jude the Obscure,* and *Winter Words,* Hardy's last poems, tracing in the patterns of his work his heroic endurance at bearing the sorrows of the Will to Live.

The chronological sequence of criticism commences with Roy Morrell's study of *The Dynasts,* Hardy's approach to epic, with its curious hope that the Will might yet improve. J. Hillis Miller, who seems to me the most eminent of living critics of Hardy, follows with an overview of the consciousness of Hardy the novelist, emphasizing that his mind confronts the world in detachment, refusing involvement, despite the ambiguous attraction of the world's dangerous energies.

That world is described in the essay by Jean R. Brooks on *The Return of the Native,* a novel seen by Brooks as "concerned with the Promethean struggle of conscious life against the unconscious 'rayless' universe from which it sprang." Ian Gregor, writing on *The Woodlanders,* categorizes it as an elegiac novel with touches of bizarre comedy, a rare combination in Hardy.

Hardy's poetry, in an overview by Dennis Taylor, is described as a dramatized pattern portraying deliberate rigidity, showing organic forms stiffening into decay and death in a tragic rhythm. A parallel rhythm, in which an absence in familial continuity is tragically reconstituted, is traced in Jan B. Gordon's essay on *Tess,* which finds that for Hardy a crisis in history always leads to a crisis for the self.

Hardy's own repressed sense of personal crisis, emergent in his poetry, moves from the self's pain to a sense of shared suffering, partly under the influence of Swinburne, according to the analysis of Ross C. Murfin. Margaret Mahar, reading the poetry as a mode of renunciation, establishes Hardy as a conscious dualist, both in matter and in method.

This book's remaining essays center upon the major novels. The eminent feminist critic Elaine Showalter studies what she calls Henchard's "unmanning" in *The Mayor of Casterbridge* and concludes that: "In Henchard the forces of male rebellion and female suffering ultimately conjoin." Another current mode of criticism, deconstructive rather than feminist, is exemplified by Ramón Saldívar's reading of *Jude the Obscure,* in which the novel "signifies the laws of language over which neither Hardy nor his readers can exercise complete control."

The final essay in this volume, by Susan Beegel, analyzes male sexuality in *Far from the Madding Crowd,* and refuses to read the novel as "a tragedy of reduced expectations." Instead, Beegel proposes a vitalistic reading in which Gabriel's love, stronger than death, rejuvenates Bathsheba. Without following D. H. Lawrence, Beegel returns us to the sense in which the vitalist Lawrence was Hardy's true son, and so reminds us also that Hardy's vision is comprehensive enough to escape the confinements of any single critical tradition.

# Introduction

I

For Arthur Schopenhauer, the Will to Live was the true thing-in-itself, not an interpretation but a rapacious, active, universal, and ultimately indifferent drive or desire. Schopenhauer's great work, *The World as Will and Representation,* had the same relation to and influence upon many of the principal nineteenth- and early twentieth-century novelists that Freud's writings have in regard to many of this century's later, crucial masters of prose fiction. Zola, Maupassant, Turgenev, and Tolstoy join Thomas Hardy as Schopenhauer's nineteenth-century heirs, in a tradition that goes on through Proust, Conrad, and Thomas Mann to culminate in aspects of Borges and Beckett, the two most eminent living writers of narrative. Since Schopenhauer (despite Freud's denials) was one of Freud's prime precursors, one could argue that aspects of Freud's influence upon writers simply carry on from Schopenhauer's previous effect. Manifestly, the relation of Schopenhauer to Hardy is different in both kind and degree from the larger sense in which Schopenhauer was Freud's forerunner or Wittgenstein's. A poet-novelist like Hardy turns to a rhetorical speculator like Schopenhauer only because he finds something in his own temperament and sensibility confirmed and strengthened, and not at all as Lucretius turned to Epicurus, or as Whitman was inspired by Emerson.

The true precursor for Hardy was Shelley, whose visionary skepticism permeates the novels as well as the poems and *The Dynasts.* There is some technical debt to George Eliot in the early novels, but Hardy in his depths was little more moved by her than by Wilkie Collins, from whom he also learned elements of craft. Shelley's tragic sense of eros is pervasive throughout Hardy, and ultimately determines Hardy's understanding of his strongest heroines: Bathsheba Everdene, Eustacia Vye, Marty South, Tess Durbeyfield, Sue Bridehead. Between desire and fulfillment in Shelley falls the shadow of

1

the selfhood, a shadow that makes love and what might be called the means of love quite irreconcilable. What M. D. Zabel named as "the aesthetic of incongruity" in Hardy and ascribed to temperamental causes is in a profound way the result of attempting to transmute the procedures of *The Revolt of Islam* and *Epipsychidion* into the supposedly naturalistic novel.

J. Hillis Miller, when he worked more in the mode of a critic of consciousness like Georges Poulet than in the deconstruction of Paul de Man and Jacques Derrida, saw the fate of love in Hardy as being darkened always by a shadow cast by the lover's consciousness itself. Hugh Kenner, with a distaste for Hardy akin to (and perhaps derived from) T. S. Eliot's in *After Strange Gods,* suggested that Miller had created a kind of Proustian Hardy, who turns out to be a case rather than an artist. Hardy was certainly not an artist comparable to Henry James (who dismissed him as a mere imitator of George Eliot) or James Joyce, but the High Modernist shibboleths for testing the novel have now waned considerably, except for a few surviving high priests of Modernism like Kenner. A better guide to Hardy's permanent strength as a novelist was his heir D. H. Lawrence, whose *The Rainbow* and *Women in Love* marvelously brought Hardy's legacy to an apotheosis. Lawrence, praising Hardy with a rebel son's ambivalence, associated him with Tolstoy as a tragic writer:

> And this is the quality Hardy shares with the great writers, Shakespeare or Sophocles or Tolstoi, this setting behind the small action of his protagonists the terrific action of unfathomed nature; setting a smaller system of morality, the one grasped and formulated by the human consciousness within the vast, uncomprehended and incomprehensible morality of nature or of life itself, surpassing human consciousness. The difference is, that whereas in Shakespeare or Sophocles the greater, uncomprehended morality, or fate, is actively transgressed and gives active punishment, in Hardy and Tolstoi the lesser, human morality, the mechanical system is actively transgressed, and holds, and punishes the protagonist, whilst the greater morality is only passively, negatively transgressed, it is represented merely as being present in background, in scenery, not taking any active part, having no direct connexion with the protagonist. Œdipus, Hamlet, Macbeth set themselves up against, or find themselves set up against, the unfathomed moral forces of nature, and out of this unfathomed force comes their death. Whereas Anna Karenina, Eustacia, Tess, Sue, and Jude find themselves up against the established system

of human government and morality, they cannot detach themselves, and are brought down. Their real tragedy is that they are unfaithful to the greater unwritten morality, which would have bidden Anna Karenina be patient and wait until she, by virtue of greater right, could take what she needed from society; would have bidden Vronsky detach himself from the system, become an individual, creating a new colony of morality with Anna; would have bidden Eustacia fight Clym for his own soul, and Tess take and claim her Angel, since she had the greater light; would have bidden Jude and Sue endure for very honour's sake, since one must bide by the best that one has known, and not succumb to the lesser good.

("Study of Thomas Hardy")

This seems to me powerful and just, because it catches what is most surprising and enduring in Hardy's novels—the sublime stature and aesthetic dignity of his crucial protagonists—while exposing also his great limitation, his denial of freedom to his best personages. Lawrence's prescription for what would have saved Eustacia and Clym, Tess and Angel, Sue and Jude, is perhaps not as persuasive. He speaks of them as though they were Gudrun and Gerald, and thus have failed to be Ursula and Birkin. It is Hardy's genius that they are what they had to be: as imperfect as their creator and his vision, as impure as his language and his plotting, and finally painful and memorable to us:

> Note that, in this bitterness, delight,
> Since the imperfect is so hot in us,
> Lies in flawed words and stubborn sounds.

## II

I first read *The Return of the Native* when I was about fifteen, forty years ago, and had reread it in whole or in part several times through the years before rereading it now. What I had remembered most vividly then I am likely to remember again: Eustacia, Venn the red man, the Heath. I had almost forgotten Clym, and his mother, and Thomasin, and Wildeve, and probably will forget them again. Clym, in particular, is a weak failure in characterization, and nearly sinks the novel; indeed ought to capsize any novel whatsoever. Yet *The Return of the Native* survives him, even though its chief glory, the sexually enchanting Eustacia Vye, does not. Her suicide is so much the waste of a marvelous woman (or representation of a woman, if you insist upon being a formalist) that the reader finds Clym even more intolerable than he is, and is likely not to forgive Hardy, except that Hardy clearly suffers the loss quite as much as any reader does.

Eustacia underwent a singular transformation during the novel's composition, from a daemonic sort of female Byron, or Byronic witch-like creature, to the grandly beautiful, discontented, and human—all too human but hardly blameworthy—heroine, who may be the most desirable woman in all of nineteenth-century British fiction. "A powerful personality uncurbed by any institutional attachment or by submission to any objective beliefs; unhampered by any ideas"—it would be a good description of Eustacia, but is actually Hardy himself through the eyes of T. S. Eliot in *After Strange Gods*, where Hardy is chastised for not believing in Original Sin and deplored also because "at times his style touches sublimity without ever having passed through the stage of being good."

Here is Eustacia in the early "Queen of Night" chapter:

> She was in person full-limbed and somewhat heavy; without ruddiness, as without pallor; and soft to the touch as a cloud. To see her hair was to fancy that a whole winter did not contain darkness enough to form its shadow: it closed over her forehead like nightfall extinguishing the western glow.
>
> Her nerves extended into those tresses, and her temper could always be softened by stroking them down. When her hair was brushed she would instantly sink into stillness and look like the Sphinx. If, in passing under one of the Egdon banks, any of its thick skeins were caught, as they sometimes were, by a prickly tuft of the large *Ulex Europaeus*—which will act as a sort of hairbrush—she would go back a few steps, and pass against it a second time.
>
> She had Pagan eyes, full of nocturnal mysteries, and their light, as it came and went, and came again, was partially hampered by their oppressive lids and lashes; and of these the under lid was much fuller than it usually is with English women. This enabled her to indulge in reverie without seeming to do so: she might have been believed capable of sleeping without closing them up. Assuming that the souls of men and women were visible essences, you could fancy the colour of Eustacia's soul to be flame-like. The sparks from it that rose into her dark pupils gave the same impression.

Hardy's Eustacia may owe something to Walter Pater's *The Renaissance,* published five years before *The Return of the Native,* since in some ways she makes a third with Pater's evocations of the Botticelli Venus and Leonardo's Mona Lisa, visions of antithetical female sexuality. Eustacia's flame-like quality precisely recalls Pater's ecstacy of passion in the "Conclusion" to *The Renaissance,* and the epigraph to *The Return of the Native* could well have been:

> This at least of flame-like our life has, that it is but the concurrence, renewed from moment to moment, of forces parting sooner or later on their ways.

This at least of flame-like Eustacia's life has, that the concurrence of forces parts sooner rather than later. But then this most beautiful of Hardy's women is also the most doom-eager, the color of her soul being flame-like. The Heath brings her only Wildeve and Clym, but Paris doubtless would have brought her scarce better, since as Queen of Night she attracts the constancy and the kindness of sorrow.

If Clym and Wildeve are bad actors, and they are, what about Egdon Heath? On this, critics are perpetually divided, some finding the landscape sublime, while others protest that its representation is bathetic. I myself am divided, since clearly it is both, and sometimes simultaneously so! Though Eustacia hates it fiercely, it is nearly as Shelleyan as she is, and rather less natural than presumably it ought to be. That it is more overwritten than overgrown is palpable:

> To recline on a stump of thorn in the central valley of Egdon, between afternoon and night, as now, where the eye could reach nothing of the world outside the summits and shoulders of heathland which filled the whole circumference of its glance, and to know that everything around and underneath had been from prehistoric times as unaltered as the stars overhead, gave ballast to the mind adrift on change, and harassed by the irrepressible New. The great inviolate place had an ancient permanence which the sea cannot claim. Who can say of a particular sea that it is old? Distilled by the sun, kneaded by the moon, it is renewed in a year, in a day, or in an hour. The sea changed, the fields changed, the rivers, the villages, and the people changed, yet Egdon remained. Those surfaces were neither so steep as to be destructible by weather, nor so flat as to be the victims of floods and deposits. With the exception of an aged highway, and a still more aged barrow presently to be referred to—themselves almost crystal-

lized to natural products by long continuance—even the trifling irregularities were not caused by pickaxe, plough, or spade, but remained as the very finger-touches of the last geological change.

Even Melville cannot always handle this heightened mode; Hardy rarely can, although he attempts it often. And yet we do remember Egdon Heath, years after reading the novel, possibly because something about it wounds us even as it wounds Eustacia. We remember also Diggory Venn, not as the prosperous burgher he becomes, but as we first encounter him, permeated by the red ochre of his picturesque trade:

> The decayed officer, by degrees, came up alongside his fellow-wayfarer, and wished him good evening. The reddleman turned his head and replied in sad and occupied tones. He was young, and his face, if not exactly handsome, approached so near to handsome that nobody would have contradicted an assertion that it really was so in its natural colour. His eye, which glared so strangely through his stain, was in itself attractive—keen as that of a bird of prey, and blue as autumn mist. He had neither whisker nor moustache, which allowed the soft curves of the lower part of his face to be apparent. His lips were thin, and though, as it seemed, compressed by thought, there was a pleasant twitch at their corners now and then. He was clothed throughout in a tight-fitting suit of corduroy, excellent in quality, not much worn, and well-chosen for its purpose; but deprived of its original colour by his trade. It showed to advantage the good shape of his figure. A certain well-to-do air about the man suggested that he was not poor for his degree. The natural query of an observer would have been, Why should such a promising being as this have hidden his prepossessing exterior by adopting that singular occupation?

Hardy had intended Venn to disappear mysteriously forever from Egdon Heath, instead of marrying Thomasin, but yielded to the anxiety of giving the contemporary reader something cheerful and normative at the end of his austere and dark novel. He ought to have kept to his intent, but perhaps it does not matter. The Heath endures, the red man either vanishes or is transmogrified into a husband and a burgher. Though we see Clym rather uselessly preaching to all comers as the book closes, our spirits are elsewhere, with the wild image of longing that no longer haunts the Heath, Hardy's lost Queen of Night.

## III

Of Hardy's major novels, *The Mayor of Casterbridge* is the least flawed and clearly the closest to tragic convention in Western literary tradition. If one hesitates to prefer it to *The Return of the Native, Tess,* or *Jude,* that may be because it is the least original and eccentric work of the four. Henchard is certainly the best articulated and most consistent of Hardy's male personages, but Lucetta is no Eustacia, and the amiable Elizabeth-Jane does not compel much of the reader's interest. The book's glory, Henchard, is so massive a self-punisher that he can be said to leap over the psychic cosmos of Schopenhauer directly into that of Freud's great essay on the economics of masochism, with its grim new category of "moral masochism." In a surprising way, Hardy reverses, through Henchard, one of the principal *topoi* of Western tragedy, as set forth acutely by Northrop Frye:

> A strong element of demonic ritual in public punishments and similar mob amusements is exploited by tragic and ironic myth. Breaking on the wheel becomes Lear's wheel of fire; bear-baiting is an image for Gloucester and Macbeth, and for the crucified Prometheus the humiliation of exposure, the horror of being watched, is a greater misery than the pain. *Derkou theama* (behold the spectacle; get your staring over with) is his bitterest cry. The inability of Milton's blind Samson to stare back is his greatest torment, and one which forces him to scream at Delilah, in one of the most terrible passages of all tragic drama, that he will tear her to pieces if she touches him.

For Henchard "the humiliation of exposure" becomes a terrible passion, until at last he makes an exhibition of himself during a royal visit. Perhaps he can revert to what Frye calls "the horror of being watched" only when he knows that the gesture involved will be his last. Hence his Will, which may be the most powerful prose passage that Hardy ever wrote:

> They stood in silence while he ran into the cottage; returning in a moment with a crumpled scrap of paper. On it there was pencilled as follows:—

> "Michael Henchard's Will

> "That Elizabeth-Jane Farfrae be not told of my death, or made to grieve on account of me.
> "& that I be not bury'd in consecrated ground.
> "& that no sexton be asked to toll the bell.

"& that nobody is wished to see my dead body.

"& that no murners walk behind me at my funeral.

"& that no flours be planted on my grave.

"& that no man remember me.

"To this I put my name.

"MICHAEL HENCHARD."

That dark testament is the essence of Henchard. It is notorious that "tragedy" becomes a very problematical form in the European Enlightenment and afterwards. Romanticism, which has been our continuous Modernism from the mid-1740s to the present moment, did not return the tragic hero to us, though from Richardson's Clarissa Harlowe until now we have received many resurgences of the tragic heroine. Hardy and Ibsen can be judged to have come closest to reviving the tragic hero, in contradistinction to the hero-villain who, throughout Romantic tradition, limns his night-piece and judges it to have been his best. Henchard, despite his blind strength and his terrible errors, is no villain, and as readers we suffer with him, unrelievedly, because our sympathy for him is unimpeded.

Unfortunately, the suffering becomes altogether *too* unrelieved, as it does again with Jude Fawley. Rereading *The Mayor of Casterbridge* is less painful than rereading *Jude the Obscure,* since at least we do not have to contemplate little Father Time hanging the other urchins and himself, but it is still very painful indeed. Whether or not tragedy should possess some catharsis, we resent the imposition of too much pathos upon us, and we need some gesture of purification if only to keep us away from our own defensive ironies. Henchard, alas, *accomplishes nothing,* for himself or for others. Ahab, a great hero-villain, goes down fighting his implacable fate, the whiteness of the whale, but Henchard is a self-destroyer to no purpose. And yet we are vastly moved by him and know that we should be. Why?

The novel's full title is *The Life and Death of the Mayor of Casterbridge: A Story of a Man of Character.* As Robert Louis Stevenson said in a note to Hardy, "Henchard is a great fellow," which implies that he is a great personality rather than a man of character. This is, in fact, how Hardy represents Henchard, and the critic R. H. Hutton was right to be puzzled by Hardy's title, in a review published in *The Spectator* on June 5, 1886:

Mr. Hardy has not given us any more powerful study than that of Michael Henchard. Why he should especially term his hero in his title-page a "man of character," we do not clearly understand. Properly speaking, character is the stamp graven on a man, and character therefore, like anything which can be graven, and

which, when graven, remains, is a word much more applicable to
that which has fixity and permanence, than to that which is fitful
and changeful, and which impresses a totally different image of
itself on the wax of plastic circumstance at one time, from that
which it impresses on a similarly plastic surface at another time.
To keep strictly to the associations from which the word "character" is derived, a man of character ought to suggest a man of
steady and unvarying character, a man who conveys very much
the same conception of his own qualities under one set of circumstances, which he conveys under another. This is true of many
men, and they might be called men of character *par excellence*.
But the essence of Michael Henchard is that he is a man of large
nature and depth of passion, who is yet subject to the most fitful
influences, who can do in one mood acts of which he will never
cease to repent in almost all his other moods, whose temper of
heart changes many times even during the execution of the same
purpose, though the same ardour, the same pride, the same
wrathful magnanimity, the same inability to carry out in cool
blood the angry resolve of the mood of revenge or scorn, the
same hasty unreasonableness, and the same disposition to swing
back to an equally hasty reasonableness, distinguish him throughout. In one very good sense, the great deficiency of Michael Henchard might be said to be in "character." It might well be said
that with a little *more* character, with a little more fixity of mind,
with a little more power of recovering *himself* when he was losing
his balance, his would have been a nature of gigantic mould;
whereas, as Mr. Hardy's novel is meant to show, it was a nature
which ran mostly to waste. But, of course, in the larger and wider
sense of the word "character," that sense which has less reference
to the permanent definition of the stamp, and more reference to
the confidence with which the varying moods may be anticipated,
it is not inadmissible to call Michael Henchard a "man of character." Still, the words on the title-page rather mislead. One looks
for the picture of a man of much more constancy of purpose, and
much less tragic mobility of mood, than Michael Henchard. None
the less, the picture is a very vivid one, and almost magnificent
in its fullness of expression. The largeness of his nature, the unreasonable generosity and suddenness of his friendships, the depth
of his self-humiliation for what was evil in him, the eagerness of
his craving for sympathy, the vehemence of his impulses both for

good and evil, the curious dash of stoicism in a nature so eager
for sympathy, and of fortitude in one so moody and restless,—
all these are lineaments which, mingled together as Mr. Hardy
has mingled them, produce a curiously strong impression of reality, as well as of homely grandeur.

One can summarize Hutton's point by saying that Henchard is stronger
in pathos than in ethos, and yet ethos is the daimon, character is fate, and
Hardy specifically sets out to show that Henchard's character is his fate. The
strength of Hardy's irony is that it is also life's irony, and will become
Sigmund Freud's irony: Henchard's destiny demonstrates that there are no
accidents, meaning that nothing happens to one that is not already oneself.
Henchard stares out at the night as though he were staring at an adversary,
but there is nothing out there. There is only the self turned against the self,
only the drive, beyond the pleasure principle, to death.

The pre-Socratic aphorism that character is fate seems to have been
picked up by Hardy from George Eliot's *The Mill on the Floss*, where it is
attributed to Novalis. But Hardy need not have gleaned it from anywhere in
particular. Everyone in Hardy's novels is over-determined by his or her past,
because for Hardy, as for Freud, everything that is dreadful has already
happened and there never can be anything absolutely new. Such a specula-
tion belies the very word "novel," and certainly was no aid to Hardy's
inventiveness. Nothing that happens to Henchard surprises us. His fate is
redeemed from dreariness only by its aesthetic dignity, which returns us to
the problematical question of Hardy's relation to tragedy as a literary form.

Henchard is burdened neither with wisdom nor with knowledge; he is
a man of will and of action, with little capacity for reflection, but with a
spirit perpetually open and generous towards others. J. Hillis Miller sees him
as being governed erotically by mediated desire, but since Miller sees this as
the iron law in Hardy's erotic universe, it loses any particular force as an
observation upon Henchard. I would prefer to say that Henchard, more even
than most men and like all women in Hardy, is hungry for love, desperate
for some company in the void of existence. D. H. Lawrence read the tragedy
of Hardy's figures not as the consequence of mediated desire, but as the fate
of any desire that will not be bounded by convention and community.

This is the tragedy of Hardy, always the same: the tragedy of
those who, more or less pioneers, have died in the wilderness,
whither they had escaped for free action, after having left the
walled security, and the comparative imprisonment, of the established convention. This is the theme of novel after novel: remain

quite within the convention, and you are good, safe, and happy in the long run, though you never have the vivid pang of sympathy on your side: or, on the other hand, be passionate, individual, wilful, you will find the security of the convention a walled prison, you will escape, and you will die, either of your own lack of strength to bear the isolation and the exposure, or by direct revenge from the community, or from both. This is the tragedy, and only this: it is nothing more metaphysical than the division of a man against himself in such a way: first, that he is a member of the community, and must, upon his honour, in no way move to disintegrate the community, either in its moral or its practical form; second, that the convention of the community is a prison to his natural, individual desire, a desire that compels him, whether he feel justified or not, to break the bounds of the community, lands him outside the pale, there to stand alone, and say: "I was right, my desire was real and inevitable; if I was to be myself I must fulfil it, convention or no convention," or else, there to stand alone, doubting, and saying: "Was I right, was I wrong? If I was wrong, oh, let me die!"—in which case he courts death.

The growth and the development of this tragedy, the deeper and deeper realisation of this division and this problem, the coming towards some conclusion, is the one theme of the Wessex novels.

("Study of Thomas Hardy")

This is general enough to be just, but not quite specific enough for the self-destructive Henchard. Also not sufficiently specific is the sympathetic judgment of Irving Howe, who speaks of "Henchard's personal struggle—the struggle of a splendid animal trying to escape a trap and thereby entangling itself all the more." I find more precise the dark musings of Sigmund Freud, Hardy's contemporary, who might be thinking of Michael Henchard when he meditates upon "The Economic Problem in Masochism":

The third form of masochism, the moral type, is chiefly remarkable for having loosened its connection with what we recognize to be sexuality. To all other masochistic sufferings there still clings the condition that it should be administered by the loved person; it is endured at his command; in the moral type of masochism this limitation has been dropped. It is the suffering itself that matters; whether the sentence is cast by a loved or by an indifferent person is of no importance; it may even be caused by

impersonal forces or circumstances, but the true masochist always
holds out his cheek wherever he sees a chance of receiving a blow.

The origins of "moral masochism" are in an unconscious sense of guilt,
a need for punishment that transcends actual culpability. Even Henchard's
original and grotesque "crime," his drunken exploit in wife-selling, does not
so much engender in him remorse at the consciousness of wrongdoing, but
rather helps engulf him in the "guilt" of the moral masochist. That means
Henchard knows his guilt not as affect or emotion but as a negation, as the
nullification of his desires and his ambitions. In a more than Freudian sense,
Henchard's primal ambivalence is directed against himself, against the authority principle in his own self.

If *The Mayor of Casterbridge* is a less original book than *Tess* or *Jude,*
it is also a more persuasive and universal vision than Hardy achieved elsewhere. Miguel de Unamuno, defining the tragic sense of life, remarked that:
"The chiefest sanctity of a temple is that it is a place to which men go to to
weep in common. A *miserere* sung in common by a multitude tormented by
destiny has as much value as a philosophy." That is not tragedy as Aristotle
defined it, but it is tragedy as Thomas Hardy wrote it.


## IV

Of all the novels of Hardy, *Tess of the D'Urbervilles* now appeals to the
widest audience. The book's popularity with the common reader has dis-
placed the earlier ascendancy of *The Return of the Native.* It can even be
asserted that Hardy's novel has proved to be prophetic of a sensibility by no
means fully emergent in 1891. Nearly a century later, the book sometimes
seems to have moments of vision that are contemporary with us. These tend
to come from Hardy's intimate sympathy with his heroine, a sympathy that
verges upon paternal love. It is curious that Hardy is more involved with
Tess than with Jude Fawley in *Jude the Obscure,* even though Jude is closer
to being Hardy's surrogate than any other male figure in the novels.

J. Hillis Miller, in the most advanced critical study yet attempted of
*Tess,* reads it as "a story about repetition," but by "repetition" Miller appears to mean a linked chain of interpretations. A compulsion to interpret
may be the reader's share, and may be Hardy's own stance towards his own
novel (and perhaps even extends to Angel Clare's role in the book), but seems
to me fairly irrelevant to Tess herself. Since the novel is a story about Tess,
I cannot regard it as being "about" repetition, or even one that concerns a
difference in repetitions. Hardy's more profound ironies are neither classical

nor Romantic, but Biblical, as Miller himself discerns. Classical irony turns upon contrasts between what is said and what is meant, while Romantic irony inhabits the gap between expectation and fulfillment. But Biblical irony appears whenever giant incongruities clash, which happens when Yahweh, who is incommensurate, is closely juxtaposed to men and women and their vain imaginings. When Yahweh devours roast calf under the terebinths at Mamre, or when Jacob wrestles with a nameless one among the Elohim at Penuel, then we are confronted by an irony neither classical nor Romantic.

Hardy, like his master Shelley, is an unbeliever who remains within the literary context of the Bible, and again like Shelley he derives his mode of prophetic irony from the Bible. A striking instance (noted by Hillis Miller) comes in chapter 11:

> In the meantime Alec d'Urberville had pushed on up the slope to clear his genuine doubt as to the quarter of The Chase they were in. He had, in fact, ridden quite at random for over an hour, taking any turning that came to hand in order to prolong companionship with her, and giving far more attention to Tess's moonlit person than to any wayside object. A little rest for the jaded animal being desirable, he did not hasten his search for landmarks. A clamber over the hill into the adjoining vale brought him to the fence of a highway whose contours he recognized, which settled the question of their whereabouts. D'Urberville thereupon turned back; but by this time the moon had quite gone down, and partly on account of the fog The Chase was wrapped in thick darkness, although morning was not far off. He was obliged to advance with outstretched hands to avoid contact with the boughs, and discovered that to hit the exact spot from which he had started was at first entirely beyond him. Roaming up and down, round and round, he at length heard a slight movement of the horse close at hand; and the sleeve of his overcoat unexpectedly caught his foot.
>
> "Tess!" said d'Urberville.
>
> There was no answer. The obscurity was now so great that he could see absolutely nothing but a pale nebulousness at his feet, which represented the white muslin figure he had left upon the dead leaves. Everything else was blackness alike. D'Urberville stooped; and heard a gentle regular breathing. He knelt and bent lower, till her breath warmed his face, and in a moment his cheek was in contact with hers. She was sleeping soundly, and upon her eyelashes there lingered tears.

Darkness and silence ruled everywhere around. Above them rose the primeval yews and oaks of The Chase, in which were poised gentle roosting birds in their last nap; and about them stole the hopping rabbits and hares. But, might some say, where was Tess's guardian angel? where was the providence of her simple faith? Perhaps, like that other god of whom the ironical Tishbite spoke, he was talking, or he was pursuing, or he was in a journey, or he was sleeping and not to be awaked.

Why it was that upon this beautiful feminine tissue, sensitive as gossamer, and practically blank as snow as yet, there should have been traced such a coarse pattern as it was doomed to receive; why so often the coarse appropriates the finer thus, the wrong man the woman, the wrong woman the man, many thousand years of analytical philosophy have failed to explain to our sense of order. One may, indeed, admit the possibility of a retribution lurking in the present catastrophe. Doubtless some of Tess d'Urberville's mailed ancestors rollicking home from a fray had dealt the same measure even more ruthlessly towards peasant girls of their time. But though to visit the sins of the fathers upon the children may be a morality good enough for divinities, it is scorned by average human nature; and it therefore does not mend the matter.

As Tess's own people down in those retreats are never tired of saying among each other in their fatalistic way: "It was to be." There lay the pity of it. An immeasurable social chasm was to divide our heroine's personality thereafter from that previous self of hers who stepped from her mother's door to try her fortune at Trantridge poultry-farm.

The ironical Tishbite is the savage Elijah the prophet, who mocks the priests of Baal, urging them: "Cry aloud: for he is a god; either he is talking, or he is pursuing, or he is in a journey, or peradventure he sleepeth, and must be awaked." Elijah's irony depends upon the incommensurateness of Yahweh and the human—all too human—Baal. Hardy's irony cannot be what Hillis Miller deconstructively wishes it to be when he rather remarkably suggests that Tess herself is "like the prophets of Baal," nor does it seem right to call Yahweh's declaration that He is a jealous (or zealous) God "the divine lust for vengeance," as Miller does. Yahweh, after all, has just given the Second Commandment against making graven images or idols, such as the Baal whom Elijah mocks. Hardy associates Alec's "violation" of Tess with a destruction of pastoral innocence, which he scarcely sees as Baal-worship or idolatry. His emphasis is precisely that no mode of religion, revealed or natural, could defend Tess from an over-determined system in which the only thing-in-itself is the rapacious Will to Live, a Will that itself is, as it were, the curse of Yahweh upon the hungry generations.

Repetition, in *Tess,* is repetition as Schopenhauer saw it, which is little different from how Hardy and Freud subsequently saw it. What is repeated, compulsively, is a unitary desire that is rapacious, indifferent, and universal. The pleasures of repetition in Hardy's *Tess* are not interpretive and per-spectival, and so engendered by difference, but are actually masochistic, in the erotogenic sense, and so ensue from the necessity of similarity. Hardy's pragmatic version of the aesthetic vision in this novel is essentially sado-masochistic, and the sufferings of poor Tess give an equivocal pleasure of repetition to the reader. The book's extraordinary popularity partly results from its exquisitely subtle and deeply sympathetic unfolding of the torments of Tess, a pure woman because a pure nature, and doomed to suffer merely because she is so much a natural woman. The poet Lionel Johnson, whose early book (1895) on Hardy still seems to me unsurpassed, brought to the reading of *Tess* a spirit that was antithetically both Shelleyan and Roman Catholic:

> as a girl of generous thought and sentiment, rich in beauty, rich in the natural joys of life, she is brought into collision with the harshness of life. . . . the world was very strong; her conscience was blinded and bewildered; she did some things nobly, and some despairingly: but there is nothing, not even in studies of criminal anthropology or of morbid pathology, to suggest that she was wholly an irresponsible victim of her own temperament, and of adverse circumstances. . . . She went through fire and water, and made no true use of them: she is pitiable, but not admirable.

Johnson is very clear-sighted, but perhaps too much the Catholic mor-alist. To the common reader, Tess is both pitiable and admirable, as Hardy wanted her to be. Is it admirable, though, that, by identifying with her, the reader takes a masochistic pleasure in her suffering? Aesthetically, I would reply yes, but the question remains a disturbing one. When the black flag goes slowly up the staff and we know that the beautiful Tess has been executed, do we reside in Hardy's final ironies, or do we experience a plea-sure of repetition that leaves us void of interpretive zeal, yet replete with the gratification of a drive beyond the pleasure principle?

V

Alone among Hardy's novels, *Jude the Obscure* has three strong figures, all triumphs of representation: Sue, Jude, Arabella. Unfortunately, it also has little Father Time, Hardy's most memorable disaster in representation. Even more unfortunately, it is a book in which Hardy's drive to go on telling stories gives way to his precursor Shelley's despair that there is one story and one story only, the triumph of life over human integrity. As the most Shelleyan of Hardy's novels (except perhaps for *The Well-Beloved,* which precedes it in initial composition, though not in revision and publication), *Jude the Obscure* has a complex and perhaps crippling relation to *Epipsychidion.* Sue Bridehead is more Shelleyan than even Shelley's Emilia in that poem, and would have been better off married to Shelley than to Jude Fawley, which is not to say that poor Shelley could have survived the union any better than the unhappy Jude.

D. H. Lawrence, inevitably, was Sue's most articulate critic:

> Her female spirit did not wed with the male spirit: she could not prophesy. Her spirit submitted to the male spirit, owned the priority of the male spirit, wished to become the male spirit.

Sue needs no defense, least of all in 1986 when she has become prevalent, a subtle rebel against any dialectic of power founded wholly upon mere gender. Yet, within the novel, Sue is less a rebel than she is Jude's Shelleyan epipsyche, his twin sister (actually his cousin) and counterpart. She can live neither with Jude, nor without him, and their love is both narcissistic and incestuous, Hardy's metaphor for the Will to Live at its most destructive, because in Jude and Sue it destroys the most transcendent beings Hardy had ever imagined.

It will not suffice to call *Jude the Obscure* a tragedy, since what is most tragic in Jude and Sue is their Shelleyan transcendence. When Shelley attempted tragedy in *The Cenci,* he succeeded only by diverting the form into a lament for the descent of Beatrice Cenci to her father's level. But Jude and Sue cannot be said to descend, any more than Eustacia, Henchard, and Tess descend. The Will to Live in Hardy's cosmos is too terrible and too incessant for us to speak of it as debasing its subjects or victims. In a world dominated by drive, a spirit like Jude's is condemned to die whispering the Jobean lament: "Let the day perish wherein I was born." *Jude the Obscure* is Hardy's Book of Job, and like Job is too dark for tragedy, while unlike Job it is just the reverse of theodicy, being Hardy's ultimate declaration that the ways of the Immanent Will towards man are unjustifiable.

Few interchanges in literature are at once so pathetic and so charming as the intricate, Shelleyan dances of scruple and desire intertwined that involve Sue and Jude:

> He laughed. "Never mind," he said. "So that I am near you, I am comparatively happy. It is more than this earthly wretch called Me deserves—you spirit, you disembodied creature, you dear, sweet, tantalizing phantom—hardly flesh at all; so that when I put my arms round you, I almost expect them to pass through you as through air! Forgive me for being gross, as you call it! Remember that our calling ourselves cousins when really strangers was a snare. The enmity of our parents gave a piquancy to you in my eyes that was intenser ever than the novelty of ordinary new acquaintance."
>
> "Say those pretty lines, then, from Shelley's 'Epipsychidion' as if they meant me," she solicited, slanting up closer to him as they stood. "Don't you know them?"
>
> "I know hardly any poetry," he replied, mournfully.
>
> "Don't you?" These are some of them:
>
> "'There was a Being whom my spirit oft
>   Met on its visioned wanderings far aloft.
>
>   . . . . . . . . . . . . . . . .
>
>   A seraph of Heaven, too gentle to be human,
>   Veiling beneath that radiant form of woman . . .'"
>
> "Oh, it is too flattering, so I won't go on! But say it's me!— say it's me!"
>
> "It *is* you, dear; exactly like you!"
>
> "Now I forgive you! And you shall kiss me just once there— not very long." She put the tip of her finger gingerly to her cheek, and he did as commanded. "You do care for me very much, don't you, in spite of my not—you know?"
>
> "Yes, sweet!" he said, with a sigh, and bade her good-night.

It is Sue, right enough, and it is disaster. The true epigraph to *Jude the Obscure* comes at the climax of *Epipsychidion*:

> In one another's substance finding food,
> Like flames too pure and light and unimbued
> To nourish their bright lives with baser prey,
> Which point to Heaven and cannot pass away:
> One hope within two wills, one will beneath

Two overshadowing minds, one life, one death,
One Heaven, one Hell, one immortality,
And one annihilation.

That "one will beneath" the "two overshadowing minds" of Sue and Jude is the Immanent Will of Thomas Hardy, and it indeed does become "one annihilation."

VI

*Only a poet challenges a poet as poet,* and so only a poet makes a poet. To the poet-in-a-poet, a poem is always *the other man,* the precursor, and so a poem is always a person, always the father of one's Second Birth. To live, the poet must *misinterpret* the father, by the crucial act of misprision, which is the re-writing of the father.

But who, what is the poetic father? The voice of the other, of the *daimon,* is always speaking in one; the voice that cannot die because already it has survived death—*the dead poet lives in one.* In the last phase of strong poets, they attempt to join the undying *by living in the dead poets* who are already alive in them. This late Return of the Dead recalls us, as readers, to a recognition of the original motive for the catastrophe of poetic incarnation. Vico, who identified the origins of poetry with the impulse towards divination (to foretell, but also to become a god by foretelling), implicitly understood (as did Emerson, and Wordsworth) that a poem is written to escape dying. Literally, poems are refusals of mortality. Every poem therefore has two makers: the precursor, and the ephebe's rejected mortality.

A poet, I argue in consequence, is not so much a man speaking to men as a man rebelling against being spoken to by a dead man (the precursor) outrageously more alive than himself. A poet dare not regard himself as being *late,* yet cannot accept a substitute for the first vision he reflectively judges to have been his precursor's also. Perhaps this is why the poet-in-a-poet *cannot marry,* whatever the person-in-a-poet chooses to have done.

Poetic influence, in the sense I give to it, has almost nothing to do with the verbal resemblances between one poet and another. Hardy, on the surface, scarcely resembles Shelley, his prime precursor, but then Browning, who resembles Shelley even less, was yet more fully Shelley's ephebe than even Hardy was. The same observation can be made of Swinburne and of Yeats in relation to Shelley. What Blake called the Spiritual Form, at once the aboriginal poetical self and the True Subject, is what the ephebe is so dangerously obliged to the precursor for even possessing. Poets need not *look* like their fathers, and the anxiety of influence more frequently than not is quite distinct from the anxiety of style. Since poetic influence is necessarily misprision, a taking or doing amiss of one's burden, it is to be expected that such a process of malformation and misinterpretation will, at the very least, produce deviations in style between strong poets. Let us remember always Emerson's insistence as to what it is that makes a poem:

> For it is not metres, but a metre-making argument, that makes a poem,—a thought so passionate and alive, that, like the spirit of a plant or an animal, it has an architecture of its own, and adorns nature with a new thing. The thought and the form are equal in the order of time, but in the order of genesis the thought is prior to the form. The poet has a new thought: he has a whole new experience to unfold; he will tell us how it was with him, and all men will be the richer in his fortune. For, the experience of each new age requires a new confession, and the world seems always waiting for its poet.
>
> ("The Poet")

Emerson would not acknowledge that meter-making arguments themselves were subject to the tyrannies of inheritance, but that they are so subject is the saddest truth I know about poets and poetry. In Hardy's best poems, the central meter-making argument is what might be called a skeptical lament for the hopeless incongruity of ends and means in all human acts. Love and the means of love cannot be brought together, and the truest name for the human condition is simply that it is loss:

> And brightest things that are theirs. . . .
> Ah, no; the years, the years;
> Down their carved names the rain-drop ploughs.

These are the closing lines of "During Wind and Rain," as good a poem as our century has given us. The poem, like so many others, is a grandchild of the "Ode to the West Wind," as much as Stevens's "The Course of a Particular" or any number of major lyrics by Yeats. A carrion-eater, Old Style, would challenge my observations, and to such a challenge I could offer, in its own terms, only the first appearance of the refrain:

> Ah, no; the years O!
> How the sick leaves reel down in throngs!

But such terms can be ignored. Poetic influence, between strong poets, works in the depths, as all love antithetically works. At the center of Hardy's verse, whether in the early *Wessex Poems* or the late *Winter Words,* is this vision:

> And much I grieved to think how power and will
> In opposition rule our mortal day—
>
> And why God made irreconcilable
> Good and the means of good; and for despair
> I half disdained mine eye's desire to fill
>
> With the spent vision of the times that were
> And scarce have ceased to be—

Shelley's *Triumph of Life* can give us also the heroic motto for the major characters in Hardy's novels: "For in the battle Life and they did wage, / She remained conqueror." The motto would serve as well for the superb volume *Winter Words in Various Moods and Metres,* published on October 2 in 1928, the year that Hardy died on January 11. Hardy had hoped to publish the book on June 2, 1930, which would have been his ninetieth birthday. Though a few poems in the book go back as far as the 1860s, most were written after the appearance of Hardy's volume of lyrics *Human Shows* in 1925. A few books of twentieth-century verse in English compare with *Winter Words* in greatness, but very few. Though the collection is diverse, and has no central design, its emergent theme is a counterpoise to the burden of poetic incarnation, and might be called the Return of the Dead, who haunt Hardy as he faces towards death.

In his early poem "Shelley's Skylark" (1887), Hardy, writing rather in the style of his fellow Shelleyan Browning, speaks of his ancestor's "ecstatic heights in thought and rhyme." Recent critics who admire Shelley are not particularly fond of "To a Skylark," and it is rather too ecstatic for most varieties of modern sensibility, but we can surmise why it so moved Hardy:

> We look before and after,
>     And pine for what is not—
> Our sincerest laughter
>     With some pain is fraught—
> Our sweetest songs are those that tell of saddest thought.
>
> Yet if we could scorn
>     Hate and pride and fear;
> If we were things born
>     Not to shed a tear,
> I know not how thy joy we ever should come near.

The thought here, as elsewhere in Shelley, is not so simple as it may seem. Our divided consciousness, keeping us from being able to unperplex joy from pain and ruining the presentness of the moment, at least brings us an aesthetic gain. But even if we lacked our range of negative affections, even if grief were not our birthright, the pure joy of the lark's song would still surpass us. We may think of Shelleyan ladies like Marty South, and even more Sue Bridehead, who seems to have emerged from the *Epipsychidion*. Or perhaps we may remember Angel Clare as a kind of parody of Shelley himself. Hardy's Shelley is very close to the most central of Shelleys, the visionary skeptic, whose head and whose heart could never be reconciled, for they both told truths, but contrary truths. In *Prometheus Unbound,* we are told that in our life the shadow cast by love is always ruin, which is the head's report, but the heart in Shelley goes on saying that if there is to be coherence at all, it must come through Eros.

*Winter Words,* as befits a man going into his later eighties, is more in ruin's shadow than in love's realm. The last poem, written in 1927, is called "He Resolves to Say No More," and follows directly on "We Are Getting to The End," which may be the bleakest sonnet in the language. Both poems explicitly reject any vision of hope, and are set against the Shelleyan rational meliorism of *Prometheus Unbound.* "We are getting to the end of visioning / The impossible within this universe," Hardy flatly insists, and he recalls Shelley's vision of rolling time backward, only to dismiss it as the doctrine of Shelley's Ahasuerus: "(Magians who drive the midnight quill / With brain aglow / Can see it so)." Behind this rejection is the mystery of misprision, of deep poetic influence in its final phase, which I have called *Apophrades* or the Return of the Dead. Hovering everywhere in *Winter Words,* though far less explicitly than it hovers in *The Dynasts,* is Shelley's *Hellas.* The peculiar strength and achievement of *Winter Words* is not that we are compelled to remember Shelley when we read in it, but rather that it makes us read much of Shelley as though Hardy were Shelley's ancestor, the dark father whom the revolutionary idealist failed to cast out.

Nearly every poem in *Winter Words* has a poignance unusual even in Hardy, but I am moved most by "He Never Expected Much," the poet's reflection on his eighty-sixth birthday, where his dialogue with the "World" attains a resolution:

> "I do not promise overmuch,
>        Child; overmuch;
> Just neutral-tinted haps and such,"
>        You said to minds like mine.

Wise warning for your credit's sake!
Which I for one failed not to take,
And hence could stem such strain and ache
    As each year might assign.

The "neutral-tinted haps," so supremely hard to get into poems, are the staple of Hardy's achievement in verse, and contrast both to Wordsworth's "sober coloring" and Shelley's "deep autumnal tone." All through *Winter Words* the attentive reader will hear a chastened return of High Romantic Idealism, but muted into Hardy's tonality. Where Yeats malformed both himself and his High Romantic fathers Blake and Shelley in the violences of *Last Poems and Plays,* Hardy more effectively subdued the questing temperaments of his fathers Shelley and Browning in *Winter Words.* The wrestling with the great dead is subtler in Hardy, and kinder both to himself and to the fathers.

ROY MORRELL

# The Dynasts

*The Dynasts* has a curious position on the list of Hardy's books. Few people read it; but many uproot from it—or cull from other critical books—quotations about the "Immanent Will" which they use to explain Hardy's pessimism. The poem, they believe, is a final formulation of his "philosophy" and provides the key to understanding the novels. "What finally became explicit," says S. C. Chew, "had always been implicit." And the same view is strongly argued in *The History of the English Novel* by Baker, who feels that Hardy had always been groping towards a conception of the universe which should give coherence to his impressions, and that he reached it at last in *The Dynasts*.

Baker's reaction has to be taken seriously because, first, he seems to start with some sympathy for Hardy; second, he pursues his argument to a conclusion which, if his premises were correct, would damn Hardy completely; and, third, he quotes many other authorities, and thus seems to have a weight of critical opinion on his side. He is following, and to some extent commenting on, the verdicts of others; and a little reflection will, I think, confirm the impression that even when critics are less explanatory than Chew and Baker, they none the less habitually rely on *The Dynasts* and the "Will" for the language of their interpretation of Hardy. Thus Chapman attacks Hardy's phrase about "the President of the Immortals" on the grounds that Hardy here deserts his "own conception" of the Immanent Will—ignoring

From *Thomas Hardy: The Will and the Way*. © 1965 by the University of Malaya Press.

the fact that he did not formulate that conception until years later, and, in the actual sense understood by this critic, never formulated it; and many others make the same mistake of assuming that the "Will" was something much more than a part of the mythological framework of *The Dynasts*, that it had for long been a real belief of Hardy's, a basic conception underlying the novels.

That Hardy should have written the novels without being fully conscious of their "meaning" is not, in itself, absurd; what *is* absurd is the fact that a questionable interpretation of *The Dynasts* should be used, not to make the novels more coherent, but to destroy any coherence they seemed previously to possess. Baker himself follows his statement that Hardy's determinism gives coherence to the novels, by saying it cripples their tragic force; whereas, surely, whatever cripples their tragic force cannot give them more coherence. "Where is the tragic conflict when Tess, Jude, Sue and their fellow combatants are reduced to mere automata?" he asks. Where, indeed? If this complete fatalistic determinism were Hardy's brand of pessimism we could all agree to ignore him. But it is not; and Baker himself gives away his whole case by admitting that until the novels are read in the "full light" of this determinism, the tragic figures seem to have a measure of freedom; as of course they do. And when Baker goes further and includes Gabriel Oak among the victims of Fate (Oak, who so signally proves himself more than Fate's match!) the flimsiness of his theory is shown. It may be that when we *recall* Hardy's novels, a deterministic interpretation can be made to seem plausible; but it is very different when we read or reread them.

At all events, the purpose of this chapter is not just to question the propriety of using *The Dynasts* as a key to the novels, when all that the key has done is to jam the lock. It is, in part, to use our reading of the novels to help elucidate *The Dynasts*; to throw doubt, at least, upon the usual superficial interpretations; to ask whether the human beings in the poem are depicted as always and necessarily puppets of the Will, or whether there is any suggestion that they ought to have, and could have, a measure of freedom. Do not some of the people succeed in acting more effectively than others? Surely if some men lose battles, others must—sometimes—win? Would it not be almost beyond the bounds of possibility for Hardy to depict the Will as frustrating equally the endeavours of *all* men, and *all* types of human activity?

The fact that such obvious and basic questions are seldom asked is itself significant: for from many casual critical references, we might infer that *The Dynasts* had nothing to do with human beings at all.

It was once a commonplace of criticism to point to the two scales employed by Hardy: first he showed human beings seemingly dwarfed against a vast universal background; second, he showed these "smaller" figures close up, insisting upon their greater significance; imparting "to readers the sentiment that the smaller might be the greater to them as men." It is very unlikely that Hardy would have reversed his procedure in *The Dynasts,* or that we shall reach his intention by concentrating upon the Will and the aerial choruses and ignoring the human beings completely.

It is upon the humans, then, that we shall concentrate. But first a word about the Will and puppetry. While Hardy was still writing *The Dynasts,* he began a poem, published much later, in which he said he could forgive all mankind's follies and wickednesses, save the one absurdity of their

> Acting like puppets
> Under Time's buffets

An early note foreshadowing *The Dynasts,* moreover, shows that Hardy intended to

> Write a history of human automatism, or impulsion—viz., an account of human action in spite of human knowledge, showing how far conduct lags behind the knowledge that should really guide it.

Hardy blames man, in short, for *choosing* to be a puppet: the Will does not make him so. Even in some of the most hackneyed passages in the Fore Scene, the real subject appears to be not the Will Itself, but Its remoteness, Its irrelevance, Its "mindlessness of earthly woes." When the Spirit of the Pities suggests that

> though Its consciousness
> May be estranged, engrossed afar, or sealed,
> Sublunar shocks may wake Its watch anon?

The Spirit of the Years replies,

> Nay . . .
> The Will has woven with an absent heed
> Since life first was; and ever will so weave.

The Will, as First Cause, started life going; but it does not now intervene to comfort, to guide, to set things straight. Man's one hope, Hardy thought, was to realize this fact, and to rely on himself. The Pities' description of the Will, "Its consciousness . . . estranged, engrossed afar, or sealed," is an unmistakable paraphrase of Hardy's ironical description of "the Providence of

Tess's humble faith" that was "talking, or pursuing, or in a journey, or
sleeping and not to be awaked" when she desperately needed some protection. It is clear that although at the end of *The Dynasts* Hardy is faintly
mythopoeic, writing of the Will as if It might one day conceivably develop
a mind or a conscience, Hardy's usual references to It are mythoclastic: It
is Something that, literally, isn't there. Even his more definite references—
before the After Scene—depersonalize the Will; they describe It as so amor-
phous that everyone is a part of It. Hardy is presenting Something which
cannot be relied upon for help: It can help you only if you help yourself.

Hardy once remarked that classical philosophers made the mistake of
assuming that the world had been created as "a comfortable place for man."
It is interesting to note that an orthodox philosopher, Professor John Laird,
makes precisely this assumption even about the world Hardy shows us in
*The Dynasts*. It is not surprising that, with this view of Hardy's intentions,
he should decide that the poem is a failure. He attacks it for inconsistency
and because, as he says, it offers but "a troubled perspective to every serious
reader who is eager for a clue and a philosophy." It does not occur to him
that Hardy might be *trying* to give the reader a "troubled perspective," that
he might be *refusing* to hand out a "clue and a philosophy." In the Preface
Hardy says the doctrines of the "supernatural spectators" are "advanced
with little eye to a systematised philosophy warranted to lift 'the burden of
the mystery' of this unintelligible world." When Hardy quotes Wordsworth
it is more often than not to dissociate himself; at all events, he is gently
doing so here. He had no sympathy for the Wordsworth who found in Nature
a "holy plan" protecting the Blind Highland Boy and the Idiot Boy better
than their friends or parents could. To Hardy, human care and effort were
never superfluous; for humans to bear the "burthen" bravely alone was always better than to wait for Someone or Something to lift it from their
shoulders. The world is not made comfortable *for* man. Too often, however,
"man makes life worse than it need be"—as Hardy once remarked to William Archer.

Let us see what man makes of the chances left him in *The Dynasts*. For
the most part we are not, as in the novels, in the sphere of individual freedom,
exploring man's loss or gain of love or happiness; we are in that of social,
political and military manoeuvring, exploring actions that win or lose battles,
win or lose empires. But we are still concerned with human beings.

Few of Hardy's humans, however, are exactly "heroic." Even in the
scenes leading up to the battle of Waterloo, we are reminded continually of
the sufferings of the common soldiers, even of the women and children camp-
followers. Even the leaders, amidst their desperate efforts and anxieties, are

men rather than dramatic heroes or history-book figures. Blücher, for instance, has been wounded, and has risen from a sickbed to lead his forces. His army has marched since five in the morning, but he leads it on, checking the rumour of a French interception post before advancing across the Lasne valley, exhorting his troops on, encouraging them, but also insisting on strict discipline, and keeping the whole army together (3.7.3). All this reminds one of Gabriel Oak rather than a warrior hero. But if there is an absence of the "heroic," there is also an absence of the mockery that often goes with the word: only rarely and tragically do the soldiers appear less than men. Even in the most sordid and unheroic scene in the drama (2.3.1), during the Peninsula retreat, where the demoralized deserters, men and women, half-naked, some wounded and dying, some dead-drunk, hide in the wine cellar, we find Hardy still asserting their humanity. The Spirit Ironic exclaims, seemingly with justice,

> Quaint Poesy, and real romance of war!

But he is reproved by the Spirit of the Pities:

> Mock on, Shade, if thou wilt! But others find
> Poesy ever lurk where pitpats poor mankind.

Hardy is determined, even here, that we shall not forget the importance of mankind.

But *The Dynasts* is not just about man's plight: it is also about what man can do, and how and when. We shall postpone the question of the comparative helplessness of "the Managed" in the hands of "the Managers," and see the subordinates, even common soldiers, as sharing the aims of commanders and rulers, and wishing to contribute loyally to those aims, although not always succeeding.

One condition of effective action may most easily be explained by recalling something we noticed in the novels: Bathsheba loses something of her independence when she realizes she has been seen and judged by Gabriel Oak; Tess's resolution is fatally weakened when she sees herself in the eyes of Angel's brothers. . . . Free and effective action always becomes more difficult if a person allows an image of himself to come between him and what has to be done. The most striking instance in *The Dynasts* is that of Villeneuve. Napoleon plans to invade England; he can do this only if the English fleet is kept out of the channel. He orders Villeneuve to engage them. Villeneuve need not win: if he fights and loses, that will suffice to keep the English fleet occupied. But Villeneuve does not like the idea of being beaten: his ships are rotten, crews are rebellious, and on board two ships there is fever. Perhaps he does not want Napoleon to know how bad things are; at all events, to save his navy's prestige, and his own, he refuses to give battle. He bows to "the inevitable" as Decrès says, trying to excuse him. The whole invasion plan has been wrecked to save Villeneuve's face; and Napoleon, who sees the excuse of "the inevitable" for what it is, is justifiably bitter about

> This traitor—
> Of whom I asked no more than fight and lose,
> Provided he detained the enemy.
>
> (1.3.1)

Later, Villeneuve tries to redeem himself from disgrace by fighting the English at Trafalgar. He is hopelessly defeated. Previously, in the Channel, a defeat for Villeneuve would have meant a conquest for France. But at Trafalgar it was unnecessary and wasteful for the French to fight. Better to have kept the fleet intact, even than to have gained a victory. Napoleon sees the real meaning of Villeneuve's second mistake as easily as he saw through his earlier excuses:

> Thuswise Villeneuve, poor craven, quitted him!
> Thus are my projects for the navy dammed
>
> (1.4.1)

Villeneuve's unconscious motive was to prove that he was not a coward. Concern for this image of himself, in his own and others' eyes, destroyed his ability to act freely and effectively in the service of France.

Early in *The Dynasts*, the Will is said to be on Napoleon's side: a metaphorical way of saying he has the secret of effective action. Hardy does not explain, but he none the less clearly shows, how the secret is lost: when Napoleon starts to regard himself as a "man of destiny," his power is on the wane:

> Some force within me, baffling mine intent,
> Harries me onward
>
> (2.1.8)

This seems, at least in part, Napoleon's excuse to Queen Louisa for doing what he wants to do; but such references become more insistent in part 3, and Napoleon's actions become less and less effective. Instead of *doing*, he becomes conscious of *being*. He becomes preoccupied with himself, his importance, his family affairs. Begetting an heir changes his attitude to the whole war, at least for a time. Bad news from Spain evokes protests from him, and the remark,

> O well—no matter:
> Why should I linger on these haps of war
> Now that I have a son!
>
> (2.6.3)

And the chorus, "The Will itself is slave to him," follows immediately, sung by the Spirits Ironic. Later, this son's portrait is displayed "to cheer the hearts" of his troops before Moscow (3.1.4), and they all parade before it: a pathetic egocentric lapse just before the whole tide of the disastrous Russian campaign turns against him.

It is just this kind of personal weakness that Napoleon is quick to see in others; indeed he has just blamed Marmont for losing a battle at Salamanca, because he had

> forced a conflict to cull laurel crowns
> Before King Joseph should arrive to share them.
>
> (Ibid.)

And what had angered him about Villeneuve was a comparable preoccupation with kudos. At that earlier stage, however, Napoleon's own conduct had been in marked contrast: he had even accepted Decrès's excuses in his impatience to get back to practical policy:

> Well, have it so!—What are we going to do?
> My brain has only one wish—to succeed!
>
> (1.3.1)

And succeed he does: until his objective political aims give way before the image of himself.

For the second mode of effective action I shall use Napoleon's own word "contrivance." The Napoleon of the earlier part of the poem is essentially a contriving man. He has a clear idea of his ultimate objective, and he is prepared to reach it by any method, however roundabout or unorthodox. He can look ahead, allow for contingencies, adapt himself to changed circumstances, and, above all, he knows the importance of timing.

Hearing of Villeneuve's failure to engage the English fleet, he abandons the invasion boats, and adopts another plan:

> Instead of crossing, thitherward I tour
> By roundabout contrivance not less sure,
>
> (1.3.1)

he says: and marches quickly east to surprise the Austrians at Ulm, and defeat them. Even after Trafalgar he still retains his aim of beating the English sea power, but by still more "roundabout contrivance." Asked to explain how "ships can be wrecked by land," he says he will prevent other nations from trading with England, and so

> slowly starve
> Her bloated revenues and monstrous trade,
> Till all her hulls lie sodden in their docks,
> And her grey island eyes in vain shall seek
> One jack of hers upon the ocean plains!
>
> (1.6.1)

It is Napoleon's unorthodox contrivance which upsets General Mack:

> The accursed cunning of our adversary
> Confounds all codes of honourable war,
> Which ever have held as granted that the track
> Of armies bearing hither from the Rhine—
> Whether in peace or strenuous invasion—
> Should pierce through Schwarzwald, and through Memmingen
> And meet us in our front. But he must wind
> And corkscrew meanly round, where foot of man
> Can scarce find pathway, stealing up to us
> Thiefwise, by our back door!
>
> (1.4.3)

It is the sort of comically pathetic protest an old-fashioned wrestler might make if his opponent use jiu-jitsu. Indeed "jiu-jitsu" is an accurate name for Napoleon's tactics in many later battles: he directs and times his attacks according to his enemies' decisions, and turns the mistakes and weight of the enemy against that enemy himself.

Before Austerlitz (1.6.1) Napoleon's whole approach is marked by flexibility. He does not commit himself to a definite course; the French position is described rather as "*Rich in chance* for opportune attack"; and he announces not a definite plan, but what he will do in this or that contingency. Once the battle has begun (1.6.3) he concentrates upon timing, holding back his forces until the moment comes:

> Leave them alone! Nor stick nor stone we'll stir
> To interrupt them. Nought that we can scheme
> Will help us like their own stark sightlessness!

At Jena too (2.1.4) when the soldiery are impatient to attack, Napoleon says,

> Nay, caution, men! 'Tis mine to time your deeds
> By light of long experience; yours to do them.

The reader can trace in the poem a definite evolution of such tactics—a new resourcefulness and timely contrivance replacing the old methods of fighting. "Being taught" by Napoleon, they "return to plague the inventor." Indeed the supreme instance of such unorthodox resourcefulness is the firing of Moscow (3.1.6–8).

Wellington's fortifications known as "the lines of Torres Vedras" anger and disconcert Massena partly by their unorthodoxy and partly for another reason. He sneers at such "prim ponderosities"; and Loison explains:

> They are Lord Wellington's select device,
> And like him, heavy, slow, laborious, sure.
>
> (2.6.2)

A third type of action Hardy regards as effective is here exemplified: action taken without reliance upon good luck, but, on the contrary, after a laborious "full look at the Worst" that could happen. Hardy's successful generals are all realists or "pessimists" in this sense.

Moore, dying at Corunna, replies to a suggestion of Hope's that the English would have won, if they had been lucky enough to induce the French to give battle at Lugo:

> Yes . . . Yes—But it has never been my lot
> To owe much to good luck; nor was it then.
> Good fortune has been mine, but (*bitterly*) mostly so
> By the exhaustion of all shapes of bad.
>
> (2.3.3)

Napoleon says,

> Things that verge nigh, my simple Joséphine,
> Are not shoved off by wilful winking at,
> Better quiz evils with too strained an eye
> Than have them leap from disregarded lairs.
>
> (2.2.6)

Wellington, too, praises Brunswick particularly because

> He is of those brave men who danger see,
> And seeing front it,—not of those, less brave
> But counted more, who face it sightlessly.
>
> (3.6.2)

The lines of Torres Vedras were the fruit of this attitude in Wellington himself. They were his guarantee against another retreat and evacuation as disastrous as that which ended with Corunna.

Corunna, however, could have been worse. Moore's success in covering the evacuation of his troops reminds us of the type of action to which Hardy gives, perhaps, final emphasis: simple dogged persistence, in which every individual is prepared to give his last effort. Corunna is a "last shot" stand. At the start of the battle, Hardy shows us two stragglers, full of excuses, about to desert. But somehow they do not. They pull themselves together, and again enter the fight. They are not heroes, but they are men (2.3.3). Hardy seems to show, thus, that a stiffening in the whole army's resistance was due to the decision taken by such men—as individuals. A similar emphasis upon ". . . every man . . ." reinvests Nelson's Trafalgar signal with meaning (1.5.1). At Albuera, too, the battle is going against the British— even the weather (a characteristic touch of Hardy's!) seems against them. A fatalist would certainly assume that the "Will" was against Beresford and his harassed, almost defeated army; but they are not defeated, simply because they refuse to accept defeat (2.6.4).

This doggedness Hardy seems to regard as an especially English virtue. In many battles the French gain an initial tactical advantage which they gradually lose, and the final issue is decided by simple endurance. This, much elaborated, is the pattern of the Waterloo scenes. Napoleon has an advantage, and fails to maintain it. Manoeuvres give way to more primitive fighting. As Wellington says,

> Manoeuvring does not seem to animate
> Napoleon's methods now. Forward he comes,
> And pounds away on us in the ancient style;
> Till he is beaten back in the ancient style;
> And so the see-saw sways!
>
> (3.7.7)

Ney attacks the English key position again and again, and is repulsed; all units are desperate and are calling for reinforcements for the deciding phase of the battle. Neither Napoleon nor Wellington has a single reserve, and Wellington, asked by Kempt's Aide for more men, can only advise that

> Those he has left him, be they many or few,
> Fight till they fall, like others on the field.
>
> (Ibid.)

Hill, with a "full look at the Worst," asks Wellington for his last commands in case Wellington himself is shot, and is told,

> These simply: to hold out unto the last,
> As long as one man stands on one lame leg
> With one ball in his pouch!—then end as I.
>
> (Ibid.)

Again Wellington receives a plea for reinforcements: the Aide is told:

> Inform your General
> That his proposal asks the impossible!
> That he, I, every Englishman afield,
> Must fall upon the spot we occupy,
> Our wounds in front.
>
> (Ibid.)

The final impression is that simple endurance was the most important factor at Waterloo. Victory is made possible only by desperate and heart-breaking stands and struggles, the squares holding out, fighting for time, until all the various forces, including the belated armies under von Bülow and Blücher, can be brought into action.

But endurance is not the only factor: the main contrast between Napoleon and Wellington is that Napoleon tries to keep up his men's morale by false optimism, by deceiving them into thinking that Blücher's army, seen in the distance, are French troops under Grouchy. Ney protests in vain; and the truth, when it finally becomes known, breaks the French. Wellington gives *his* men a "full look at the Worst," and still relies on them "to fight till they fall." He gives them no false hopes. Indeed he keeps an actual asset, a Guards regiment, hidden; and throws these into the attack when the soldiers of both sides are nearing exhaustion; and their effect is decisive in breaking the French attack, and giving the English cavalry its chance. Thus, careful timing and realistic or "pessimistic" fact-facing cannot easily be separated from the endurance that finally wins battles.

Hardy's *Dynasts* certainly does not present us with a world in which human endeavour counts for nothing. The value of discipline, cooperation, and carefully timed effort is recognized clearly. It is a world, too, in which individual decisions count. At Wagram (2.4.3) despite careful manoeuvring and desperate tactics, Napoleon only just turns the scales to victory, and only because the Archduke John, arriving in time, but not realizing how even is "the poise of forces," turns tail instead of attacking. Hardy again and again makes a special effort to show the component parts—even individual parts—of any success or failure, of any movement of the "Will," which is indeed only "the will of all conjunctively" (3.1.5).

When we speak of "discipline" and "cooperation," we are, indeed, talking of individuals, of "every man doing his duty." The stand at Corunna—we noticed how Hardy tells the story of the two stragglers—was made possible by the resolves of individuals:

> This harassed force now appears as if composed of quite other than the men observed in the Retreat insubordinately straggling along like vagabonds. Yet they are the same men, suddenly stiffened and grown amenable to discipline by the satisfaction of standing to the enemy at last.
>
> (2.3.3)

But the most striking evidence of the potentiality of the individual occurs earlier in that same Retreat, when the English were fleeing from the French in Spain. That even the most wretched creatures of that demoralized rout could have done something, is shown by the success of such platoons as did periodically rally, and fire, and hold up the enemy advance (2.3.1). And, most significant of all, two deserters who managed to escape discovery by the British officer in the same scene, found themselves, in the next scene, still hidden beneath straw in the cellar, within point-blank range of Napoleon himself! Had they not thrown away their arms, they could have shot him!

Here, as often with most effect, Hardy points his moral ironically and negatively: unpreparedness showing the value of remaining prepared. But he uses the positive method too: Napoleon has a single night when it may be possible to escape from Elba—if only the wind rises. He waits till long after others would have given up hope; the wind comes just in time, and he gets away (3.5.1).

That one man who is prepared to take any stray chance that comes his way is able to divert the whole course of the "Will" is also shown in *The Peasant's Confession*. This poem, though published separately, derives from Hardy's Waterloo research. It tells how a messenger from Napoleon with detailed instructions to Grouchy about engaging the Prussian troops and preventing their coming to Wellington's aid, was murdered. It will be remembered that the messenger's disappearance, with the consequent uncertainty over Grouchy's movements, causes Napoleon and his generals much anxiety in *The Dynasts*. It is worth noting in passing, however, that Hardy does not make Napoleon so foolish as to blame chance or fate; he blames negligence. When Soult gives him his personal assurance that a messenger has been sent, Napoleon exclaims,

A messenger! Had my poor Berthier been here
Six would have insufficed

(3.7.2)

*The Peasant's Confession* tells how the peasant is told of the messenger's mission, calculates that a battle between Grouchy and Blücher would destroy his crops, and so misdirects the messenger and kills him. The main point of the poem, undeniably, lies in the Peasant's remorse; but it is also undeniable that the earlier part of the poem reflects something of the excitement of possessing, and using, the power to change the course of history.

We are told in the Fore Scene of *The Dynasts* that the Will has no aim. That we imagine It to have an aim is a pathetic fallacy, or an inescapable weakness in our language. The Will is but a neutral "consequence": the sum of all the causes and wills, conscious and unconscious, in the web of organic life. And, as Hardy wrote to Edward Wright, "Whenever it happens that all the rest of the Great Will is in equilibrium" then even "the minute portion of it called one person's will is free." Even this one person's "share in the sum of sources" can "Bend a digit the poise of forces, And a fair desire fulfil." In the world of *The Dynasts* Hardy shows us many occasions when opposing forces are evenly matched, or when there is otherwise scope for the contrivers, the plodders, the careful watchers. And traitor and coward, as well as loyal supporters, have their effect upon the outcome.

Hardy makes, however, another and different point about the individual. There are larger aims, the aims of common humanity, which cut across national and dynastic interests. Just as in some of the later novels, Hardy suggests that common humanity has to contend with an unsympathetic universe *and also* with an unsympathetic man-made structure of convention and society, so too in *The Dynasts,* common humanity, "the Managed" (3.7.8), have pathetically less freedom than "the Managers" for whom the war is plied:

On earth below
Are men—unnatured and mechanic-drawn—
Mixt nationalities in row and row,
Wheeling them to and fro
In moves dissociate from their souls' demand,
For dynasts' ends that few even understand.

(2.6.4)

The "souls' demand" of ordinary human beings is shown by the way the rank and file of opposing armies, between engagements, drink together and shake hands across a brook (2.4.5); and when the Spirit Ironic laughs at this "spectacle of [the Will's] instruments, set to riddle one another through," drinking "together in peace and concord," the Spirit Sinister replies:

> Come, Sprite, don't carry your ironies too far, or you may wake up the Unconscious Itself, and tempt it to let all the gory clockwork of the show run down to spite me!

Unhappily humanity does not always behave thus. The impotent rage of a defeated army and the vindictive plundering of the victorious, "driven to demonry by the Immanent Unrecking" (3.7.8) after a battle, are sorrier but equally true aspects of common humanity. But it is in some such context that we must take Hardy's suggestion at the very close of the poem that the Will may one day develop a mind, events may "wake up the Unconscious Itself": even mass man may develop something like a mass conscience, a sense of restraint, a mind. It seems almost as though Hardy imagined temporarily—and uncharacteristically—that human nature itself might change. More usually he conveys the impression that human nature, as it is, would be good enough if only its potentialities were properly used.

"War is doomed" Hardy had told William Archer, about the time he was writing *The Dynasts,* explaining that men were becoming too civilized to resort to this absurd way of settling differences. The Great War and the Treaty of Versailles disillusioned Hardy, and he then regretted having given the end of *The Dynasts* this optimistic turn. But let us be clear that what Hardy regretted was having suggested that there might be an improvement in the Will itself—something automatic and independent of human effort. The more characteristic belief that a way through all the difficulties that beset us might still exist, if we regarded those difficulties honestly and courageously, he never retracted: a belief in—

> The fact of life with dependence placed
> On the human heart's resource alone,
> In brotherhood bonded close and graced
>
> With loving-kindness fully blown,
> And visioned help unsought, unknown.

# J. HILLIS MILLER

# *The Refusal of Involvement*

Nowhere in Hardy's writings is there a description of an originating act in which the mind separates itself from everything but itself. His self-awareness and that of his characters are always inextricably involved in their awareness of the world. Their minds are turned habitually outward. Almost every sentence Hardy ever wrote, whether in his fiction, in his poetry, or in his more private writings, is objective. It names something outside the mind of which that mind is aware. A man, in his view, should even look at his own interior life as something detached and external, not as something known from the inside with special intimacy. "A naturalist's interest in the hatching of a queer egg or germ is the utmost introspective consideration you should allow yourself," he says in a private notebook entry of 1888.

In spite of this distaste for introspection, there is a passage in Florence Emily Hardy's *Life* which takes the reader close to the intrinsic quality of his mind. This text, like most of the *Life,* was probably composed by Hardy himself:

> One event of this date or a little later [when Hardy was about six] stood out, he used to say, more distinctly than any [other]. He was lying on his back in the sun, thinking how useless he was, and covered his face with his straw hat. The sun's rays streamed through the interstices of the straw, the lining having disappeared. Reflecting on his experiences of the world so far as

From *Thomas Hardy: Distance and Desire.* © 1970 by the President and Fellows of Harvard College. The Belknap Press of Harvard University Press, 1970.

he had got, he came to the conclusion that he did not wish to grow up. Other boys were always talking of when they would be men; he did not want at all to be a man, or to possess things, but to remain as he was, in the same spot, and to know no more people than he already knew (about half a dozen).

This episode does not constitute a genetic moment. Two events have preceded it and are reflected in it. The first is certain "experiences of the world." The nature of these is suggested by a passage at the opening of *Jude the Obscure* which so closely resembles the text in the *Life* that it may be called an anticipatory comment on it. The young Jude, like the young Hardy, finds that a man is not born free. Each person is ushered into the world in a certain spot in space and time. He has certain ancestors. He finds himself with a certain role to play in his family, in his community, in his social class, in his nation, even on the stage of world history. Like the young Jude, who is shown in the middle of a "vast concave" cornfield which goes "right up towards the sky all round, where it [is] lost by degrees in the mist that shut[s] out the actual verge and accentuate[s] the solitude," each man finds himself at the center of a receding series of contexts which locates him and defines him. This imprisonment is all the more painful for being so intangible. Jude stands alone and in the open, but he is nonetheless bound by the situation he has inherited. Like Pip in Dickens's *Great Expectations,* he is an orphan. Like Pip, he has been told by his foster mother that he is "useless" and would be better dead. Along with so many other heroes of nineteenth-century novels, Hardy's protagonists find themselves "living in a world which [does] not want them." Though Hardy himself was not an orphan and seems to have had a fairly happy childhood, he too, in the passage from the *Life,* broods over how "useless" he is. The conventional motifs of the orphan hero and the indifferent foster parent express his general sense that no man's situation is of his making or satisfies his desire.

Hardy's response to this experience of life is so instinctive that it is never recorded, but always precedes any record, though it is repeated again and again in his own life and in that of his characters. It precedes any record because it makes consciousness and the recording of consciousness possible. This response is a movement of passive withdrawal. Like a snail crawling into its shell, or like a furtive animal creeping into its burrow, he pulls his hat over his face and looks quietly at what he can see through the interstices of the straw. The gesture objectifies an act of detachment which, for him, is involuntary and antedates any gesture which embodies it. The separation which is natural to the mind may be lost by a man's absorption in the world or it may be maintained by a willful standing back, but initially it is given with consciousness itself. To be conscious is to be separated. The mind has a native clarity and distinctness which detaches it from everything it registers.

Though Hardy finds that his consciousness separates him from the world, he does not turn away from what he sees to investigate the realm of interior space. He and his characters are distinguished by the shallowness of their minds. They have no profound inner depths leading down to the "buried self" or to God. They remain even in detachment oriented toward the outside world and reflecting it, mirrorlike. Though Hardy remains turned toward the exterior, looking at it or thinking about it, his movement of retraction separates him from blind engagement and turns everything he sees into a spectacle viewed from the outside.

A passage in *The Mayor of Casterbridge* demonstrates further this superficiality of consciousness. The act of coming to self-awareness does not lead to a recognition of the intrinsic quality of the mind. It is a revelation about the outside world, a recognition of the mute detachment of external objects and of the inexplicable fact that this particular power of knowing, which might be anywhere or beholding any scene, happens to be imprisoned by one environment rather than by another. The mind is held entranced by a vision of objects which seem themselves entranced, constrained. The passage describes Elizabeth-Jane Henchard's experience as she sits late at night by the bedside of her dying mother. She hears one of those odd sounds audible in a silent house in the small hours: one clock ticking against another clock, "ticking harder and harder till it seemed to clang like a gong." This revelation of the fact that a clock's ticking is a mechanical noise, not a natural expression of the passage of time, leads her to recognize the paradoxical nature of her situation. She is both within her immediate environment and outside it. She is in bondage to it in the sense that if she looks at anything she must look at what happens to be there to see. She is free of it in the sense that what she sees has no necessary connection to her watching mind. Seeing this causes her consciousness to spin incoherently with unanswerable questions about why things around her are as they are. Though the passage registers as acute an awareness of self as is expressed anywhere in Hardy's writing, it shows the mind still turned chiefly toward the outside world, still asking why things are as they are rather than why the mind is as it is. The question of the nature of the mind arises only after a confrontation of the helpless objectivity of external things:

> and all this while the subtle-souled girl [was] asking herself why
> she was born, why sitting in a room, and blinking at the candle;

why things around her had taken the shape they wore in preference to every other possible shape. Why they stared at her so
helplessly, as if waiting for the touch of some wand that should
release them from terrestrial constraint; what that chaos called
consciousness, which spun in her at this moment like a top,
tended to, and began in.

The spontaneous withdrawal of the mind to a position of detached
watchfulness is ratified by an act of will. Rather than choosing to lose himself
in one or another of the beguiling forms of engagement offered by the world,
Hardy, like many of his characters, chooses to keep his distance. Like Her-
man Melville's Bartleby, he decides he "would prefer not to"—prefer not to
grow up, prefer not to take responsibility, prefer not to move out of his own
narrow circle, prefer not to possess things, prefer not to know more people.
The young Jude also experiences this desire to remain on the periphery of
life. He too pulls his hat over his eyes and lies "vaguely reflecting": "As you
got older, and felt yourself to be at the centre of your time, and not a point
in its circumference, as you had felt when you were little, you were seized
with a sort of shuddering, he perceived. All around you there seemed to be
something glaring, garish, rattling, and the noises and glares hit upon the
little cell called your life, and shook it, and warped it. If he could only prevent
himself growing up! He did not want to be a man." The motif recurs once
more when the speaker in a late poem, a poem characteristically craggy in
diction, remembers as a child crouching safely in a thicket of ferns and asking
himself: "Why should I have to grow to man's estate, / And this afar-noised
World perambulate?" ("Childhood among the Ferns"). The world is noise
and glare, the threat of an engulfing violence which will shake and twist a
man's life. Only if he can remain self-contained, sealed off from everything,
can he escape this violence. He must therefore refuse any involvement in the
world. Hardy's fundamental spiritual movement is the exact opposite of
Nietzsche's will to power. It is the will not to will, the will to remain quietly
watching on the sidelines.

Having given up the virile goals which motivate most men, Hardy can
turn back on the world and watch it from a safe distance, see it clearly with
a "full look at the Worst" ("In Tenebris, II"), and judge it. This way of
being related to the world is the origin of his art. Such an attitude determines
the habitual stance of his narrators, that detachment which sees events from
above them or from a time long after they have happened. Or it might be
better to say that these spatial and temporal distances objectify a separation
which is outside of life, outside of time and space altogether, as the speaker

in "Wessex Heights" seems "where I was before my birth, and after death may be." The tone of voice natural to a spectator who sees things from such a position imparts its slightly acerb flavor throughout his work as a compound of irony, cold detachment, musing reminiscent bitterness, an odd kind of sympathy which might be called "pity at a distance," and, mixed with these, a curious joy, a grim satisfaction that things have, as was foreseen, come out for the worst in this worst of all possible worlds.

Such a perspective is also possessed by many of the protagonists of Hardy's novels, those watchers from a distance like Gabriel Oak in *Far from the Madding Crowd*, Christopher Julian in *The Hand of Ethelberta*, Diggory Venn in *The Return of the Native*, or Giles Winterborne in *The Woodlanders*. The detachment of such characters is expressed in the recurrent motif of spying in his fiction. He frequently presents a scene in which one character sees another without being seen, watches from an upper window or a hill, peeks in a window from outside at night, or covertly studies a reflection in a mirror.

In the lyric poetry too a stance of detachment is habitual. The speaker of the poems is "The Dead Man Walking," to borrow the title of one of them. He is withdrawn from the present, "with no listing or longing to join" ("In Tenebris, III"). From this separation he focuses his attention on the ghosts of the past. He sees things from the perspective of death, and as a consequence is so quiet a watcher, so effaced, that birds, animals, and forlorn strangers pay no attention to him, knowing that his vision is as distant as the stars ("'I Am the One'"). This detachment is most elaborately dramatized in the choruses of spirits in *The Dynasts*. These spirits, says Hardy, are not supernatural beings. They "are not supposed to be more than the best human intelligences of their time in a sort of quint-essential form." From this generalization he excludes the Chorus of Pities. They are "merely Humanity, with all its weaknesses." The careful attention to details of optical placement in *The Dynasts*, which John Wain has associated with cinematic technique, is more than a matter of vivid presentation. It is an extension of the implicit point of view in the novels and in the lyric poems. It has a thematic as well as technical meaning. The choruses in *The Dynasts* are able to see the whole expanse of history at a glance. When they focus on a particular event they see it in the context of this all-encompassing panoramic vision. The spirits in the "General Chorus of Intelligences" at the end of the "Fore Scene" boast that they are everywhere at once and can contract all time and space to a single spot of time:

> We'll close up Time, as a bird its van,
> We'll traverse Space, as spirits can,

> Link pulses severed by leagues and years,
> Bring cradles into touch with biers;
> So that the far-off Consequence appears
> Prompt at the heel of foregone Cause.

The narrative voice and perspective in the fiction, the attitude natural to many characters in the novels, the location of the speaker habitual in the poems, the epic machinery of *The Dynasts*—all these express the detachment of consciousness which is fundamental to Hardy's way of looking at the world. Such separation allows him and his spokesmen to see reality as it is. From a detached point of view the environment no longer seems so close that one can only be aware of its dangerous energy, its glare and garish rattling. The man who is pursuing some immediate goal is too close to life to see it whole. Only from a distance are its patterns visible. In *Desperate Remedies,* for example, Aeneas Manston is paradoxically granted by the intensity of his involvement the insight born of a momentary detachment. From the point of view of the man involved in a concrete situation, such a perspective is trivial, a momentary wandering of the mind. The narrator and the reader, however, can see that the character has by a fortuitous inattention been briefly granted a glimpse of the true pattern of existence. Here the view of the protagonist approaches, in a moment of vision which recurs in Hardy's fiction, the wide view of the narrator:

> There exists, as it were, an outer chamber to the mind, in which, when a man is occupied centrally with the most momentous question of his life, casual and trifling thoughts are just allowed to wander softly for an interval, before being banished altogether. Thus, amid his concentration did Manston receive perceptions of the individuals about him in the lively thoroughfare of the Strand; tall men looking insignificant; little men looking great and profound; lost women of miserable repute looking as happy as the days are long; wives, happy by assumption, looking careworn and miserable. Each and all were alike in this one respect, that they followed a solitary trail like the inwoven threads which form a banner, and all were equally unconscious of the significant whole they collectively showed forth.

The same image appears in *The Woodlanders*. Though Giles Winterborne and Marty South walking in the early morning are completely "isolated" and "self-contained," their lives form part of the total fabric of human actions being performed all over the globe: "their lonely courses formed no detached design at all, but were part of the pattern in the great web of human doings then weaving in both hemispheres from the White Sea to Cape Horn."

What Manston has for an instant, Hardy and his narrators have as a permanent possession. They see each individual life in the context of the whole cloth of which it is part. This superimposition of the engaged view and the detached, wide view pervades Hardy's writing and is the source of its characteristic ironies. If much of his work is made up of careful notation of immediate particulars—the weather, the landscape, a house or a room, the colors of things, apparently irrelevant details, what the characters say, think, or do as they seek satisfaction of their desires—the narrative perspective on these particulars, present in the steady and cool tone of the language, is a vision so wide that it reduces any particular to utter insignificance. Such a view reveals the fact that "winning, equally with losing," in any of the games of life, is "below the zero of the true philosopher's concern."

The nature of the universe seen from this perspective is expressed figuratively in the key images of *The Dynasts*. The motif of the single thread in a cloth reappears there when the Spirit of the Years says that the story of the Napoleonic Wars is "but one flimsy riband" of the "web Enorm" woven by the Immanent Will through "ceaseless artistries in Circumstance / Of curious stuff and braid." Along with this image goes another, that of a monstrous mass in senseless motion. The writhing of the whole includes in its random movement all men and women driven by their desires and intentions. *Desperate Remedies* anticipates this motif too. In one scene Aeneas Manston looks into a rain-water-butt and watches as "hundreds of thousands of minute living creatures sported and tumbled in its depth with every contortion that gaiety could suggest; perfectly happy, though consisting only of a head, or a tail, or at most a head and a tail, and all doomed to die within the twenty-four hours." Perfect image of man's life as Hardy sees it! In *The Dynasts*, published over thirty years after *Desperate Remedies*, the image reappears in Hardy's picture of the people of the earth, "distressed by events which they did not cause," "writhing, crawling, heaving, and vibrating in their various cities and nationalities," or "busying themselves like cheese-mites," or advancing with a "motion . . . peristaltic and vermicular" like a monstrous caterpillar, or "like slowworms through grass." The actions of man are controlled by the unconscious motion of the universe, "a brain-like network of currents and ejections, twitching, interpenetrating, entangling, and thrusting hither and thither the human forms." Dreaming brain, network, web, mass of writhing, intertwined creatures—these images describe a universe in which each part is a helpless victim of the weaving energy which unconsciously knits together the whole.

Hardy's conception of human life presupposes a paradoxical form of dualism. There is only one realm, that of matter in motion, but out of this "unweeting" movement human consciousness, that "mistake of God's" ("'I Travel as a Phantom Now'"), has arisen accidentally, from the play of physical causes. Though the detached clarity of vision which is possible to the human mind has come from physical nature, it is radically different from its source. It sees nature for the first time as it is, has for the first time pity for animal and human suffering, and brings into the universe a desire that events should be logical or reasonable, a desire that people should get what they deserve. But of course the world does not correspond to this desire. This is seen as soon as the desire appears. Knowledge of the injustice woven into the texture of things does not require extensive experience. The young Jude musing under his hat perceives already the clash of man's logic and nature's: "Events did not rhyme quite as he had thought. Nature's logic was too horrid for him to care for. That mercy towards one set of creatures was cruelty towards another sickened his sense of harmony." Like little Father Time in *Jude the Obscure,* Hardy is already as old as the hills when he is born, foresees the vanity of every wish, and knows that death is the end of life. To see the world clearly is already to see the folly of any involvement in it.

In Hardy's world there is no supernatural hierarchy of ideals or commandments, nor is there any law inherent in the physical world which says it is right to do one thing, wrong to do another, or which establishes any relative worth among things or people. Events happen as they do happen. They have neither value in themselves nor value in relation to any end beyond them. Worse yet, suffering is certain for man. In place of God there is the Immanent Will, and this unthinking force is sure to inflict pain on a man until he is lucky enough to die. Birth itself is "an ordeal of degrading personal compulsion, whose gratuitousness nothing in the result seemed to justify." Best of all would be not to be born at all, as Hardy affirms poignantly in "To an Unborn Pauper Child."

Both halves of the term "Immanent Will" are important. The supreme power is immanent rather than transcendent. It does not come from outside the world, but is a force within nature, part of its substance. It is a version of the inherent energy of the physical world as seen by nineteenth-century science: an unconscious power working by regular laws of matter in motion. Though what happens is ordained by no divine lawgiver, the state of the universe at any one moment leads inevitably to its state at the next moment.

Existence is made up of an enormous number of simultaneous energies each doing its bit to make the whole mechanism move. If a man had enough knowledge he could predict exactly what will be the state of the universe ten years from now or ten thousand. All things have been fated from all time.

The term "Will" is equally important. Hardy's use of this word supports Martin Heidegger's claim that a dualistic metaphysics leads to the establishment of volition as the supreme category of being. Hardy recognizes that his nomenclature may seem odd, since what he has in mind is not conscious willing. Nevertheless he defends "will" in a letter of 1904 to Edward Clodd as the most exact word for his meaning: "What you say about the 'Will' is true enough, if you take the word in its ordinary sense. But in the lack of another word to express precisely what is meant, a secondary sense has gradually arisen, that of effort exercised in a reflex or unconscious manner. Another word would have been better if one could have had it, though 'Power' would not do, as power can be suspended or withheld, and the forces of Nature cannot." Though the Immanent Will is not conscious, it is still will, a blind force sweeping through the universe, urging things to happen as they do happen, weaving the web of circumstances, shaping things in patterns determined by its irresistible energy.

The only hope for a change from this situation would be a gradual coming to consciousness of the Immanent Will. This odd version of "evolutionary meliorism," which Hardy considered himself to have invented, is expressed in a number of his poems, most powerfully in *The Dynasts,* where the Spirit of the Years, after the reader has been shown all the senseless carnage of the Napoleonic Wars, foresees a time when all will be changed— "Consciousness the Will informing, till It fashion all things fair!" Hardy takes great pleasure in a number of his poems, for example, in "The Blow," or in "Fragment," in describing the anguish of the Immanent Will if it should become conscious and understand what exquisite tortures of suffering it has unwittingly imposed on man and on the animals over the centuries:

> Should that morn come, and show thy opened eyes
> All that Life's palpitating tissues feel,
> How wilt thou bear thyself in thy surprise?—
>
> Wilt thou destroy, in one wild shock of shame,
> Thy whole high heaving firmamental frame,
> Or patiently adjust, amend, and heal?
>
> ("The Sleep-Worker")

"If Law itself had consciousness, how the aspect of its creatures would terrify it, fill it with remorse!" At this point in world history, however, the long expected event has not yet occurred. Mankind is "waiting, waiting, for God *to know it*" ("Fragment"). This earnest expectation may or may not be fulfilled. Meanwhile man must endure things as they are. This endurance is made more painful by knowledge that if the Immanent Will does not come to consciousness the best man can hope for is that he will be lucky enough to "darkle to extinction swift and sure." The development of man is a mistake on the part of the vital energy of earth. Man is no more fit for survival than the dinosaur or the saber-toothed tiger.

This vision of the universe is presupposed throughout Hardy's writing. The philosophical passages in *The Dynasts* only make explicit what is implicit in his novels and early poems. His vision of things is one version of a world view widely present in the late nineteenth century. Its sources in his reading of Tyndall, Huxley, Darwin, Spencer, Schopenhauer, Comte, and others have been often discussed. It is impossible to demonstrate, however, that any one of these sources is uniquely important in determining Hardy's view of things. He read many of the writers who formulated the late Victorian outlook, and his notions were undoubtedly also acquired in part from newspapers, periodicals, and other such reading. What matters most is to identify the idiosyncratic emphases in his version of a current view, the personal elements in his response to this view, and the way all the aspects of his world view are involved with one another.

They are involved not in the sense that all flow from some single presupposition, but in the sense that the various elements might be spoken of as implying one another. Beginning with any one of them leads to the others as natural if not inevitable accompaniments. They form a system or structure. If consciousness is a lucid, depthless, anonymous awareness of what is outside it, a "point of view," a reflecting mirror, then the mind sees the world from a distance as something different from it in nature. The wider, the more detached, the more impersonal, the more disinterested, the more clear and objective a man's view is the closer he will come to seeing the truth of things as they are. This is the scientific or historical point of view, a natural associate of the bifurcation of the world into subject and object. Mind is seen as detached lucidity watching a world of matter in motion.

This motion in things appears to be caused by an intrinsic power within them, a power to which Hardy, like Schopenhauer or Nietzsche, gives the name will. If man is separated from the universe by the detached clarity of his mind, he participates in the motion of nature through his body, through the emotions that body feels, and through the energy of desire which engages him in the world. This energy seems to be within his control, but is actually only the working through his body of the universal will in its unconscious activities of self-fulfillment. For Hardy, man has a double nature, a power of thinking and understanding, and a power of doing, feeling, and willing. If through the latter he takes part in the endless physical changes of the world, through the former he recognizes that these transformations, even those "willed" by man, leave nature still indifferent to human needs, unstructured by any inherent system of value. If the world view of nineteenth-century science accompanies naturally the separation of mind from world, along with the scientific view goes that draining of value from the essence of matter of fact which Alfred North Whitehead has described in *Science and the Modern World*. Objects are merely objects. They behave as they do behave, according to universal and impersonal laws. Any human value they may appear to have is a subjective illusion cast over them by man's instinctive desire that the world should provide him with an environment corresponding to his needs.

The emptying of human significance from things is often associated with loss of religious faith. Only a world of hierarchical levels in participation easily allows for a God who is both within His world and outside it. In the dispersal which is likely to accompany the separation of existence into two realms, subject and object, mind and world, God may at first be seen as separating himself from his creation. He withdraws to a distant place and watches the universe from afar. The scientist in his all-embracing objectivity apes this conception of God. If the division of realms of existence appears complete, if there seems no inherence of God in my consciousness, in nature, or in other people, if there remain open no more avenues of mediation by which a distant God may be reached, however indirectly, as in the forlorn echo from an infinite distance in Matthew Arnold's "The Buried Life," then I may experience not the "disappearance of God" but the death of God, that death which Hardy announces in "God's Funeral."

The experience of the death of God seems a natural concomitant of a definition of man as pure consciousness and of everything else as the object of that consciousness. To the "deicide eyes of seers" ("A Plaint to Man") God seems no more than a "man-projected Figure" ("God's Funeral"). God is killed by the attainment of that all-embracing vision which makes man a seer. The span of perfected human consciousness, separate, pure, clear-seeing, is as wide as the infinite universe it beholds, a universe now revealed to be made of blazing suns in a black void. Such a universe is shown to Lady Constantine by the young astronomer, Swithin St. Cleeve, in *Two on a Tower*. "Until a person has thought out the stars and their interspaces," says Swithin, "he has hardly learnt that there are things much more terrible than monsters of shape, namely, monsters of magnitude without known shape. Such monsters are the voids and waste places of the sky." In such a view the detachment of the watching mind corresponds to the infinite breadth of the universe it beholds. Both are equally null, nullity reflecting nullity, man and all his concerns reduced by the terrible impersonality of space to infinitesimal specks in a measureless hollow. "There is a size," says Swithin,

> at which dignity begins . . . ; further on there is a size at which grandeur begins; further on there is a size at which solemnity begins; further on, a size at which awfulness begins; further on, a size at which ghastliness begins. That size faintly approaches the size of the stellar universe. . . . [If] you are restless and anxious about the future, study astronomy at once. Your troubles will be reduced amazingly. But your study will reduce them in a singular way, by reducing the importance of everything . . . It is quite impossible to think at all adequately of the sky—of what the sky substantially is, without feeling it as a juxtaposed nightmare.

Such a sense of man's place in the universe is not too different from that of his contemporary, Friedrich Nietzsche, but Hardy's response to this vision is radically different. It is in this response that his special quality must be sought. As a number of critics have seen, his attitude is in some ways strikingly similar to that of Nietzsche's predecessor, Arthur Schopenhauer, the philosopher whose dissertation *On the Four-fold Root of the Principle of Sufficient Reason* Hardy read in 1889 or 1890 in Mrs. Karl Hillebrand's translation. Nietzsche defines man as the will to power. In a world of amoral determinism man should take matters into his own hands, become a center of force organizing the world into patterns of value. The man of relentless will can turn his life from fated repetition into willed repetition and so escape into a paradoxical freedom. Hardy, like Schopenhauer's saint or artist who has lifted the veil of Maya, is more passive and detached. Like so many of his countrymen, like Dickens for example, he fears the guilt involved in becoming the value-giving center of his world. Willing means yielding to those emotions which orient a man toward other people. The longing for power and ownership involves a man in the swarming activity of the Immanent Will, and so alienates him from himself, as Napoleon in *The Dynasts*, surely a man of will, is nevertheless only an instrument of impersonal forces working through him.

Each man, in Hardy's view, has a paradoxical freedom. His own power of willing is, as in Schopenhauer's system, only his embodiment of a tiny part of the vast energy of the Immanent Will. Even so, a man's will is apparently under the control of his mind, or at least it expresses the intentions of that mind. This means that if the other powers around him are in a momentary equilibrium he can act freely rather than being pushed by external energies. Hardy returns frequently to this notion and always expresses it in the language of physical forces in interaction, as when he speaks of "the modicum of free will conjecturally possessed by organic life when the mighty necessitating forces—unconscious or other—that have 'the balancings of the clouds,' happen to be in equilibrium," or as in a stanza from a poem of 1893, "He Wonders about Himself":

> Part is mine of the general Will,
> Cannot my share in the sum of sources
> Bend a digit the poise of forces,
> And a fair desire fulfil?

The language here reveals how little free Hardy's concept of free will is. As part of the general will his individual will expresses that of which it is a part. It is moved with the whole, even though in unusual circumstances of balance it may be the part of the general will which gives the push to things. His freedom is in fact servitude, as the note of interrogation in this poem suggests. Another text on the theme makes this even clearer. It uses an odd metaphor which suggests that the free will of the individual is no more than his power to move independently, but automatically, according to patterns that have been implanted previously by the "Great Will": "whenever it happens that all the rest of the Great Will is in equilibrium the minute portion called one person's will is free, just as a performer's fingers are free to go on playing the pianoforte of themselves when he talks or thinks of something else and the head does not rule them." Once more the image of the digit occurs. Man is at best no more than a forefinger of the universal sleep-walking giant. Another such text describes the Will as "like a knitter drowsed, / Whose fingers play in skilled unmindfulness." Even when the individual will acts with the paradoxical freedom of a self-acting finger it is still no more than a portion of the universal Will. As a result, the more powerfully a man wills or desires, the more surely he becomes the puppet of an all-shaping energy, and the quicker he encompasses his own destruction. As soon as he engages himself in life he joins a vast streaming movement urging him on toward death and the failure of his desires.

Safety therefore lies in passivity, in secrecy, in self-effacement, in reticence, in the refusal of emotions and of their temptations to involvement. These temptations, however, are almost irresistibly strong, even for a man naturally so clear-headed as Hardy. Though the mind is different in essence from the physical motion of things as they are driven by the Immanent Will, it does not constitute a realm altogether apart. The mind of even the most detached and far-seeing man is still oriented toward the world, watching it, dwelling within it, open to its solicitations, subject to its glare and garish rattling. Like Joseph Conrad in *Victory* and elsewhere, Hardy frequently turns to a theme which is for both writers not without its grimly comic aspects: the story of a man who by luck or by deliberate effort of will has kept himself apart from other men and women, but is in spite of his aloofness lured into involvement and suffering. Boldwood in *Far from the Madding Crowd* is a good example of such a character. Nor was Hardy himself exempt from such experiences, in spite of his reticence and self-control.

In his fiction and in his life this loss of self-possession takes two principle forms: falling in love and yielding to the magical power of music. His love affair with his cousin Tryphena Sparks, if this indeed took place, and his love for his first wife seem to have been, in their ambiguous complexity, the central events of his personal life. These events are reflected with varying degrees of obliquity in his writing, most directly in the poem "Thoughts of Phena, at News of Her Death" and in the poems he wrote after the death of his wife, the "Poems of 1912–13." Certainly these infatuations were the most important cases in which Hardy broke his instinctive reserve. The suffering which seems to have followed in both cases can be glimpsed here and there in the sparse evidence about his private life. This suffering gives his life a pattern much like the recurrent form of his fiction. It was not only Tryphena Sparks or Emma Gifford to whom he responded, however. A number of examples are given in the *Life* of his penchant, as a boy and as a young man, for falling passionately in love with girls he had glimpsed from a distance. The poem "To Lizbie Browne" commemorates one of these episodes:

> But, Lizbie Browne,
> I let you slip;
> Shaped not a sign;
> Touched never your lip
> With lip of mine,
> Lost Lizbie Browne!

As for Hardy's response to music, a curious passage in the *Life*, a passage almost adjacent to the text describing the young boy's retreat under his hat, shows how he shared with the characters in his fiction a strong susceptibility to it:

> He was of ecstatic temperament, extraordinarily sensitive to mu-
> sic, and among the endless jigs, hornpipes, reels, waltzes, and
> country-dances that his father played of an evening in his early
> married years, and to which the boy danced a *pas seul* in the
> middle of the room, there were three or four that always moved
> the child to tears, though he strenuously tried to hide them. . . .
> This peculiarity in himself troubled the mind of "Tommy" as he
> was called, and set him wondering at a phenomenon to which he
> ventured not to confess. He used to say in later life that, like
> Calantha in Ford's *Broken Heart,* he danced on at these times to
> conceal his weeping. He was not over four years of age at this
> date.

An admirably suggestive and revealing passage! He was of "ecstatic temperament"—the phrase is a strong one. In spite of his self-enclosure, his cultivation of a watchful detachment, Hardy was so subject to the lure of the outside world that music could draw him out of himself, destroy his self-control, and reduce him to helpless tears. His response to music, however, is more than a reaction to the objective beauty of a moving melody. It is also a mediated reaction to other people, those who have invented the tune or who play it. The boy weeping as he listens to music is as much subject to his father as to the melody. It is this double enslavement which so troubles him. The power of music is like the power of a beautiful woman. In both cases an overwhelming emotional reaction draws his soul involuntarily out of his body and makes him the puppet of someone outside himself, as the children were entranced by the Pied Piper of Hamelin.

This association between music and love is dramatized in that admirable short story, "The Fiddler of the Reels" (1893). The Fiddler, "Mop" Olla-moor, plays so magically that he could "well-nigh have drawn an ache from the heart of a gate-post. He could make any child in the parish, who was at all sensitive to music, burst into tears in a few minutes by simply fiddling one of the old dance-tunes he almost entirely affected—country jigs, reels, and 'Favourite Quick Steps' of the last century." Mop's power is also sexual, and his sexual magnetism works by way of his music. Like a young girl Hardy once heard whose singing had the power of "drawing out the soul of listeners in a gradual thread of excruciating attention like silk from a co-coon," Mop can "play the fiddle so as to draw your soul out of your body like a spider's thread." The story tells how he enthralls a young country girl, Car'line, steals her away from her betrothed, seduces her, and some years later once more hypnotizes her with his playing so that he can abduct the

child born of their union. Music and love—both are an irresistible fascination.

Rather than yielding in complete abnegation of will to the lure of music
and love, as does Car'line, Hardy fights for his independence. This is not
easy to do. It is one thing to withdraw under his hat in a moment of solitude
and decide not to involve himself in the world. It is quite another to remain
in possession of himself while his father is plaaying the fiddle or when he
sees a pretty girl. In fact it is impossible. The tears flow involuntarily; his
soul goes out of his body. The best he can do is to hide his tears, keep his
love secret, as he did from the various girls he loved when he was an ado-
lescent.

This hiding takes a curious form. In the passage cited above Hardy
dances on to conceal his weeping. The dancing is a response to the emotive
power of the music, but it is an indirect, covert response, a transposition of
the helpless and self-betraying tears into a more or less impersonal and socially accepted form of behavior. In dancing the uncontrolled tears and the
lax flowing out of the soul into the world are turned into the controlled
expression of art. This art is a way of being involved in the world and of
responding to it without being swallowed up by it. It holds things at a
distance and imitates in another pattern the objective patterns in the outside
world which have held his attention through their power to generate an
emotional fascination. Such an art is at once a reaction to the external world,
and a protection against it. It is a transformation of the reaction into a shape
which imitates it at a distance.

Exactly this pattern can be seen in another passage from the early pages
of the *Life*. Once more there is a strong emotional response to the qualitative
aspects of an experience. The experience is accepted and yet held at arm's
length through its change into the objective form of a work of art. The text
comes between the one about the young Hardy's response to music and the
one about his desire not to grow up:

> In those days the staircase at Bockhampton (later removed) had
> its walls coloured Venetian red by his father, and was so situated
> that the evening sun shone into it, adding to its colour a great
> intensity for a quarter of an hour or more. Tommy used to wait
> for this chromatic effect, and, sitting alone there, would recite to
> himself "And now another day is gone" from Dr. Watts's Hymns,
> with great fervency, though perhaps not for any religious reason,
> but from a sense that the scene suited the lines.

The same elements are here: the bright red wall which draws him to watch for its special intensity at sunset; the holding back from the danger of his response not by destroying the response or by turning away from it, but by transmuting it into another form which matches it at a distance, the fervency of the singing corresponding to the intensity of the red wall at sunset. The fundamental structure of Hardy's relation to the world may be identified through the juxtaposition of these homologous texts. In all of them the mind confronts in detachment a world which is seen as possessing dangerous energies, energies which are yet ambiguously attractive. There is a refusal of direct involvement, but there is also discovery of a means of indirect response. Hardy's preference for such responses may help to explain why he became a writer and what relation to the world his writing expresses.

JEAN R. BROOKS

# The Return of the Native:
## *A Novel of Environment*

*The Return of the Native* strikes a harsher note than *Far from the Madding Crowd*. Egdon Heath, the resistant matter of the cosmos on which the action takes place, bears, shapes, nourishes, and kills conscious organisms possessed of its striving will without its unconsciousness of suffering. The six main characters take their key from Egdon. They all feel its pull through some affinity of temperament. Clym, Mrs Yeobright, and Diggory Venn share its look of isolation; Thomasin, Clym, and Venn its endurance; Eustacia and Wildeve, though they hate it, share its primal vitality and indifference to others. The rustics, too, take a more subdued tone from the heath. The accent of their talk falls on time passing, change and decay. Their environment is one in which change and chance, death and darkness, prevail, and "the overpowering of the fervid by the inanimate" is a recognized conclusion to human effort.

It is fashionable in this denigrating age to decry Hardy's description of the heath in chapter 1 as pretentious. An earlier critic was nearer the mark in likening it to the entry of the Gods in Wagner. Large orchestras are not out of place in making the power of cosmic forces felt on the pulse. Egdon is presented as a visual correlative of space and time and the modern view of life "as a thing to be put up with." It is characteristic of Hardy's poetic style to begin with the specific—"A Saturday afternoon in November"—and widen the local view gradually to a philosophic vision of cosmic processes which the heath has power to affect:

From *Thomas Hardy: The Poetic Structure*. © 1971 by Jean R. Brooks. Cornell University Press, 1971.

The face of the heath by its mere complexion added half an hour to evening; it could in like manner retard the dawn, sadden noon, anticipate the frowning of storms scarcely generated, and intensify the opacity of a moonless midnight to a cause of shaking and dread.

The description of the heath in terms of a face, "a face on which time makes but little impression," which will later be recalled by the face (Clym's) on which time has recorded disillusive experience, introduces the theme of shape that opposes the chaos of Egdon's primal matter. But in this first chapter the details emphasize storm and darkness. Jungians will recognize in Hardy's hint of the tragic climax the subconscious hinterland of elemental myth that presents man's painful predicament in relation to a demonic landscape of barren earth, isolating wind, stormy water, and creative/destructive fire.

The storm was its lover, and the wind its friend. Then it became the home of strange phantoms; and it was found to be the hitherto unrecognized original of those wild regions of obscurity which are vaguely felt to be compassing us about in midnight dreams of flight and disaster, and are never thought of after the dream till revived by scenes like this.

Its "Titanic form" widens the perspective still further to invest the heath with heroic echoes of classical myth; particularly the Prometheus myth of rebellion against darkness. There is a swing back again, characteristic of Hardy's poetic method, from these long philosophical perspectives to "intelligible facts regarding landscape," its emotional and practical connection with man and his efforts to civilize it. The evocation ends with another swing from localized human vision to a vista of geological aeons. The Latinate dignity of the language, the balanced pauses, the unhurried rhythm, the slow build-up of paragraph structure, enact a persistent hammering at intractable physical substance which is part of the character and theme of Egdon.

The great inviolate place had an ancient permanence which the sea cannot claim. Who can say of a particular sea that it is old? Distilled by the sun, kneaded by the moon, it is renewed in a year, in a day, or in an hour. The sea changed, the fields changed, the rivers, the villages, and the people changed, yet Egdon remained. Those surfaces were neither so steep as to be destructible by weather, nor so flat as to be the victims of floods and deposits.

With the exception of an aged highway, and a still more aged barrow . . . themselves almost crystallized to natural products by long continuance—even the trifling irregularities were not caused by pickaxe, plough, or spade, but remained as the very finger-touches of the last geological change.

*The Return of the Native* is concerned with the Promethean struggle of conscious life against the unconscious "rayless" universe from which it sprang. The poetic-dramatic structure of the first chapters initiates the underlying metaphor of the novel, the ancient conflict of light and darkness. The white man-made road that crosses the brown heath, the red glow of bonfires, the "blood-coloured" figure of Diggory Venn, challenge the dark drabness of the earth.

To light a fire is the instinctive and resistant act of man when, at the winter ingress, the curfew is sounded throughout Nature. It indicates a spontaneous, Promethean rebelliousness against the fiat that this recurrent season shall bring foul times, cold darkness, misery and death. Black chaos comes, and the fettered gods of the earth say, Let there be light.

The almost supernatural figure of Diggory Venn modulates between the heath and the human beings whose desire for joy and purpose troubles the scene. He is dyed into an identification of the heath and its products. Yet his conspicuous fiery colour suggests a character that will master reality through involvement with it.

Chapter 2 begins with one of Hardy's familiar images of the human condition, the meeting of two lonely figures on a deserted road. One wonders about the meaning of the two walking figures and the woman concealed in the van. The chapter ends with another anonymous figure rising from the central point of Rainbarrow as the apex of plain, hill, and tumulus. Between the two scenes of human interest stands the modulating chord of the heath. Hardy is careful to plant his descriptions of scene where they will direct emotion. The reader's eye is forced to follow the reddleman's musing survey upwards from the "speck on the road" that defines the vanishing Captain to the protruberance of the barrow and the ambiguous potential of the crowning figure to make or mar human significance.

The shifting perspective, that enlarges and diminishes the human figure ("a spike from a helmet," "the only obvious justification of [the hills'] outline," "it descended . . . with the glide of a water-drop down a bud"), and transforms the barrow itself from "a wart on an Atlantean brow" to "the pole and axis of this heathery world," leaves in suspension the comparative significance of scene and human actors. The figure of unknown potential has been associated with the Celts who built the barrow as a bulwark of order against chaos; but what it marks is a place of death. It gives a perfect aesthetic finish to the mass; yet the Greek ideal of perfect beauty has been defined in chapter 1 as an anachronism. As it disappears, the surprise of the movement where all seemed fixity stresses the function of human consciousness on the natural scene. It can change and be changed.

Change is the keynote of the distanced "sky-backed pantomime of silhouettes" which replaces the composition of barrow and lonely figure. In chapter 3 the focus shifts from the permanent mass of the heath, with solitary wanderers crawling like ants over its surface and the still figure on its central point, to a firelit impression of movement and evanescence.

> All was unstable; quivering as leaves, evanescent as lightning. Shadowy eye-sockets, deep as those of a death's head, suddenly turned into pits of lustre: a lantern-jaw was cavernous, then it was shining; wrinkles were emphasized to ravines, or obliterated entirely by a changed ray.

Stillness gives way to motion; the solitary figure reaching for the sky to several "burdened figures" bowed down under the furze they carry, playing out the next stage of human development. The pyramid-shaped bonfire they build to top the barrow enacts a wordless ritual of human function to shape and control. The heath, detached from them by the radiant circle of light they have created, becomes the "vast abyss" of Milton's, Dante's and Homer's hell. By implication, the distorted human features evoke tormented souls acting out a timeless doom.

Hardy modulates from ritual to the human plane by bringing the fragmented Grandfer Cantle gradually forward from the composition to speak and act as a mortal limited by time and the need for warmth and self-assertion. The elemental ritual of light and darkness recedes as the kindly rustic voices gather strength. But it remains in the imagination to colour the talk of local human concerns with its larger rhythms. The conflict of wills that emerges from the gossip about Mrs Yeobright forbidding the banns, Tamsin's rash choice of Wildeve, Wildeve's character and attainments, the criticism of Eustacia's non-communal bonfire, the anticipation of Clym's Promethean role—"What a dog he used to be for bonfires!"—the nostalgia for youth and quiet acceptance of death as part of the seasonal cycle: all are marked with the preceding evocation of the limitations of the earth and the desire to transcend them; the fire of life and passion and the distortion of reality it brings with its comfort; the double vision of man's speck-like in-significance on the face of the heath and the poetic light that gives his ephem-eral features the eternal grandeur of ravines and caverns.

The human drama evolves, as it were, from the scene and its implica-tions. The character of Egdon encourages resistance and determines the kind of action that can take place within its bounds. Isolation fosters Eustacia's attraction to Clym and to a man of inferior calibre, the misunderstanding between Clym and his mother, the misapprehension about Mrs Yeobright's guineas. The openness of the country enables bonfire signals to be seen for miles; and kills Mrs Yeobright after her exhausting walk from one isolated cottage to another. Much of the action consists of solitary journeys across the heath to keep up communications or assignations, to spy out the land, or pursue erring mortals who have lost their way literally and figuratively on the dark criss-crossing paths that become symbolic of their antagonistic purposes. The presence of the vast passionless heath puts the human move-ments into perspective as the scurrying of ephemeral ants.

The plot resembles *Far from the Madding Crowd* in the tragic chain of love relationships and the situation of Wildeve, the gay man vacillating be-tween the innocent girl he is engaged to and the woman of greater passion and complexity. The pattern is again complicated by an idealist with an obsession, though Clym Yeobright's ambition, unlike Boldwood's, is uncon-nected with the irrational force of sexual love. Mrs Yeobright adds another colour to the figure in the carpet in the conflict between generations and their ideals of progress. As usual, the poetic stylization contributes to mean-ing. Douglas Brown [in *Thomas Hardy*] notes that

> the very grouping of the protagonists tells much. On one far side is Thomasin ("All similes concerning her began and ended with birds") and on the other, Wildeve, the ineffectual engineer, in-vading the country to become a publican. Clym (the native home from exile) and Eustacia (seeking exile, and confusing that with home) stand between them. At the centre, between Clym and Eustacia, Mrs Yeobright is subtly placed, a countrywoman up-holding urban attitudes whose true nature and effect she cannot perceive.

R. W. Stallman, in his ingenious article "Hardy's Hour-Glass Novel" (*Se-wanee Review* 55 [1947]) sees in the novel a chain of seven "hourglass" plots, in which Fate keeps turning the hourglass over to reverse events, sit-uations, and partners.

The tragic action was designed originally to lead to the double death in

the weir, involving the earlier tragedy of Mrs Yeobright's death. The original
five-part structure, the strict regard for unities of place, time (the year and
a day of folklore quest) and action, may recall Shakespearean and Classical
drama. The two signal fires are the novel's poles of time and action, and
Rainbarrow its axis in space. But such stylization is part of Hardy's normal
poetic technique. The five parts clearly graph the stages in the inter-related
love affairs, and the disillusionment which reality brings to Eustacia's romantic dreams of happiness and Clym's dreams of finding a purpose.

Book 1 introduces the three women whose relationship to the two men
is to promote a tragic antagonism of ideals. The wedding complications of
Tamsin and Wildeve introduce the blind obstructiveness of things (the marriage licence, and the subconscious reluctance of Wildeve that allowed the
mistake to happen; Mrs Yeobright's "Such things don't happen for nothing"
anticipates the psychology of Freudian error), and the countermoves of human intelligence (Mrs Yeobright's unscrupulous use of Venn as a rival lover
to bring Wildeve to heel, and Venn's active determination to look after Tamsin's interests). Book 2, "The Arrival," resolves the marriage complications
and changes the emotional current by the return of Clym Yeobright. Interest
is sustained by the potential of conflict and attraction between a man who
has rejected the worldly vanity of Paris and a woman for whom he represents
an avenue of escape to its delights. Book 3, "The Fascination," charts the
blind sexual attraction between Clym and Eustacia, each a distorted projection of fulfilment to the other, and the serious division it causes between
Clym and his mother. Mrs Yeobright's attempt to heal the breach by her gift
of money to Tamsin and Clym sows the seeds of the catastrophe by a combination of carelessness (she entrusts the money to the weak-witted Christian
Cantle), blind chance (Wildeve wins the guineas from Cantle), and ignorance
(Venn does not know that half the money he wins back from Wildeve was
destined for Clym).

Book 4, "The Closed Door," shows more than one door closing on
human possibilities. Clym's blindness limits his ambitions to knowledge of
a few square feet of furze. Simultaneously it dashes Eustacia's hopes of
escaping Egdon through Clym, and sends her back to Wildeve. Wildeve's
presence in the cottage with Eustacia when Mrs Yeobright calls keeps the
door closed against her, and Clym's heavy sleep is another closed door. Hope
of reconciliation is closed for ever by Mrs Yeobright's lonely death on the
heath. But Johnny Nunsuch's dramatic restatement of Mrs Yeobright's
words, "she said I was to say that I had seed her, and she was a broken-
hearted woman and cast off by her son" opens the door to Clym's painful

discovery in book 5 of the circumstances of her death and Eustacia's part in it. "The Discovery" charts the steps Clym takes to find out the truth, and the Oedipus-like irony that each step he takes drives him deeper into a hell of remorse, self-knowledge, and division from the other woman he loves. The final step drives Eustacia from his anger to seek escape through Wildeve, and to a despairing death with him in storm and darkness.

Hardy gave way to editorial necessity and common probability to add Book 6, which presents "the inevitable movement onward" that restores order after tragic catastrophe. Tamsin and Diggory Venn find happiness in marriage, and Clym partial fulfilment as an itinerant preacher, to the accompaniment of the rituals of May Day and the waxing of a feather bed for the married pair, which involve them all in the seasonal rite of fertility and regeneration.

One can point to the usual incidents in the working out of plot which compel comparisons vital to structure. The different purposes, selfish and altruistic, which motivate the characters to seek conflicting manifestations of fulfilment; which animate the various figures who crown Rainbarrow, and inspire the lonely journeys taken across the heath, are worth close study. The different attitudes to Egdon and its limitations and traditions are embodied, as Dr Beatty has shown, in Hardy's descriptions of Mistover Knap and Blooms-End. Captain Vye's house at Mistover Knap has "the appearance of a fortification." Blooms-End is separated from the heath only by a row of white palings and a little garden (which orders nature by control, not defence). The traditional mummers find a warm welcome at Blooms-End, the family home of the Yeobrights; while "for mummers and mumming Eustacia had the greatest contempt." At Blooms-End, the loft over the fuel-house "was lighted by a semicircular hole, through which the pigeons crept to their lodgings in the same high quarters of the premises," and the sun irradiated Tamsin as she selected apples from their natural packing of fern, with "pigeons . . . flying about her head with the greatest unconcern." At the fuel-house of Mistover Knap, the outsider Eustacia looks in from the darkness at the mummers' rehearsal to relieve her boredom, through "a small rough hole in the mud wall, originally made for pigeons," but now disused, and the building is lit from the inside.

What the contrasts reveal is that all the stylizations draw their meaning from the underpattern of conflicting light and dark. This central opposition moves the conflict between Clym and Eustacia, to which all the other characters stand in dramatic relationship. Their association with the elemental forces in conflict is defined by the fire and light images which identify them with the Promethean myth, and the images of darkness and death that endow Eustacia additionally with some of the attributes of Persephone Queen of the Shades.

The different manifestations of light and fire which define the characters also define their responses to the leitmotif question "What is doing well?" Wildeve has the "curse of inflammability"; Eustacia is a smouldering sub-terranean fire reaching by blind instinct for the sun; they snatch at the heat of momentary passion in a rebellion that speaks to the twentieth-century rebellion against the permanence of things. Clym's way of opposing the gods of darkness is to bring light rather than fire to mankind. (The name "Yeo-bright" is significant in both its parts.) Tamsin is marked by the image of benevolent sunshine. Mrs Yeobright, who has ignored the primitive power of the cosmos in her "civilized" desires for Clym's advancement, meets death by fire in a parched waste land with a poisonous serpent and a sun that foreshadows the hostile antagonist of Camus's *The Outsider*. Diggory Venn is permeated with the colour of fire, and shares the craft and symbolic am-biguity of the early fire-god Loki. Fire as an answer to darkness can be creative or destructive; an instrument of mastery or chaos. The scenes that carry the underpattern show the characters acting out their ritual roles as bringers of light or darkness to the pattern of human fate.

Clym Yeobright plays the double role of Promethean hero and ironic parody of primitive heroic attitudes. There is no doubt about his altruistic Promethean aspirations. "The deity that lies ignominiously chained within an ephemeral human carcase shone out of him like a ray." His absence has taught him that Egdon realities are realities the world over. Yet the context in which we first see Clym at close quarters (bk. 2, chap. 6) qualifies our approval of his aim to teach the Egdon eremites "how to breast the misery they are born to." At the Blooms-End Christmas party the snug picture framed by the settle does not show much evidence of misery.

> At the other side of the chimney stood the settle, which is the necessary supplement to a fire so open that nothing less than a strong breeze will carry up the smoke. It is, to the hearths of old-fashioned cavernous fireplaces, what the east belt of trees is to the exposed country estate, or the north wall to the garden. Out-side the settle candles gutter, locks of hair wave, young women shiver, and old men sneeze. Inside is Paradise. Not a symptom of a draught disturbs the air; the sitters' backs are as warm as their faces, and songs and old tales are drawn from the occupants by the comfortable heat, like fruit from melon-plants in a frame.

Hardy's selection of concrete detail to build up poetic mood and sequence takes us from the physical effects of the coldness outside to the simple statement that sums up human yearning for fulfilment, "Inside was Paradise." The simile of melon-plants in a frame clinches the natural sequence of comfort and growth that order this earthly Paradise—which Clym would jump in his ascetic plans for higher development.

> To argue upon the possibility of culture before luxury to the
> bucolic world may be to argue truly, but it is an attempt to disturb
> a sequence to which humanity has been long accustomed.

Outside the ordered frame of unreflective comfort are Clym, who has passed beyond it, and Eustacia, who has not yet reached it. The conjunction of traditional scene of conviviality, blind animal will to enjoy that has motivated Eustacia's presence, and Clym's "typical countenance of the future" marked by consciousness of man's tragic predicament in an uncaring universe, questions whether modern perceptiveness may be an unmixed blessing to men untouched by the disillusive centuries and adapted to the world they live in.

Clym's troubles spring from his failure to respect the laws of physical reality. His blindness is both a natural consequence of ignoring physical strain on his eyes, a simplification of the modern complexity of life which denies him "any more perfect insight into the conditions of existence," and a complex poetic symbol of the figurative blindness displayed by this representative of "modern perceptiveness" who "loved his kind," to the needs of the individuals closest to him, and to the nature of his illusions. He is blind to the reality which is in the heath, himself, his mother, Eustacia, and the "Egdon eremites" he had come to teach how to bear it. He meets its obstructiveness in the common resistance to the kind of progress that jumps the stage of social advance, in the irrational demands of sexual love, in the reality of Eustacia's primitive nature that runs counter to his projected image of her (a fault that makes him brother to Angel Clare and Knight). His sense of affinity with the dead and virgin moonscape (bk. 3, chap. 4), and the appearance of the "cloaked figure" of Eustacia, who is repeatedly associated with night, death, and the moon, at the base of Rainbarrow simultaneously with the eclipse ("for the remote celestial phenomenon had been pressed into sublunary service as a lover's signal") are correlative to his destructive and self-destructive attachment to Absolute Reality.

The failure of Clym's Promethean aim leads one to consider his role as an ironic reversal of the traditional hero-myth. R. Carpenter, in *Thomas Hardy,* sees the heroic archetype in Clym's quest for meaning. His originality is recognized at an early age, he serves his apprenticeship in a foreign land guarding treasure, and becomes possessed of deeper knowledge which he wishes to pass on to his people. His temporary withdrawal from the world suggests the initiation of a sun-god-hero into a religious cult. He returns to his birthplace, a dark and fallen world (Tartarus, the prison of the exiled Titans) but is not really recognized. He is diverted from his quest by a dark and beautiful enchantress against the wishes of his goddess mother, undergoes a period of spiritual trial and is symbolically blinded, like Oedipus and Milton's Samson, so that he may achieve true insight. The counterpointing strain of the hero who triumphs over obstacles to shape destiny, questions the validity, to the modern mind aware of "the obstructive coil of things," of simple heroic resistance. To Louis Crompton ("The Sunburnt God: Ritual and Tragic Myth in *The Return of the Native*," Boston University Studies in English, no. 6, 1960) Clym is a compound of the free hero of romance, the hero of classical tragedy, subject to fate and moral judgement, whose *hubris* leads to his downfall, and the diminished hero of modern realism, subject to biological and economic laws which limit human responsibility. But the wry comment on ancient heroic standards should not hide the genuine heroism achieved by a man who must painfully scale down his notions of progress to the limitations that condition the slow rate of evolutionary change. ("This was not the repose of actual stagnation, but the apparent repose of incredible slowness.")

The new concept of heroic action redefines Clym's quest as the quest of fallen man to re-establish harmony with nature. Clym takes his first steps towards Paradise regained when he accepts his primitive roots, puts on his old brown clothes, and becomes of no more account than a parasitic insect fretting the surface of the heath. Knowledge is redefined, in a poetic passage that emphasizes each unit of the physical scene with a major stress and pause, as "having no knowledge of anything in the world but fern, furze, heath, lichens, and moss." His movements over the heath, feeling, sensing through the dark, bring an intense regenerative contact with the physical world that is a source of strength in misery, even though conscious man can never achieve complete harmony. Hardy's description of Clym working among the small heath creatures, with its details of colour and movement, its varying rhythms of natural activity, its acceptance of the sun's meaning as simple warmth and beauty for the earth's creatures, its delight in vitality, and its superbly simple climax, celebrates like his poetry an enlargement of the horizon within those limited areas where man can still find certainty.

> His daily life was of a curious microscopic sort, his whole world
> being limited to a circuit of a few feet from his person. His

familiars were creeping and winged things, and they seemed to enrol him in their band. Bees hummed around his ears with an intimate air, and tugged at the heath and furze-flowers at his side in such numbers as to weigh them down to the sod. The strange amber-coloured butterflies which Egdon produced, and which were never seen elsewhere, quivered in the breath of his lips, alighted upon his bowed back, and sported with the glittering point of his hook as he flourished it up and down. Tribes of emerald-green grasshoppers leaped over his feet, falling awkwardly on their backs, heads, or hips, like unskilful acrobats, as chance might rule; or engaged themselves in noisy flirtations under the fern-fronds with silent ones of homely hue. Huge flies, ignorant of larders and wirenetting, and quite in a savage state, buzzed about him without knowing that he was a man. In and out of the fern-dells snakes glided in their most brilliant blue and yellow guise, it being the season immediately following the shedding of their old skins, when their colours are brightest. Litters of young rabbits came out from their forms to sun themselves upon hillocks, the hot beams blazing through the delicate tissue of each thin-fleshed ear, and firing it to a blood-red transparency in which the veins could be seen. None of them feared him.

Clym has recently been demoted from protagonist, and Eustacia promoted, on the grounds that she has the heroic force which he lacks. But it is surely intentional that a character possessing the animal vitality of a more primitive era should make a greater sensuous impact than the new heroic type, "slighted and enduring," distinguished by contemplative rather than active heroism. The two characters are perfectly balanced in their vital opposition to carry the meaning of the story.

Eustacia's delineation as "Queen of Night" indicates her function as a reverse parallel to Clym. Her first and last appearance is on the barrow, house of the dead. She shares, while she suffers from, the heath's darkness, "Tartarean dignity," indifference, and slumbrous vitality. But her relation to Clym is not a simple opposition of darkness to light. It is also the antagonism of illumination at different stages of development.

The first sentence of chapter 7, book 1, where she is defined as Queen of Night, stresses the two qualities that associate her on one side with the heath and on the other with the Promethean Clym. "Eustacia Vye was the raw material of a divinity." Her animal nature, unreflecting and unpurposive ("she would let events fall out as they might sooner than wrestle to direct them") partakes of the blind chaos of the heath's raw material, which has not yet reached Promethean forethought. The many Classical and Romantic metaphors and the "geometric precision" of her perfect beauty define Eustacia as an anachronistic reincarnation of the Hellenic age whose "old-fashioned revelling in the general situation" is being replaced by the record of disillusive time (destroyer of beauty) that scars the other faces, of Clym and the heath. But the subterranean fire of divinity is there, chained to an ideal of fulfilment antagonistic to Clym's and out of tune with the haggard times.

Her poetic context in chapter 6 defines the sun she seeks for her soul. The cumulative evocation of the wind over the heath, that begins in distinguishing the special notes of the "infinitesimal vegetable causes" which harmonize to produce "the linguistic peculiarity of the heath," and rises to a philosophical contemplation of Infinity as it is made sensuously manifest in the sound of the combined multitudes of mummied heath-bells scoured by the wind, is a rich image that evokes simultaneously the timelessness of nonhuman time that diminishes human importance, against which Eustacia rebels, and the absolute loneliness that is the price of her god-like rejection of human compromise. Her challenge to the forces that render beauty ephemeral is "a blaze of love, and extinction, . . . better than a lantern glimmer . . . which should last long years," and a too thorough identification, suggested by hourglass and telescope, with the metaphysic of transience.

Eustacia's will to enjoy in the present moment is the universal thrust of life to grow out of the primal stage of blind, self-absorbed groping towards the sun to a state of being where light, form, and meaning are imposed on matter. But she is false to her humanity by acquiescing in the lower state, as Clym is false to his by wanting to jump the intermediate stage of evolution to reach the higher. Consequently her environment controls her as it controls the ear of corn in the ground. The two movements down from and up beyond the human norm meet in a god-like desire for absolute reality, which Hardy's poetic transformations of light into darkness define as a form of the death-wish.

Eustacia's dream (bk. 2, chap. 3) is the first of a series of related ritual enactments of her subconscious drive to self-destruction. A comparison with her mumming adventure (bk. 2, chaps. 5, 6), the Egdon gipsying (bk. 4, chap. 3) and her death (bk. 6, chaps. 7–9) reveals the fantastic action of the dream ironically transformed and realized in a complex love/death sequence. The shining knight with whom she dances and plunges into the water is transformed from her Paradisal Clym to the commonplace Wildeve. The visor that hides his face turns into the mummers' ribbons that hide hers, as their true natures are concealed by their projected roles. The ecstatic dance becomes a Dionysiac revel that replaces a "sense of social order" with the self-destructive sexual impulse. The expected consummation under the pool is revealed first as her ritual death at the hands of the Christian Knight in the mummers' play, and finally as the real embrace of death with Wildeve in the weir, for which her ideal knight is partly responsible. The woman who feels she is in Paradise becomes the woman who is excluded, with Clym, from the earthly Paradise inside the settle. The brilliant rainbow light modulates to the moonlight of the mumming and the gipsying, the familiar illusory moonlight existence of Eustacia's imagination, which stresses the fantastic, trance-like ritual aspect of movement and mask-like features. It resolves finally into the hellish red glow from Susan Nunsuch's cottage that reveals the "splendid woman" who arraigns the Prince of the World as a mere waxen image of pride and vanity, and reconciles Eustacia's death by water to the death by fire consuming her in effigy. The heath that is only dimly felt in the dream looms larger and blacker in the following scenes to block her desire for absolute heroic existence. The shining knight who falls into fragments as the dreamer's translation of "the cracking . . . of the window-shutter downstairs, which the maid-servant was opening to let in the day," foreshadows the disintegration of her ideal world in face of the obstructive reality of Clym's nature and the world's daylight triviality. Her death sets her in her only "artistically happy background," where her conflicting drives to darkness and sunlight are reconciled. "Pallor did not include all the quality of her complexion, which seemed more than whiteness; it was almost light."

Clym and Eustacia each have a partial truth that bears on the question of how to live. Mrs Yeobright provides another. Her conception of doing well is coloured by Egdon, which she neither loves nor hates, but tries to ignore in her desire to civilize the wilderness. She is one of T. S. Eliot's women of Canterbury, fearful of the "disturbance of the quiet seasons" and human order from the ultimate powers of the cosmos which Clym and Eustacia know as light and heat and darkness.

Mrs Yeobright is related poetically to the heath and to the elemental struggle of light and darkness by Hardy's visual presentation. When she steps forward into the light of the bonfire in book 1, chapter 3, "her face, encompassed by the blackness of the receding heath, showed whitely, and without half-lights, like a cameo." The profile etched distinctly on a dark ground, repeated in our first sight of Clym's face (bk. 2, chap. 6) and Eustacia's (bk. 1, chap. 6) suggests inflexible resistance to cosmic darkness.

Her journey across the heath to her death builds up a complex poetic image of her confrontation by the ultimate reality of the cosmos which civilization does not cope with. Its absurdity and hostility to human purpose are demonstrated in the action of the closed door. Poetically, they are embodied in the merciless sun and the parched obstructive earth she has to cross; major symbols of the elemental conflict between Clym and Eustacia which destroys her in its working out. Every image, every word, is selected for sound and sense to evoke a harsh waste land on fire with the blazing sun that "had branded the whole heath with his mark": the scorched and flagging plants, the air "like that of a kiln," the "incineration" of the quartz sand, the "metallic mirrors" of smooth-fleshed leaves, the moan of lightning-blasted trees. Echoes of Lear and his Fool on the stormy heath in Johnny Nunsuch's innocent questions and statements of fact and Mrs Yeobright's answers charged with experience of human misery, heighten the poetic emotion. But it is controlled by the changing perspective that measures Mrs Yeobright's human effort objectively against the lowly species of the heath "busy in all the fulness of life" and indifferent to her prostration.

> Independent worlds of ephemerons were passing their time in mad carousal, some in the air, some on the hot ground and vegetation, some in the tepid and stringy water of a nearly dried pool. All the shallower ponds had decreased to a vaporous mud amid which the maggoty shapes of innumerable obscure creatures could be indistinctly seen, heaving and wallowing with enjoyment.

Human isolation from primal harmony is complete. The "vaporous mud" and "maggoty shapes . . . heaving and wallowing" evoke a preconscious world in which human emotion and purpose are anachronisms. If these lowly creatures recall Eustacia's preconscious will to enjoy, the gleaming wet heron who flies towards the sun recalls the unworldly aspirations of Clym, equally antagonistic to Mrs Yeobright's desire for civilization. The ants who share with her the shepherd's-thyme where she lies dying, "where they toiled a never-ending and heavy-laden throng" in a miniature city street, define the futile bustle of her "doing well" in face of the sun, which "stood directly in her face, like some merciless incendiary, brand in hand, waiting to consume her."

Wildeve's relationship to Egdon and the Promethean light that rebels against it denotes a man who is not great enough to become a force of nature instead of a helpless instrument. Even his vices are petty; his little meannesses about Tamsin's allowance, his trumpery schemes of revenge. Our first sight of him through the window of the Quiet Woman is not of a sharp profile, but an indeterminate "vast shadow, in which could be dimly traced portions of a masculine contour." His tendency "to care for the remote, to dislike the near" recalls Eustacia's and Clym's dissatisfaction with human limitations. But Wildeve cannot initiate rebellion. He can only respond to Eustacia's fire, and be consumed in her flame, like the moth-signal he releases to her.

Tamsin Yeobright and Diggory Venn are grouped together to reflect the passive and active principle of acquiescence in the human condition that is Egdon. Tamsin, the gentle point of rest between the major antagonists, has no awkward ideas about doing well to thrust her out of her environment. Doing simply means marrying for Tamsin, and her firmness on this point helps to retrieve the error of the unfulfilled wedding that begins the novel. The sun-lighted ritual of braiding her hair on the wedding day stresses her adherence to the traditional ordering of birth, marriage, children, and death—one of the few ambitions that tally with the Egdon rate of progress. The images of light and music which introduce her (bk. 1, chap. 4) imply a relationship to the earth that has not yet become discordant. Benevolent sunshine is her natural form of light, but even on the night of storm and chaos which is a perfect complement to the chaos within Eustacia, Tamsin's sense of proportion and lack of that pride which demands a personal antagonist preserves her from harm.

> To her there were not, as to Eustacia, demons in the air, and malice in every bush and bough. The drops which lashed her face were not scorpions, but prosy rain; Egdon in the mass was no monster whatever, but impersonal open ground. Her fears of the place were rational, her dislikes of its worst moods reasonable.

Diggory Venn, acquiescing in human limitations while working at the same time, like Oak, with the grain of his environment, has a link with darkness and fire that is ambiguous. When action depends on intimate knowledge of the heath—when he uses the camouflage of turves to eavesdrop on the plans of Eustacia and Wildeve, or when his familiarity with Shadwater Weir enables him to devise a plan of rescue—his triumph is due to the light of human intelligence controlling events. But his sudden appearances and disappearances, his colour, his devil's luck in gambling, his tricksy pranks with their unpredictable outcome, invest him with the poetry of a supernatural folklore character; not so much a "Mephistophilian visitant" of the Christian era as a primitive fire daemon capable of good or evil. John Hagan points out ("A Note on the Significance of Diggory Venn," *Nineteenth Century Fiction* 17 [1961–62]) that his well-intentioned interventions solve immediate problems, but initiate unwittingly the long-range tragedy of cosmic cross-purposes: Eustacia's decision to abandon Wildeve for Clym, and the events connected with the closed door.

Hardy's extended description of the reddleman stresses the ambiguity in his character which mirrors the ambiguity of the cosmos. The domestic picture (bk. 1, chap. 8) of a peaceful red man smoking a red pipe and darning a red stocking, kindly binding Johnny's wounds with a red bandage, gives way in chapter 9 to an evocation of his shadow side. His link with the heath is stressed in the "blood-coloured figure" which is, like Egdon in storm, "a sublimation of all the horrid dreams" of the human race. "Blood-coloured," an alteration from the simple "red" of the manuscript, takes up the theme of guilt suggested in "the mark of Cain" simile which defines the effects of reddle, and amplified in the evocation of the reddleman as an isolated "Ishmaelitish" character (the same adjective describes both the heath and the reddleman) who had taken to the trade as a lifelong penance for criminal deeds. The imaginative details of a legendary inheritance of guilt superimposed on the good and well-balanced human character of Diggory Venn suggest, paradoxically, a harmony with what Egdon means through acceptance of isolation and the guilt inherent in existence. After Clym's agonized self-reproach at Eustacia's death, it is Venn who puts it into perspective.

> "But you can't charge yourself with crimes in that way," said Venn. "You may as well say that the parents be the cause of a murder by the child, for without the parents the child would never have been begot."

The heightened poetic tone of chapter 8, book 3, where Venn wins back the Yeobright guineas, defines his ambiguous relation to light and darkness in a brilliant sensuous correlative. The overpowering darkness of the heath at night is fitfully broken by various forms of light which illuminate the flat stone, reminiscent of the flatness of the heath, and human participation in a game of chance, which becomes an image of the human predicament. It is natural that Venn's familiarity with the heath should give him an advantage over the excitable Wildeve, who is disturbed by the humbler heath-dwellers. Wildeve's confused actions and Venn's calmness, chance and direction, range themselves with the antagonisms of darkness and light that motivate the novel. The visual presentation of Venn as a "red automaton" raises him to the plane of a supernatural agent of fate. But his human lack of knowledge that half the guineas were destined for Clym qualifies his control of the situation.

The ritual patterns in the scene intensify its effect as a glimpse of destiny working itself out on another plane. In the heightened poetic tension, Venn's ballad-like incantation of the incremental phrases of Wildeve's gambling stories as the money coils in in reverse direction; the night moths which circle the lantern twice; the heath-croppers who encircle the gamblers twice, "their heads being all towards the players, at whom they gazed intently"; the thirteen glowworms placed in a circle round the dice, take on the aspect of mechanical functions of fate controlled by the "red automaton." The moths attracted to the light and the death's-head moth which extinguishes the lantern to the accompaniment of "a mournful whining from the herons which were nesting lower down the vale," foreshadow in symbol and detail the deaths of Wildeve and Mrs Yeobright.

The transformation of a folklore character into a mundane dairy farmer with a bank balance in book 6 worries some critics. While Hardy's note to chapter 3 indicates that his "austere artistic code" did not originally plan such a transformation, Venn's change tallies with the laws that condition Egdon's rate of progress. The cycle of aeons as well as the cycle of seasons directs his evolution from a "nearly perished link between obsolete forms of life and those which generally prevail." It is part of the movement of the novel from primitive darkness to conscious understanding appropriate to the modern era.

The poetic development of the novel is completed by a return to the visual image of "a motionless figure standing on the top of the tumulus, just as Eustacia had stood on that lonely summit some two years and a half before." But the transformation of Eustacia into Clym has replaced the dark winter night with summer afternoon, isolation with relationship to man and the lower species, and the self-absorbed unconscious drives of nature with hope of redemption through man's consciousness of the roots from which he sprang. Clym's suffering has taught him that love of place or woman is not enough without understanding, and that in order to move forward on Egdon one must move back.

To know Egdon is to know the great forces that move the world. It is not isolated from the rest of space, and time. Vapours from other continents arrive upon the wind, and rare migrants as well as native species watch the alien movements of man in a setting that "seemed to belong to the ancient carboniferous period." Egdon contains all the elements of the world before the Fall, including a secluded Paradise and a serpent. All its Promethean characters are seeking a place where they will feel at home after the development of isolating consciousness. Their survival depends on their reassessment of the place where they are. Hardy's sensuous evocation of the heath and its effect on human fate makes its physical presence impossible to ignore.

At moments of crisis its "oppressive horizontality" gives Clym, and others, "a sense of bare equality with, and no superiority to, a single living thing under the sun." There is no special place in nature for man. But from the heath's dark negation springs that affirmation of its raw vitality and that yearning for the light which combine to enable conscious man, as part of the general Will, to

> Bend a digit the poise of forces,
> And a fair desire fulfil.
>                    ("He Wonders
>                    about Himself ")

IAN GREGOR

# *The Great Web:* The Woodlanders

No matter on what terms we leave *The Mayor of Casterbridge,* it is difficult not to feel a reasonableness in the claim that the novel has an epic quality about it. We may, in using that description, intend a variety of things—the authority with which Henchard dominates the reader's imagination, the scope and implications of his conflict with Farfrae, the compelling bleakness of his death—but whatever reason we offer, we would find it hard to dissent from the proposition that the novel makes a claim to deal with tragedy on the grand scale, and whether or not it succeeds in making good that claim, we are not puzzled as to why it should have been made. When, however, we find a similar claim being made by Hardy's next novel, *The Woodlanders,* then I think we must feel much less sure.

The claim is made early in the first chapter, when the narrator moves outside his tale and offers a description of its scope. It is to be a novel which is set in one of those "sequestered spots outside the gates of the world," but where, nevertheless, "dramas of a grandeur and unity truly Sophoclean are enacted in the real, by virtue of the concentrated passions and closely-knit interdependence of the lives therein." Even if we consent not to lean too hard upon the word "Sophoclean," "dramas of grandeur and unity" seems over-pitched for the novel which follows. Reference to Greek tragedy inevitably makes us think of a central figure grandly conceived with a theme to match, but in *The Woodlanders,* most strikingly of all Hardy's major novels, we find

From *The Great Web: The Form of Hardy's Major Fiction.* © 1974 by Ian Gregor. Faber & Faber, 1974.

such a figure quite absent. The mood of the novel seems elegiac, rather than heroic, and though we may be moved by its low-keyed pathos, we would seem far away from the mood which produced *Oedipus* and *Antigone*.

If I raise the matter in this way it is not in a pedantic spirit, trying to keep the record of literary lineage clear, but rather as a way of indicating a crucial difference between *The Mayor* and *The Woodlanders*. It is a difference which marks out a new phase in Hardy's development as a novelist, but it is a development which, at first sight, looks like a loss of power, and it is not hard to see how that loss might be described.

Starting from the absence of a central and dominating figure, an unsympathetic account of the novel would go on to argue that Hardy barely justifies such a dangerous dispersal of his interest. Grace and Melbury come through as static and idealised creations, Grace as frivolous and petty in her interests, Melbury as a well-meaning but naïvely snobbish father, Mrs. Charmond and Fitzpiers as the stereotypes of rakish and self-regarding outsiders who first destroy others only to go on and destroy themselves. It is only in Melbury's case, the account might continue, that we have any sense of a deeply felt personal conflict which makes us feel that the character is "alive"—alive to the author and to his readers. The setting of the novel, as both woodland and orchard, has an undeniable presence, but it is hardly a dramatic presence like Egdon or like Casterbridge, an inseparable part of the action of the novel; it is there as a mood, and it reminds us more that Hardy was a poet than that he was a novelist. Presumably, such an unsympathetic account would go on to indicate certain failures in plotting, such as the lightning exits and entrances of the "South Carolina gentleman of very passionate nature," and what might be thought of as the near-farce of Giles lying fatally ill outside his own hut for days on end for fear of offending Grace's sense of propriety. Of course, even such an account of the novel would not feel prevented from conceding a measurement of achievement, and this would almost certainly include, in addition to the rather ambiguous praise of "the setting," the striking reality that is given to work—as always in Hardy—and the impressive incarnation of that sense in the stoical figure of Marty South. But these, the critic would probably argue, are moments in a novel which, in terms of its total movement and structure, fails to convince, the more so if we have just finished reading *The Mayor,* which immediately preceded it.

If I begin my discussion of *The Woodlanders* by sketching in an unfavourable reaction to the novel, this is not because I see my own account in terms of a counter-case. Indeed in the assumptions which my putative account makes—that the characters should have a strongly defined inner life and a plot to articulate that life—the case is persuasive. What I want to argue is that if *The Woodlanders* strikes us as a better novel than my "sketch" suggests, this is because it is a different kind of novel to *The Mayor*, aiming at a different kind of unity, even if we freely concede it is not Sophoclean. It emerges from a significantly different set of interests, interests which have been in Hardy's mind for some years, but are now related to a shift in his views about the nature of fiction. To talk of Hardy "shifting his views" is always hazardous, because the expression of these views as they occur in the *Life* is invariably random, and the chronology dubious. But to say the least, we can indicate from the entries in the *Life* for the years 1885–87, during the time he was at work on *The Woodlanders,* an unusual degree of self-awareness about the relationship between fiction and reality, and this casts light on what he was attempting to do in that novel.

It would seem that the idea for a novel, at least resembling *The Wood-landers,* came to Hardy in the mid-1870s, and came to him presumably very much in the pastoral terms of *Under the Greenwood Tree.* For various rea-sons the project was shelved, or, more accurately, allowed to remain dormant in his mind. During the next ten years Hardy's attention was absorbed in writing two major novels, *The Return of the Native,* and *The Mayor of Casterbridge.* In the first of these, I have tried to show [elsewhere], he became concerned with self-estrangement, as it expressed itself in a dialectic between the impersonality and timelessness of the Heath and the individual history of the Yeobrights. In the second, *The Mayor of Casterbridge,* the perspective was significantly altered. A single character dominated the novel, a character who already belonged to history, and this released in the novel a dialectic, not between the timeless opposites of man and nature, but within a precise crisis in the history of southwest England in the 1840s. In that crisis Hardy found an archetypal dimension. When Hardy returned to *The Woodlanders* in the mid-1880s he had then behind him *The Return of the Native,* and *The Mayor,* and though the "issues" with which those novels deal exist more as tendencies, preoccupations, they are nevertheless distinctly present, and when they become operative within the simple pastoral framework of the early version of "my woodland novel," we get the distinctive character of *The Woodlanders* as we now know it. "Looking back"—that is a phrase which summons up the mood of the novel—and Hardy is encouraged to take that stance both from the point of view of the pastoral form itself, with its built-in distinction between the sophistication of the narrator and the simplicity of the material, and also from the point of view of his own de-velopment as a novelist, at work on a novel conceived at a much earlier stage in his career. Recollection, the remembrance of things past, a concern to render a consciousness increasingly susceptible to the tensions of the present, these elements give the peculiar colour to *The Woodlanders*. The role of "place" in *The Return of the Native,* of "character" in *The Mayor,* is now occupied by "time," and it is this which enables us to get rather different bearings on the novel from those suggested in my preliminary sketch. All Hardy's novels are concerned in one way or another with "time," but *The Woodlanders* is marked out from the others by the detachment of its narration, and in that detachment we find implied a dimension of time which is peculiar to that novel, enabling us to see the particular details I singled out earlier for unsympathetic attention, but to see them now at one remove.

On 17 November 1885 we find Hardy recording in his diary, "Have gone back to my original plot for *The Woodlanders* after all," and from then, until 4 February 1887, he is at work on the novel. To read through the entries in the *Life* for that period is to find a remarkable consistency in his remarks on art and reality; I begin with an entry which contains a less abstract reflection:

> *2 January 1886:* Cold weather brings out upon the faces of people the written marks of their habits, vices, passions, and memories, as warmth brings out on paper a writing in sympathetic ink.
>
> *3 January:* My art is to intensify the expression of things . . . so that the heart and inner meaning is made vividly visible.
>
> *4 March:* Novel-writing as an art cannot go backward. Having reached the analytic stage it must transcend it by going still further in the same direction.
>
> The human race to be shown as one great network or tissue which quivers in every part when one point is shaken, like a spider's web if touched.

In December he records with approval a visit to an Impressionist Exhibition in London. The diary continues:

> *January 1887:* I don't want to see landscapes, i.e., scenic paintings of them, because I don't want to see the original realities—as optical effects, that is. I want to see the deeper reality underlying the scenic, the expression of what are sometimes called abstract imaginings.
>
> The "simply natural" is interesting no longer. The much decried, mad, late-Turner rendering is now necessary to create my interest. The exact truth as to material fact ceases to be of

importance in art . . . when it does not bring anything to the object that coalesces with and translates the qualities that are already there,—half-hidden, it may be—and the two united are depicted as the All.

4 *February, 8.20 p.m.:* "Finished *The Woodlanders.* Thought I should feel glad, but I do not particularly,—though relieved." In after years he often said that in some respects *The Woodlanders* was his best novel.

"The deeper reality underlying the scenic" for the painter, "the transcending of the analytic" for the novelist, the language may be vague and awkward, but the drift is clear, the rendering of a consciousness which both observes the natural world and is itself an inescapable part of all that it contemplates. This going beyond the analytic is for Hardy a fresh awareness of the recording consciousness, a consciousness interlocked with the different levels of consciousness in nature itself. This is the kind of "grandeur and unity" he is now seeking. As J. Hillis Miller puts it, "The landscape, the past, language, art; facts old and new, men and women in their living together—these for [Hardy] form a complicated structure of interpenetrating realities, a dynamic field of tensions and interactions both spatial and temporal." This, of course, has always been present in his work, but what gives it special prominence in *The Woodlanders* is that it moves from being an implication of his fictional world constituting its subject. It is a movement initiated by a heightened sense of the narrator's presence, so that at the beginning of the tale, it is *his* consciousness we are taken into.

Dramatised as a rambler pursuing a deserted coach-road, "for old association's sake," the narrator ponders the distinction between the empty highway and the empty woodlands which border it:

> The physiognomy of a deserted highway expresses solitude to a degree that is not reached by mere dales or downs, and bespeaks a tomb-like stillness more emphatic than that of glades and pools. The contrast of what is with what might be, probably accounts for this. To step, for instance, at the place under notice, from the edge of the plantation into the adjoining thoroughfare, and pause amid its emptiness for a moment, was to exchange by the act of a single stride the simple absence of human companionship for an incubus of the forlorn.

That distinction between solitude and loneliness is one that is to play a considerable part in the novel. It is a distinction which turns on memory:

the wood lives because of "old associations," the highway only when it is being actively used, somewhere to go to, not merely come from. We can see that distinction at work both in the lives of the characters and in the narrator who reveals those lives. There is the community of Little Hintock sustained by memory and its routine of work, but it is a community which can no longer cohere; in the sense that it is vulnerable to forces beyond its control, it is devoured by its isolation. The narrator too, is able to weave his tale out of old association, summon up memory, but it is a tale which derives its pathos and power from the dissolution of those memories, the growing necessity of recognising a world elsewhere. At one point Marty and Giles are seen in terms which reveal a continuity of related perspectives; we see the characters in relation to each other, the narrator in relation to his characters, the reader in relation to the narrator. It is a moment which distils the mood of the novel and suggests why, in this novel, the individual character and the individual plot are there to serve a wider purpose:

> Hardly anything could be more isolated or more self-contained than the lives of these two walking here in the lonely hour before day, when grey shades, material and mental, are so very grey. And yet their lonely courses formed no detached design at all, but were part of the pattern in the great web of human doings then weaving in both hemispheres from the White Sea to Cape Horn.

"The great web," the phrase describes the manner and the matter of the novel which follows it, and initiates a pondered meditation on that barely veiled antithesis, "Hardly anything could be more isolated or more self-contained."

If this account of the mood and structure of *The Woodlanders* be allowed, then it will follow that such a mood and structure can only be apprehended obliquely, when indeed the whole pattern of human doings is complete. To sense the web, we have to forget it—at least for a time. We might, in fact, begin outside the novel altogether with that singularly graceless sentence with which Hardy opens his Preface:

> In the present novel, as in one or two others of this series which involve the question of matrimonial divergence, the immortal puzzle—given the man and woman, how to find a basis for their sexual relation—is left where it stood.

It is an odd sentence, odd in tone as well as substance, as if Hardy wished to draw attention to an issue which might escape the reader's notice and then felt absolved from pursuing it. Finding a basis for sexual relationships is more likely to bring twentieth-century writers to mind than Hardy's contemporaries, and indeed there is one major work of the twentieth century which does, I think, cast considerable light on Hardy's concerns in *The Woodlanders,* and that is Eliot's *The Waste Land.* Like that poem, Hardy's novel is concerned with sterility, a sterility which can be imaged in terms which are at once personal, communal, and located within nature itself; it is to preoccupy itself with calculatedly juxtaposing past and present; it creates a context in which incidents suggestive of mythic ritual can be accommodated with those of daily living; above all, it allows a voice to be heard from time to time of one who, like Tiresias, has foresuffered all.

There is in *The Woodlanders* the sterility of self-abnegation—an abnegation which can never be confined to the self but is common to the whole way of life. This finds its clearest expression in the characters of Marty and Giles. It is however a sterility of a very particular kind, and to get the sense of it, we can turn to that famous passage, celebrating their work in the woods:

> Marty South alone, of all the women in Hintock and the world, had approximated to Winterborne's level of intelligent intercourse with Nature. In that respect she had formed his true complement in the other sex, had lived as his counterpart, had subjoined her thoughts to his as a corollary.
>
> The casual glimpses which the ordinary population bestowed upon that wondrous world of sap and leaves called the Hintock woods had been with these two, Giles and Marty, a clear gaze. They had been possessed of its finer mysteries as of commonplace knowledge; had been able to read its hieroglyphs as ordinary writing.... They had planted together, and together they had felled; together they had, with the run of the years, mentally collected those remoter signs and symbols which seen in few were of runic obscurity, but all together made an alphabet.

The eloquence of the writing, the plangency of its rhythms, pays simple testimony to the value being accorded to such "intelligent intercourse" with nature. The adjective can be pondered, the sexual intimacy finding its complement in a rational acknowledgement, which appropriately seeks its expression in language. Marty and Giles find in their "reading" of Nature a bond which defies their own relationship, a relationship expressed in the rhythms of work that is shared: "They had planted together, and together they had felled." That sense of mutuality, so removed from the area of "personal relationships," is splendidly evoked and gives memorable extension to the significance of "work" for Hardy, so that it becomes not only, as in *The Mayor,* a process of learning, but a process of feeling too. But there is a price to be paid for such a feeling too exclusively pursued and Hardy does not hesitate in naming it:

> "He ought to have married *you,* Marty, and nobody else in the world!" said Grace with conviction. . . . Marty shook her head. "In all our outdoor days and years together ma'am," she replied, "the one thing he never spoke of to me was love; nor I to him."
>
> "Yet you and he could speak in a tongue that nobody else could know—not even my father, though he came nearest knowing— the tongue of the trees and fruits and flowers themselves."

"The tongue of the trees and fruits and flowers," Grace's sentimental translation of Nature's "alphabet," does not conceal Hardy's sharp point within it, that "intercourse" with Nature, however intelligent, is not to be equated with the intelligent intercourse of man with man, or man with woman, if such discourse is to include love. If there is shared feeling between Marty and Giles, it is a feeling which can blanket out the individuals, so that Marty becomes mute in the presence of someone she can only feel her superior, and Giles can become oblivious of her womanhood. The clarity of gaze they extend upon Nature is a blur when they gaze upon each other. Language deserts Marty when she tries to communicate with Giles, and gesture becomes her only expression.

Her most memorable gestures are her refusal of the barber's offer to cut her hair, and then, on finding Giles's interest lies elsewhere her acceptance of it. Like the woman in *The Waste Land*:

> Under the firelight, under the brush, her hair
> Spread out in fiery points
> Glowed into words, then would be savagely still.

The fierce assertion of her sexuality in Marty's refusal, "My hair's my own and I'm going to keep it," is followed by the ruthless self-mutilation, her plundering of her self-hood, as surely as Alec is to plunder Tess's. The hair lies "savagely still" "upon the pale scrubbed deal of the coffin-stool table . . . stretched like waving and ropy weeds." The gesture for Marty is to be a final one, so that after Giles's death, she looked "almost like a being who had rejected with indifference the attribute of sex." "The wondrous world of sap and leaves" which Marty and Giles share as their common element will not hide the private desert between them.

> "Why, Marty—whatever has happened to your head?" . . .

Her heart swelled, and she could not speak. At length she managed to groan, looking on the ground, "I've made myself ugly—and hateful—that's what I've done!"

"No, no," he answered. "You've only cut your hair—I see now."

"I see now," the irony quivers throughout the novel.

If despairing gesture is the only language that seems available for Marty as she seeks to communicate with Giles, so he, in his turn, is forced into such a gesture in his communications with Grace, and like Marty, he seeks an extinction in work. The first of these gestures is quite literal. Grace has come to tell Giles that her father feels that they should no longer marry and that she concurs in his decision. She finds Giles at work one misty day chopping down the branches of John South's tree:

> While she stood out of observation Giles seemed to recognize her meaning; with a sudden start he worked on, climbing higher into the sky, and cutting himself off more and more from all intercourse with the sublunary world.

Eventually, he disappears from view, and Grace calls out the news to him from below. At the top of the tree Giles sat "motionless and silent in that gloomy Niflheim or fogland which involved him, and she proceeded on her way." It is the companion portrait to Marty's contemplating Giles's grave. The self-enclosure is complete and the only communication between Grace and Giles is that of her disembodied voice coming out of the mist and the sound of his axe in reply. It is a poignant demonstration of the void between them.

It is a void which is not filled by the removal of Fitzpiers from Grace's life, even though there is a renewed sense of hope. The difference between Grace and Giles is not as Hardy sees it a simple matter which could have been overcome by a more generous interpretation of the divorce laws. What separates them is a difference of consciousness, that "magic web," which Walter Pater describes, "woven through and through us . . . penetrating us with a network, subtler than our subtlest nerves, yet bearing in it the central forces of the world." Theirs is the crisis of a community as much as the crisis of individuals. The mist that screens Giles from Grace is always present, as surely as the mist that screens Marty from Giles. He sees her as an ethereal being, an alien to Little Hintock, and her remoteness sustains his fascination. He feeds on her inaccessibility. For Grace, too, Giles has no human solidity;

he is seen either simply in terms of his work, or as a human distillation of nature, "autumn's brother."

It is considerations like these which lie behind that strange scene in the woods when Giles, already ill, sleeps outside his own cottage for several days rather than compromise Grace by sharing it. In the account of *The Wood-landers* which I sketched in at the beginning of this chapter, I referred to the scene as "near-farce," and if that was felt too hostile, we could alter the tone, but retain the point, by saying that it strains our credulity. And we can find even an acute and sympathetic critic like Irving Howe saying in some exasperation, "no one, neither man nor dog, should have to be that loyal."

It is not difficult to see why the scene should provoke these reactions, but I think it is important to see that the irritant is not really "the scene," but the handling of the scene. There is a precise technical failure here, in that the imaginative purpose is defeated by obdurate detail. We find a similar failure in one of Lawrence's scenes in *Lady Chatterley's Lover,* where Connie, about to go out into the woods for a rhapsodic nude encounter with Mellors, pauses to collect her rubber shoes. Like Lawrence, Hardy is in need of a greater stylisation at this point, the kind of effect he obtains so effortlessly in the scene of Marty's hair, which was "depicted with intensity and distinctness, while her face, shoulders, hands, and figure in general were a blurred mass." If Hardy had been able similarly to blur his later scene, we would see more closely that, in fact, the whole episode is an effective expression of the structure of feeling which he has established between Grace and Giles throughout the novel. It is a moral convention, not moral decorum, that Hardy is anxious to put to work in this scene, and a convention which by definition extends beyond the individuals involved. From Giles's point of view, such a convention is operative and mandatory, because what has separated Grace from him is a whole area of consciousness, which again and again has found expression in social behaviour, in manners; and if this is a frustration it is also a fascination. Grace lives most intensely for him "at a distance." From her point of view, it is convention which has enabled her to feel most sharply her differences from Little Hintock, and those "differences" have become a part of her being. More radically, with Giles in mind, they have enabled her to draw on his companionship without committing her as a lover, a relationship which instinctually she withdraws from, as his sharing of the hut would have disconcertingly revealed. Added to the proprieties of this is the fact of Giles's illness. This, too, cuts deeply back into the novel, being the result of his indifference to self now that he has lost his house and his girl. That Grace should never think of Giles's being "ill" is because she never considered him in such physical and individual terms. He is simply there as a fond presence, a wise counsellor, a family friend. Taken as a whole, the scene reveals the blankness that has always existed in the relationship between Giles and Grace—a blankness perpetuated, if not brought about, by social and economic pressures on his side, by psychological pressures on hers. If we feel that something has gone wrong with the scene, the fault lies not in the employment of the moral convention itself—a convention which indeed, as so often in Victorian fiction, enables the novelist a rich registration of elusive truths—but in the rigidity of its handling. The result is that complex shades of feeling are lost beneath a hard veneer of moral scruple, feelings, in particular, which are intimately related to the whole presentation of Grace, as I will try to show a little later in this [essay].

## II

If the words that come to us about Marty and Giles have a kindred feeling about them—control, self-effacement, denial, frustration, resignation—those which attach themselves to Mrs. Charmond and Fitzpiers have a similar kinship, though from a rival family. In both cases the characters share a common sense of isolation. The isolation which is present to Marty and Giles finds expression in their absorption in their work; the isolation of Mrs. Charmond and Fitzpiers is in their enclosure within their own fantasies. This receives its most extreme expression in Fitzpiers's analysis of "love" to Giles, for whom it is the mute worship of "the other."

> "People living insulated, as I do by the solitude of this place, get charged with emotive fluid like a Leyden jar with electric, for want of some conductor at hand to disperse it. Human love is a subjective thing . . . I am in love with something in my own head, and no thing-in-itself outside it at all."

The Proust of Little Hintock, Fitzpiers is doomed at the outset, doomed not because of his philandering—though clearly he would have felt at home with Troy and Wildeve—but because he is incapable of feeling the reality of any world outside himself, whether it is the woods or the people who live there. In common with Mrs. Charmond he sees that world as composed of discrete objects, existing for his own purposes, and where he puts down money for Grammer Oliver's brain, she puts it down for Marty's hair. Fitzpiers lives within his own Leyden jar, passively awaiting "a conductor" to activate him.

Fitzpiers's jar finds its complementary setting within the drawn curtains of Mrs. Charmond's drawing-room, where she sits at midday, with a large fire burning in the grate, "though it was not cold." They are obviously kindred spirits, but there are significant differences between them. In our first encounter with Mrs. Charmond we recognise a familiar Hardy character—the wealthy lady of mysterious origin who has surrendered to boredom in her search for life's purpose, "I think sometimes I was born to live and do nothing, nothing, nothing but float about, as we fancy we do sometimes in dreams." Idiom, tone, movement, all add up to a description of Mrs. Charmond as "theatrical" in a way in which Fitzpiers is not, or at the least, apparently not. Where she is indolent, he is restlessly energetic, bored where he is curious, arch where he is passionate. But with both of them we are aware of "a style," and in this sense Fitzpiers is as "theatrical" as Mrs. Charmond. Fitzpiers playing the part of the romantic seducer, Mrs. Charmond assuming the disdain of the lady of the manor, the roles are consciously adopted and they complement each other. There is, however, a desperation about the playing of these roles which suggests the fundamental instability of their inner selves. If they both communicate extravagantly, we feel this is because it is the only way they *can* communicate; they are the victims of a devouring restlessness, whether it takes the "analytic" form of Fitzpiers— "In the course of a year his mind was accustomed to pass in a grand solar sweep throughout the zodiac of the intellectual heaven"—or the emotional form of Mrs. Charmond,—"she was losing judgement and dignity . . . becoming an animated impulse only, a passion incarnate."

Despite her weakness and extravagance, Hardy has a sympathy for Mrs. Charmond which is not present in his treatment of Fitzpiers. Perhaps this is precisely because she feels so much more keenly, and is a natural victim in the way that Lucetta was a victim in *The Mayor of Casterbridge*. Men after all have much more scope in arranging their downfall. Mrs. Charmond feels for Melbury, in her interview with him, in a way quite alien to Fitzpiers, and when she bursts out, "O! why were we given hungry hearts and wild desires if we have to live in a world like this?" we sense the genuine pang, for all the theatrical bravura of its expression. *A Sentimental Journey* may indeed be the ideal book to accompany Mrs. Charmond on her European travels, but they are travels of keenly felt isolation.

Perhaps the relationship between the two is given its most complete expression in that moment when, following a bitter quarrel, they meet on the roadside, unaware that they are watched by Melbury. Melodrama, sexuality, indifference, fatality, all come together and reveal the opposite pole to Marty and Giles's "intelligent intercourse with nature":

They looked in each other's faces without uttering a word, an arch yet gloomy smile wreathing her lips. Fitzpiers clasped her hanging hand, and, while she still remained in the same listless attitude, looking volumes into his eyes, he stealthily unbuttoned her glove, and stripped her hand of it by rolling back the gauntlet over the fingers, so that it came off inside out. He then raised her hand to his mouth, she still reclining passively, watching him as she might have watched a fly upon her dress.

It is a passage symptomatic of a certain aspect of Hardy's prose style, awkward and cliché-ridden for much of its length, but giving none the less a quite startling sense of sexual feeling, none the less vivid for all Fitzpiers's stagey gestures and Mrs. Charmond's indifference. It is a striking passage in that the acuteness of feeling, which is almost palpably present, is not in the least compromised by "the acting" of the protagonists. Indeed, it only serves to enforce the sense of sexual feeling, so purely expressed that it does nothing to disturb the barren isolation of the people involved. This is a moment which italicises the nature of the relationship between Fitzpiers and Mrs. Charmond in the way that Marty cutting off her hair, Giles lying out in the rain, italicises theirs. All four relationships, so radically different in nature, have in common an acute sense of self-estrangement seeking expression in terms of "theatrical" gesture. The sterile abnegation of Marty and Giles, the sterile fulfilment of Fitzpiers and Mrs. Charmond—all four characters have complementary roles to play in the novel, so that if we think of them as isolated "characters," rather than as versions of consciousness taking their substance from a total design, they will offer little to arrest attention. With the two remaining characters, Grace and George Melbury, the situation is very different.

It is useful to approach a consideration of Melbury and Grace with other Hardy characters in mind. To consider Melbury first. We can think of him as an epilogue to Hardy's interest in Henchard, for like him, "he was of the sort called self-made." He has risen to prosperity, but he is haunted by a foolish act in his youth and feels that his own future, and that of his family, are bound up with honouring a vow. Unlike Henchard, Melbury has learnt the lesson Farfrae had to teach. He has learnt the nature of social change, the importance of adaptation, and that what was good enough for him is no longer good enough for his daughter. The conflict between Melbury's obligation to the past, in which Grace was promised to the son of his old friend, and his awareness of the future, for which he has sought to provide her with an education which takes her out of the world of Little Hintock, constitutes his dilemma. In Melbury, Henchard and Farfrae resume their debate, with Grace as an Elizabeth-Jane—a prize possession testifying to the work of her father, but also a human being with a destiny of her own.

The point of making these comparisons between Melbury and Henchard is not just that they show the persistence of that character in Hardy's imagination, but that in the difference between the two men we can sense the increasing movement in that imagination towards the embodiment of contemporary consciousness in terms of social institutions. In Clym, this consciousness of change took the form of abstract reflection, in Farfrae of economic awareness. But with Melbury such a consciousness is aware, however dimly, of multiple implications. He can say, in a way that Farfrae might have done, "learning is better than houses or lands," but it is also already clear to him that learning is the passport to freedom of movement within the class structure, and that a suitable marriage will guarantee it. In this respect, *The Woodlanders* takes us into a much more modern world than anything in the earlier novels. Melbury himself, of course, is only fitfully aware of the implication of his perceptions, and what gives the latter half of his tale its poignancy is that the "modern world" invades his life in ways that he could hardly have calculated. Fitzpiers deserts Grace and Melbury has to resort to simple, face-to-face encounters, whether it is appealing to Mrs. Charmond to release Fitzpiers, or going to London in the belief that he can facilitate the working of the new divorce laws. He sees the institutionalising of contemporary consciousness in terms of an educational system, but he sees the process simply as an individual ascent up the rungs of the social ladder. He fails to see that the process has altered the entire social structure. The individual becomes impotent. And so we find Melbury in retreat from that world back into himself, a self which has been severely fractured in a way that Henchard's never is:

> He had entirely lost faith in his own judgement. That judgement
> on which he had relied for so many years seemed recently, like a
> false companion unmasked, to have disclosed unexpected depths
> of hypocrisy and speciousness where all had seemed solidity.

The collapse of his judgement, which had arranged the world for him and made him declare that "learning is better than houses or lands," has now made even houses and land remote phenomena to him.

> Melbury sat with his hands resting on the familiar knobbed thorn
> walking-stick, whose growing he had seen before he enjoyed its
> use. The scene to him was not the material environment of his
> person, but a tragic vision that travelled with him like an enve-

lope. Through this vision the incidents of the moment but gleamed confusedly here and there, as an outer landscape through the high-coloured scenes of a stained window.

That strange interior numbness, "when we are frozen up within, and quite the phantom of ourselves," brings Melbury, in his turn, to that self-alienation which all the other characters, in their various ways, come to know. Unlike them, however, he is able to retreat back into the company of the woodlanders, and consign Grace, his pride and hope, to Fitzpiers, with the observation, "It's a forlorn hope for her; and God knows how it will end." If Melbury's retreat into the woods seems more of a total extinction than Henchard's return to the Heath, for all the self-laceration implied by the terms of his Will, this is not primarily because of a difference in their individual characters, but because the world in which Melbury has lived has a complexity about it which Henchard's never had, not just a complexity of institutions but a complexity of character shaped by those institutions, with which "the self-made man," the man of simple vows to the past and judgement about the future, is ill-equipped to deal.

The embodiment of that complexity for Melbury is not in Fitzpiers, but in his own daughter, Grace. Perhaps the importance of the role of no other character in Hardy's major fiction has been so underestimated as Grace's, and it is difficult not to feel that this proceeds from the reader's chagrin, in that he expects a heroine and gets somebody disconcertingly less. Failure to see her significance has been the result of irritation with her character. This is a pity, because she is by far the most important character in the novel.

In saying that, we are not making a claim that she is a more sympathetic character, and Hardy himself confessed that "he was provoked with her all along. If she would have done a really self-abandoned, impassioned thing . . . he could have made a fine tragic ending to the book, but she was too commonplace and straight-laced and he could not make her." Commonplace and straight-laced Grace may be, but the obduracy with which she resists her creator's wish to turn her into a tragic heroine is testimony to the solidity of her imaginative presence; she has made the terms on which she will conduct her life, and she will drive a hard bargain with her creator. Just how hard is suggested by the despairing aside made by the narrator when he is driven, in a way unusual in Hardy, to reflect on the problem of doing justice to his character:

> It would have been difficult to describe Grace Melbury with precision, either then or at any time. Nay, from the highest point of

view, to precisely describe a human being, the focus of a universe,
how impossible!

Her little snobberies, her docile submission to her father, her school-girl
"crush" on Fitzpiers, her relative indifference to his desertion of her, her coy
resumption of a relationship with Giles, her primly fierce adherence to moral
proprieties when he is dying, her indulgent grief over his death and the arch
and tentative resumption of her relationship with Fitzpiers—it is "a biography" which can with some justice be summed up in the hollow-turner's
words when he observes her renewed relationship with Fitzpiers, "the way
she queened it, and fenced, and kept that poor feller at a distance was enough
to freeze yer blood. I should never have supposed it of such a girl." It is not
necessary to think of Fitzpiers as a "poor feller" to feel a truth in this and
that the marriage of Dr. and Mrs. Fitzpiers, whatever else it might be, will
be a marriage of equals. If then I make a claim that the creation of Grace is
of striking significance in Hardy's development as a novelist, it is not based
on her intrinsic worth, but rather on the fact that she is a creation who has
released in him a new complexity of insight into aspects of the contemporary
consciousness.

To give my claim direction, I see the significance of Grace to lie in the
fact that she provides Hardy with an opportunity to do a first sketch for Sue
Bridehead. Sue, of course, is the full-length portrait, with every detail pondered and heightened; she is a genuinely intellectual woman whereas Grace
has little more than educational gentility; she is an epicure of emotions,
whereas Grace is only timid and vacillating; and in every way Sue is the
more interesting and profound creation. If I bring them together it is not to
suggest a comparable interest, but to show where the importance of Grace
lies: that she gives Hardy a new feeling for "modern nerves" in relation to
"primitive felings," which he is to explore so thoroughly in his last novel.
Grace is the point of growth in the novel, the difficult element, and perhaps
it was this, rather than any traits of character, that was really responsible
for Hardy's being "provoked with her all along."

Earlier I suggested the *The Woodlanders* might usefully be compared to
Eliot's *The Waste Land,* and in citing the poem I was thinking not only of
a pervasive theme like sterility and its multidimensional treatment, but of
the way in which the characters reveal themselves *characteristically,* rather
than as individual studies. In doing this, they help to make transparent the
interpenetrating realities between man and man, man and nature, man and
the cosmos, the great web, which make Hardy's world so distinctively his
own. But in the case of Grace, practically alone in the novel, this way of

regarding "character" applies less. Her peculiar timbre derives very much from the fact that she *is* an individual—however much she frustrates our sympathies—and, moreover, it is her curiously wrought individuality which constitutes her particular fate.

This becomes explicit at a moment when Melbury is reflecting on her desertion by Fitzpiers:

> Besides, this case was not, he argued, like ordinary cases. Leaving out the question of Grace being anything but an ordinary woman, her peculiar situation, as it were in mid-air between two storeys of society.

This is to put "her peculiar situation" abstractly. The dramatic effect of that situation we see in a very sympathetic passage, close in feeling to that moment in Sue's life when she takes refuge in Phillotson's cupboard:

> In the darkness of the apartment to which she flew nothing could have been seen during the next half hour; but from the corner a quick breathing was audible from this impressionable creature, who combined modern nerves and primitive feelings, and was doomed by such coexistence to be numbered among the distressed, and to take her scourging to their exquisite extremity.

That is the perspective from which Sue's story is to be written, and it is not difficult to see that it is in the sexual life that the drama between "nerves" and "primitive feelings" will find its most intense expression. The conflict between "man" and "nature" can take place here; it is no longer in need of an Egdon Heath. In his later novels Hardy finds a grammar of modern consciousness in the sexual life, and it is this rather than any concern for "candour" that makes that life of increasing concern to him. It was, of course, Lawrence who perceived this most clearly, and in the long study he wrote on Hardy he took this as the substance of his argument. . . .

Though Lawrence is preoccupied in that essay with Sue, he would have understood Grace well. He would have understood that nullity at the centre which makes it so difficult for her to respond either to Fitzpiers or to Giles. And this is a nullity written into her consciousness, a part of her situation as much of as her temperament. The fact that we have no sense of Grace being married to Fitzpiers is not due to any lack of candour on Hardy's part, or to deference to his reading public, but because the marriage has no existence in any real sense, an impression which is made plain when we see Grace's indifference to Fitzpiers's departure with Mrs. Charmond. At first sight, this may look like a repetition of that familiar fate which Hardy's women suffer immediately upon a certain kind of marriage—we recall Bath-sheba's "listlessness" with Troy, Eustacia's with Clym. But although Fitzpiers acts upon Grace "like a dream," the effect on Grace is of an intensely vital kind in a way that it isn't for either Eustacia or Bathsheba. Grace's "love" is "the quality of awe towards a superior being" and once that being is shown to be the slave of his own passion, then he ceases to exist for Grace, "She was but little excited, and her jealousy was languid even to death." This is something that could never have been said about Bathsheba and Eustacia, and certainly part of the reason is that they were not involved in the hazard of self-consciousness which living "between two storeys of so-ciety" has produced in Grace.

The effect of this is seen lightly, but firmly, in the part played in this novel by "manners," which Hardy, revealing an unusual element in his work, uses as an index marking the precarious sense that Grace has of her own identity. There occurs a moment when Giles, having resumed his relationship with Grace, arranges for her to have a meal in an unobtrusive inn at Sherton:

> She was in a mood of the greatest depression. On arriving and seeing what the tavern was like she had been taken by surprise; but having gone too far to retreat she had heroically entered and sat down on the well-scrubbed settle, opposite the narrow table with its knives and steel forks, tin pepper-boxes, blue salt-cellars, posters advertising the sale of bullocks against the wall.

What that scene releases in Grace is an acute awareness of herself, merely as an object among other objects, but an awareness also that sees in objects, "knives and steel forks," "tin pepper-boxes," "a style of living." She is no longer at ease with that style, and the effect is not so much the rejection of it, as the sense of self-diminution. Her instincts are at war with each other: "While craving to be a country girl again . . . her first attempt had been beaten by the unexpected vitality of that fastidiousness." Hardy has managed here a subtle registration of complex feelings which are inextricably personal and social, and managed it the more surely for leaving it quite free from authorial irony, giving unfeigned seriousness to the overall effect that her "education," together with her association with Fitzpiers, has had upon her.

"While craving to be a country girl again . . . ," that is the other side of the story, and Hardy takes the measure of that impulse exactly. It finds clearest expression in one of the most quoted paragraphs in the novel, a paragraph invariably quoted out of context, so that it is made an authorial description of Giles, rather than Grace's reflections on Giles at the crucial moment in her relationship with Fitzpiers. Grace has seen him riding away to Mrs. Charmond, when suddenly Giles appears on the scene:

> He looked and smelt like Autumn's very brother, his face being sunburnt to wheat-colour, his eyes blue as corn-flowers, his sleeves and leggings dyed with fruit-stains, his hands clammy with the sweet juice of apples, his hat sprinkled with pips, and every-where about him that atmosphere of cider which at its first return each season has such an indescribable fascination for those who have been born and bred among the orchards. Her heart rose from its late sadness like a released bough; her senses revelled in the sudden lapse back to Nature unadorned.

This idealised version of Giles emerges directly from Grace's abandonment by Fitzpiers, and the form it takes is to emphasise everything that Fitzpiers ignored. Hungry for sensuous experience, Grace finds in Giles a rich em-bodiment of her mood, and though she names her feeling as a seeking for Nature unadorned, it is very much Nature adorned by the person who gives her the stability and the caring she craves. The "sudden lapse back" reminds us that, even here, Grace is aware of her feelings being given leave, that she is in need of a version of pastoral, and Giles is there to provide it. It is a version which soon speaks to her in classical accents: "Honesty, goodness, manliness, tenderness, devotion, for her only existed in their purity now in the breasts of unvarnished men." No tree of Evil is allowed to grow in these orchards, and Little Hintock becomes, like that "outer landscape" of her father's, a high-coloured scene of "a stained window." When Grace, claiming a kinship with the woodlanders, observes that her blood is no better than theirs, Fitzpiers's reply becomes self-evidently true: "Ah, you—you are re-fined and educated into something quite different."

Grace lives to learn the truth of that remark, and her divided conscious-ness finally assumes a visible form. Like Fitzpiers, engrossed with "something in my own head," and like Mrs. Charmond in her curtained room, Grace too will anticipate the tones of that voice in *The Waste Land*:

> I have heard the key
> Turn in the door once and turn once only
> We think of the key, each in his prison
> Thinking of the key.

"Propriety," "the unexpected vitality of the fastidious," "primitive feelings," "modern nerves," all these elements come together when Grace accepts Giles's offer that she live alone in the hut.

Without so much as crossing the threshold himself he closed the door upon her, and turned the key in the lock. Tapping at the window he signified that she should open the casement, and when she had done this he handed in the key to her. "You are locked in," he said, "and your own mistress."

Unlike the closing of the door in *The Return of the Native* this is not the separation of one person from another; it is a separation *within* the self. "You are your own mistress," the phrase takes on increasing ironies, as her will becomes assailed by all that it has excluded and "the primitive feelings" take over and exact their toll:

No sooner had she retired to rest that night than the wind began to rise, and after a few prefatory blasts to be accompanied by rain. The wind grew more violent, as the storm went on it was difficult to believe that no opaque body, but only an invisible colourless thing, was trampling and climbing over the roof, making branches creak, springing out of the trees upon the chimney, popping its head into the flue, and shrieking and blaspheming at every corner of the walls. As in the grisly story, the assailant was a spectre which could be felt but not seen. She had never before been so struck with the devilry of a gusty night in a wood, because she had never been so entirely alone in spirit as she was now. She seemed almost to be apart from herself—a vacuous duplicate only. The recent self of physical animation and clear intentions was not there.

The outer landscape becomes inner, and Grace reaches that terrible dissociation of self which Bathsheba and Eustacia undergo; but whereas for them, the conflict can be objectified and contained, Grace is the prey of an assailant who could only be felt, not seen:

Taking no further interest in herself as a splendid woman, [Bathsheba] acquired the indifferent feelings of an outsider in contemplating her probable fate as a singular wretch.

Eustacia could now, like other people at such a stage, take a standing-point outside herself, observe herself as a disinterested spectator, and think what a sport for Heaven this woman Eustacia was.

For Grace no such standpoint is available, she is driven from within by forces she cannot name—so that she sees her consciousness seemingly separated out from her body, "a vacuous duplicate only." Her experience is an intimation of Hardy's next creation:

> Tess had spiritually ceased to recognize the body before him as hers—allowing it to drift, like a corpse upon the current, in a direction dissociated from its living will.

These passages serve to make plain not only Hardy's intense preoccupation with the divided self, but the way in which that preoccupation is increasingly apprehended as something rooted within the individual, and much less in "the probable fate," "the sport for Heaven."

If Grace "recovers," it is a recovery in which the division within her is allowed to shape her behaviour. She becomes increasingly like Mrs. Charmond, submissive, demanding, impulsive, calculating, learning to live by the adoption of roles. She assumes the first of these roles unwittingly, and out of an instinctual loyalty to Giles, when she declares to Fitzpiers that she has, in fact, been his lover. If it is a deception which eventually worries her, it also gives her pleasure, re-establishing her in the eyes of Fitzpiers, who feels "he had never known her dangerously full compass if she were capable of such a reprisal." The deception encourages him to resume his relationship, and Grace allows it to develop on terms and in a manner which Mrs. Charmond would have approved. What Melbury once called their "freemasonry of education" begins, ironically, to reveal itself in an unsuspected way. For Fitzpiers, the scenario Grace arranges for their second courtship has its fascination—the carefully arranged meetings, the strict intervals between, the decorous exchanges, punctuated at times by quotations from *Measure for Measure,* and *Julius Caesar*—we can see Fitzpiers earning his description, "a subtlist in emotions, he cultivated as under glasses strange and mournful pleasures that he would not willingly let die just at present." And appropriately, when the time is right, the courtship finds its conclusion in a fine *coup de théâtre.*

Timothy Tangs, jealous of his new wife's former liaison with Fitzpiers, and seeing the resumed relationship with Grace, resolves to punish him by setting a mantrap at the place where the couple are accustomed to meet. The plan goes awry and Grace gets trapped instead, or more accurately her dress does. Fitzpiers, hearing her scream, fears the worst. In their common relief, however, at finding one another unharmed, they declare their love and life together can begin again. It is melodramatic, and the whole point of the episode is that it should be seen to be so.

Tangs's gesture takes its place, with Marty's charcoal scrawl and Melbury's visit to his lawyer in London, as an ineffectual single action belonging to an older, simpler community which persists uncomfortably in a world where cause and effect have become increasingly difficult to locate. The mantrap, once a means of dispensing rough justice and enforcing the social and economic *status quo,* has now become "a cobwebbed object." The traps for sexual offenders lie within the interpretation of the law itself. There is a sense in which Fitzpiers and Grace are "made" for each other, and when the mantrap is thrown by Grace, and Fitzpiers takes her into his arms, "the cobwebbed object" reveals itself as a mantrap indeed.

This romantic reunion is played deliberately off-key, as it has been throughout their renewed relationship, though its resolution has been nicely taken out of the control of the two individuals involved. "A probable fate" has entered. Grace appears to Fitzpiers's startled gaze "lacking the portion of her dress which the gin retained," but "By their united efforts . . . it was then possible to extract the silk mouthful from the monster's bite, creased and pierced with small holes, but not torn. Fitzpiers assisted her to put it on again; and when her customary contours were thus restored they walked on together . . ." The restoration of Grace's "customary contours" suggests, lightly but effectively, the nature of her reunion with Fitzpiers. She has drawn on her "fastidiousness" and found in it a sustaining role, the "spectre which could be felt but not seen" has been put to rest. How far this process has gone with Grace is neatly—and sardonically—suggested in her exchange with Fitzpiers, when he proposes that they leave Little Hintock straightaway and spend the night at the Earl of Wessex Hotel:

> "But that newly done-up place—the Earl of Wessex!"
> "If you are so very particular about the publicity I will stay at a little quiet one."
> "O no—it is not that I am particular—but I haven't a brush or comb or anything!"

"Appearances" are not a matter now of reputation, but of a brush and comb. Giles's hut is forgotten, Grace prepares a face to meet the world and intends to enjoy it—at least for a while.

This conversation, and indeed the whole treatment of Grace's and Fitzpiers's renewed courtship is remarkably assured, in that Hardy manages a detachment sufficient to release the comedy, but not so distant that it becomes censorious. The result is that he is able to catch, in a way unusual for him, a subtle interplay of emotion, in protagonists for whom he feels little sympathy. That Hardy was very conscious of his attempt at *comédie noire* is suggested by Grace's remark on finding herself and Fitzpiers unscathed by the mantrap: "O, Edred, there has been an Eye watching over us

tonight, and we should be thankful indeed!" The measure of the pious plat-
itude is taken in the fact that Grace is right, there has indeed been an Eye
watching over them, one belonging, however, not to the President of the
Immortals, but to Timothy Tangs. It is the point, made now in terms of
bizarre comedy—which is being made elsewhere with increasing insistence
and elaboration—that if we are victims, then we are more likely to be the
victims of men than of the gods.

DENNIS TAYLOR

# The Patterns in Hardy's Poetry

"The seer," Hardy wrote in 1882, "should watch that pattern among general things which his idiosyncrasy moves him to observe." "If you had the pattern," Blackmur wrote in criticism of Hardy, "everything else followed right. Pattern was the matrix of experience. If you could show experience as pattern, you showed all that could be shown." In this famous indictment of Hardy in 1940, Blackmur attacked the "absolutist, doctrinaire . . . totalitarian, frame of mind" evident in Hardy's poetry. Hardy's patterns of idea and plot are not organic and innate but are super-imposed "rigid frames to limit experience." This indictment of Hardy extends, in Leavis and other critics, to his prefabricated verse forms and stilted phrasing. Hardy's poems are successful only in those exceptional cases where, because of his intense sincerity or grasp of the literary tradition, they escape the obsessive mechanisms of his sensibility.

I would like to propose an alternative explanation of Hardy's success. Does not Hardy deliberately dramatize how patterns of experience develop from within both the mind and the life and then inevitably grow rigid? This rigidity—the rigidity of old ideas, completed plots, achieved rhythms, ageing language—is the last stage in Hardy's drama of the organic life and death of forms. Blackmur admonishes Hardy that the poet ideally "reveals the pattern *in* the flesh, the trope or forward stress of life." But Hardy intimates the forward stress of life by showing how the patterns which we realize in our experience grow obsolescent and vulnerable to the jar of new and unseen

From *ELH* 42, no. 2 (1975). © 1975 by The Johns Hopkins University Press.

life. Thus Blackmur and Hardy arrive at a similar conclusion—the poet does reveal "the pattern *in* the flesh, the trope . . . of life." But with Hardy Blackmur stops short, not seeing the figure in his own critique: "Some of these obsessions—for they lost the pattern-character of ideas and became virtually the objects of sensibility rather than the skeleton of attention—have to do with love, time, memory, death and nature, and have to do mainly with the disloyalty, implacability, or mechanical fatality of these." The change of love through time into mere memory is recapitulated in the style of Hardy's lyric speakers: what begins as the skeleton of attention ends as the obsessive object of sensibility, an object now grown implacably brittle and obsolescent. By dramatizing this tragic process in the very structure of his lyrics, Hardy makes organic and "heuristic" his mechanical fatalities. His ultimate "sincerity," then, and his vital relationship to the literary tradition is fully consistent with these "rigid frames to limit experience."

Oddly and somewhat inconsistently, Blackmur ends his essay by acknowledging a mysterious virtue in Hardy which transforms the bulk of his poetry: "As Theodore Spencer has remarked . . . Hardy's personal rhythm is the central problem in his poetry. Once it has been struck out in the open, it is felt as ever present." I would suggest that a key element in this personal rhythm is Hardy's pervasive dramatization of what is Blackmur's central concern: the development of patterns of experience.

Indeed, in a very concrete sense the imagery of a pattern is a subtle signature which we find in many of Hardy's poems. Like Hopkins with his inscaped networks and pied patterns, Hardy often focuses his vision on an interlacing web of branching veins. A fateful complication in human life is revealed and the revelation is like the moon irradiating the intertwining of branches. This visual pattern is more than a cliché for the pattern of fate. It embodies what Hardy sees as the tragic relation of mind and reality. That relation begins as a patterned coalescence of mind and reality and ends in a shocking discord. The image of a pattern symbolizes both the way we realize our world and what happens to that realization: it is gradually articulated in somewhat unconscious ways, it obsolesces in ways we do not immediately see, and that obsolescence is belatedly exposed by changes in the larger contexts of reality. Richard Wilbur was perhaps thinking of Hardy when he wrote in "Years-End":

> These sudden ends of time must give us pause.
> We fray into the future, rarely wrought
> Save in the tapestries of afterthought.

Similarly Valéry, who published Hardy's last poem, wrote: "We were that

something, and we did not know it. We know *now,* but we are it no longer."
For Hardy the tapestries of afterthought are ultimately the shapes of our lives
which we most clearly come to know at their most obsolescent. Since our
minds and our lives cannot avoid taking on some shape and since these
shapes persist in their increasing unadaptability, we are destined for tragedy
in a world where "nothing is permanent but change." What we "think the
real to be," the pattern motivated by our "passions, prejudices, and ambitions," becomes subject to the "gradual closing in" of a new and changed
situation. An image of a pattern, then, is Hardy's figure for our fate since
our fate is to be caught in the network of past realizations. In the full tragic
and ironic sense, Hardy's patterns represent what Blackmur calls "the skeleton of attention."

This abstract figure of a pattern underlies many concrete activities in
Hardy's world from the smallest to the most embracing. A man meditates
within a natural setting, the meditation expands away from the setting, and
suddenly the meditation is interrupted by a change in the natural setting
which exposes the obsolescence of the meditative pattern. On a larger scale,
a man has a romantic vision of a "well-beloved," the vision remains with
him throughout his life and indeed grows in intensity until the beloved
woman dies and reveals the tragic obsolescence of the dream pattern. On a
yet larger scale, a man's life develops a fund of experience and a set of
assumptions, in short, a patterned character, which grows eventually old-
fashioned until it is overwhelmed by the secret changes of the man's ageing
body. Again, an hereditary pattern is articulated in many individuals over
the years until that pattern goes to seed and becomes a stale and rigid "counterfeit" in its last exhausted member. And behind all these activities is Hardy's sense of the human species whose nervous, emotional, and intellectual
systems have over-evolved and become painfully vulnerable to life's ingrained
conditions.

All of these activities are patterning activities and each is governed by
a similar law. A fascinating topic—one too large to explore in detail here—
is the way Hardy was influenced by: a) the traditional model of a world as
a web seen or woven by the mind; b) the imagination's webs and patterns
in Shelley and Keats; c) the epistemological and personal webs of experience
imaged by George Eliot in *Middlemarch*; d) Tennyson's use of cosmic webs
and the webs of art; e) the veining networks of the immanent Will in Schopenhauer; f ) the scenic and sketchbook patterns of Ruskin; and g) the webs
of natural law in Darwin. Hardy brings together several of these aspects.
The pattern is in the world and in the mind; it is something seen, known,
or imagined; and it is that by which we see, know, or imagine; it originates

in ourselves and in the world of Will or nature working through ourselves; it is the conscious object of art and it is the unconscious instinct of the artist; it is beautiful and tragic. Perhaps the "pattern" image which most influenced Hardy was that of Herbert Spencer. According to Spencer, as every level of being or species or activity articulates itself from the whole mass of life, it grows more adaptable but eventually more obsolescent until dissolution overwhelms it. An "indefinite, incoherent homogeneity" evolves into a "definite, coherent heterogeneity" which eventually hardens and becomes brittle like a bony structure. Hardy said of Spencer: "Whether the theories are true or false, their effect upon the imagination is unquestionable."

Hardy's most common image for a belatedly revealed pattern is that of bare branches:

> The twigs of the birch imprint the December sky
>    Like branching veins upon a thin old hand;
> I think of summer-time, yes, of last July,
> When she was underneath them, greeting a gathered band
>    Of the urban and bland.
>
> Iced airs wheeze through the skeletoned hedge from the north
>    With steady snores, and a numbing that threatens snow,
> And skaters pass; and merry boys go forth
> To look for slides. But well, well do I know
>    Whither I would go!

The pattern of early romance—"When she was underneath" the birch trees—grew tragically clear as the romance died. Now Hardy and the scene have aged and become old records, old patterns of veins and branches. The shimmering veil of early romance has become a gaunt interlacing now patterning the old "summerhouse":

> The bushes that veiled it once have grown
>    Gaunt trees that interlace,
> Through whose lank limbs I see too clearly
>    The nakedness of the place.

The sterility of the physical pattern matches the vision which has now grown spectral:

> I am sure those branchways are brooding now,
> With a wistful blankness upon their face,
> While the few mute passengers notice how
> Spectre-beridden is the place.

Emma Hardy's life had "shut like a book" while Hardy had taken "light notice": now, "ten years since I saw her on the stairs," the tragic realization has grown in Hardy—its pattern, like the pattern of branches, "closing in" on Hardy and on what is now his own enthrallment by the past:

> And the trees are ten feet taller,
> And the sunny spaces smaller
> Whose bloomage would enthrall her.

Hardy looks back to the time of Emma's death when the tragic pattern first began to come clear and instinctively he places Emma in memory "At the end of the alley of bending boughs." These overhanging branches masked what now reveals itself "in darkening dankness": "The yawning blankness of the perspective." That perspective was secretly preparing itself as Hardy "saw morning harden upon the wall . . . unknowing / That your great going / Had place that moment, and altered all." Hardy now sees the pattern potentially present when he first saw Emma in Cornwall and "followed her on / By an alley bare boughs overspread." Here he explicitly defines the pattern of fate: "a Plan of the past . . . Was in working at last"; he did not "foreshadow what fortune might weave / From beginnings so small." "I was bound to obey." A little later they "caressed" "Under boughs of brushwood / Linking tree and tree / In a shade of lushwood" just as they would end: "Under bents that quiver / There shall rest we." When the romantic image ceases to correspond to the reality of their embittered marriage, Hardy adumbrates the tragic fixation of the two lovers with a familiar suggestion: "What now I see before me is a long lane overhung / With lovelessness, and stretching from the present to the grave." The beloved now lies "white, straight, features marble-keen" and so Hardy looks back to "That old romance" conducted when "the wide-faced moon looked through / The boughs at the faery lamps of the Larmer Avenue." In "A Wife Comes Back" a man indulges in "his life's one day of dreamery" and imagines that his estranged wife "freshed back" to the young beauty he once loved. He discovers the tragic obsolescence of this dream pattern when he searches for her "under the leafy pairs / Of the avenue elms" and finds only "an ancient dame . . . with features frozen and numb." At the house where his beloved lived and where the wind "blithely spoke . . . to the little sycamore tree," now "slow effacement / Is rife throughout, / While fiercely girds the wind at the long-limbed sycamore tree."

Hardy uses the branching pattern not only for the fate of a romantic vision but for the fate of his own conscious life, one whose patterns of awareness flourish until they become blind to the larger flux of things:

> I set every tree in my June time,
> And now they obscure the sky.
> And the children who ramble through here
>      Conceive that there never has been
> A time when no tall trees grew here,
>      That none will in time be seen.

So closely is the pattern of his love identified with the pattern of his own conscious life that Hardy gradually sees himself as a man who has become a "phantom": "so bare a bough / As Nature makes of me."

> Thus I; faltering forward,
> Leaves around me falling,
> Wind oozing thin through the thorn from norward,
> And the woman calling.

Hardy, bare-branched and thorn-like, strongly identifies with a tree in "The Tree and the Lady":

> I'm a skeleton now,
> And she's gone, craving warmth. The rime sticks like a skin to me;
> Through me Arcturus peers; Nor' lights shoot into me;
>      Gone is she, scorning my bough!

Hardy sees his mind as a network of memory grown quaint and brittle in the present:

> Do they know me, whose former mind
> Was like an open plain where no foot falls,
> But now is as a gallery portrait-lined,
>      And scored with necrologic scrawls,
> Where feeble voices rise, once full-defined,
>      From underground in curious calls?

He is one among "scathed and memoried men"; his heart is inscribed with "graving," with "quaint vermiculations." He is "Enchased and lettered as a tomb, / And scored with prints of perished hands, / And chronicled with dates of doom" like the "ancient lands" in which he lives. Since "life has bared its bones" to Hardy, he refuses to visit America where the tragic patterns have not yet ripened: their "riper times have yet to be" and they are still free of those tears "Which peoples old in tragedy / Have left upon the centuried years." In one of his most skillful poems about the meditative patterns, Hardy gazes at the patterned lines of his pedigree "Till the tangles troubled me." "The branches seemed to twist into a seared and cynic face" until Hardy feels "forestalled" by the hereditary past patterning his "every heave and coil and move": "I am merest mimicker and counterfeit!"

Hardy's sense for the rich complexity of human patterns gives depth to those cobweb images which we might too quickly pass over as clichés. A romance dies for reasons the speaker does not understand at the time of "the yellowing leaf; at moth and gnat / And cobweb-time." An ecstasy endures in a man now "cobwebbed, crazed." At a remembered "House of Hospitalities," "the mole now labours, / And spiders knit." "Where once we danced . . . The floors are sunken, cobwebs hang, / And cracks creep." The lines of the pattern become the cleaving lines of its dissolution. These images are more than conventional images of decay. They connote as a whole the subtle intertwining of nature and mind caught by a common spellbinding and deathbound motion. A woman cannot awake from the dream that her lover has died: "Yet stays this nightmare too appalling, / And like a web shakes me." The approach to death takes place "Through vaults of pain, / Enribbed and wrought with groins of ghastliness" where "garish spectres moved my brain"; pain is "blent / With webby waxing things and waning things." Our belated realization of pattern is caught in a beautiful image in "A Light Snow-Fall after Frost":

> The frost is on the wane,
> And cobwebs hanging close outside the pane
> Pose as festoons of thick white worsted there,
> Of their pale presence no eye being aware
> Till the rime made them plain.

For a while the window seemed clear; belatedly we realize that it is festooned with cobwebs. The rest of the poem suggests that, in a similar way, we belatedly realize the pattern of our waning age. Indeed, this belated realization is suggestively connected with the slighter time-lags in our physical perceptions of the way the snow, for example, whitens a road: "A watcher would have failed defining quite / When it transformed it so."

Once attuned, we can find different kinds of images for the dynamic motion of Hardy's mind-nature patterns: the "everlong motion / Of crisscrossing tides" encouraging the speaker to "brood" in "The Souls of the Slain"; the "target circles" of rain that "quivered and crossed" and "imprinted the step's wet shine" where the speaker lives out a determining episode in his life; ghosts who cast a spell over the speaker because they have "imprinted / Their dreams on" the walls of a house; men pursuing their spasmodic pleasures like larks singing in the "latticed hearse" of their cages.

One of the most suggestive examples is "The Ghost of the Past" where the speaker keeps a "spectral housekeeping" with "the Bygone there— / The Present once to me." As time passes and the Bygone continues to usurp the present, "its form began to fade" and now

> It looms a far-off skeleton
> And not a comrade nigh,
> A fitful far-off skeleton
> Dimming as days draw by.

Can one resist the intimate suggestion that as the past fades, Hardy fades, his own self dimming within the skeleton of what was his "present" reality, a "Bygone" pattern?

One of the paradoxes of Hardy's patterns is that they grow more clear as they grow more obsolescent; the outlines of the patterns grow sharper and simultaneously skeletal until the final definitive pattern is an epitaph of the experience in which it grew. Hardy's patterns seem to grow in on themselves, become indrawn, and emerge as engraved epitaphs on the mind or nature. "My full script," Hardy says, "is not confined / To that stone space, but stands deep lined / Upon that landscape." Hardy and his friends knew "not what lay behind" their early experience and now the friends are ghosts and Hardy is "brow-lined." On a later anniversary day, the old tree has become wind-cracked, a "multitude of white stones" has emerged on the garth, and the man's eyes are "so sunk that you saw the socket-bones." Such is the shock which strikes us at the end of "During Wind and Rain," stunning us with the last markings of once real people *and* with the obsolescent outline of those people carved in Hardy's brain: "Down their carved names the rain-drop ploughs." Hardy's poetry contains many skeletons and "tersely lined" tombstones which are suggestive in this manner. A comparable suggestiveness is present in the early "Neutral Tones"—and it could be said that Hardy's career consists in unveiling the implications of the pattern in "Neutral Tones." The sun "chidden of God," the pond and the "few leaves on the starving sod" is like a negative developed into the final print of the last stanza: the "God-curst sun" and the "pond edged with grayish leaves." As the pattern of tragic love grows belatedly clear, the edges of the landscape seem to become more deeply engraven in themselves and in the mind. Hardy often uses the word, "memoried," in the almost physical sense of "engraved." A woman grows "thin, thinner wrought" within an old "memoried spot." Hardy is bound to a "memoried place in "Concerning His Old Home." An old love stands "evermore" in his "memoried passion." The "House with a History" has a "memoried face." "Memoried" means much the same as "time-trenched" in "The Maid of Keinton Mandeville." Behind all of these figures, of course, stands the classic and Shakespearean image: "Time . . . delves the parallels in beauties brow." But Hardy uses the image to create a dramatic coalescence of inner and outer worlds.

Two other important characteristics of Hardy's dynamic patterns remain to be cited: their distinctive lighting and the distinctive shadows which they cast.

The moon has a venerable Romantic heritage since it is often associated with the half-light of imaginative vision. Hardy often makes traditional use of the moon. The speaker of "On Stinsford Hill at Midnight" sees a dream-like form of a lady "Sing-songing airly / Against the moon." "The Man Who Forgot" envisions a ghostly summer house "hidden where / You see the moonlight thrown." But in each case the moon is a muse "sans merci." The man who forgot realizes suddenly the forty year obsolescence of his vision: "My right mind woke, and I stood numb." The moon in actuality reveals only "bare ground." The moon makes the imagination expand and leads it into a stunned recognition of the loss of what is imagined. The lady in "Imaginings" lives out this irony: "in the moony night-time / She steals to stile and lea . . . And dreams of some blest bright-time / She knows can never be." The moon is therefore a compound symbol for both the shaping of imaginative vision and the circumstance which imprisons that vision. Indeed the moon can, consistently, represent that external fate which the expanding mind cannot see: "The broad bald moon edged up where the sea was wide. . . . That, behind, / My Fate's masked face crept near me I did not know!"

The dynamics of this symbolism redeems a poem like "The Telegram" which Blackmur finds typical of Hardy's obsessive use of a formula. The formula is the "crossed fidelity" of a bride and bridegroom, one mourning an old boyfriend, the other embittered by this faithlessness. First, it should be noted that the poem's obsessiveness is not Hardy's but the protagonists'. The poem is *about* the growth of a "formula," the bride's formula of sentimental nostalgia, the bridegroom's formula of self-pitying bitterness. The pattern of their visions creates the "long lane overhung / With lovelessness," and their visions obsess the present all the way to the grave. Secondly, the setting, which Blackmur admires but finds extraneous to the poem, provides Hardy's characteristic context for these tragic processes:

—The yachts ride mute at anchor and the fulling moon is fair,
And the giddy folk are strutting up and down the smooth parade,
And in her wild distraction she seems not to be aware
　　That she lives no more a maid.

These movements are blended. The moon is fulling, the folk are strutting, *and*—so the syntax suggests—her wild distraction (shadowed by the bridegroom's swelling resentment) grows. The moon symbolizes the "honeymoon" of the couple, its expanding "distraction." Yet the "fulling moon" is also external to the honeymoon and even opposed to it for the couple endures what is now a "waning honeymoon." Thus the moon represents a complex fulling of a pattern which is a human pattern within the larger pattern of reality, two patterns, one fulling and one waning, which will jar when consummation comes.

The moon is often associated with the branching patterns we have already discussed:

> And through the thin thorn hedge, by the rays of the moon,
> I can see the tree in the field, and beside it the mound—
> Now sheeted with snow—whereon we sat that June.

"I looked back as I left the house, / And . . . The moon upsidled through the boughs." "A bough outside is waving, / And that's its shade by the moon." In these cases, a betrayal of love that still traumatizes the speaker, a sundering of lovers in ways they did not realize at the time, the imprint of a ghostly vision on the living: all contribute to the fulling pattern. "A Hurried Meeting" is Hardy's most elaborate narrative example of this pattern symbolism. The poem, about a "haughty-hearted" unwed mother, describes an "August moonlight" setting where "elms . . . Outscreen the noon and eve," and where a mansion, "mute in its woodland wreathing," casts a "faint irradiation" on the slope. The woman slips "to the moonshade" and keeps brushing the "gossamer-web" off her "naked neck," but it keeps clinging to her as closely as her sad fate. At the end, "she emerged from shade to the moonlight ray." Thus the "sweet allure" of a "witching" love draws to its "heart-outeating" conclusion. Each of these poems focuses on the tragic process at different stages of its development and revelation. But all are linked by Hardy's feel for the tragic involvement of man and world, imaged in the moon-irradiated pattern. Indeed, Hardy saw his life in retrospect as dominated by the image. At the beginning of a life or a love or a vision and at their skeletal conclusions, the pattern presides in "At Moonrise and Onwards":

> —How many a year
> Have you kept pace with me,
> Wan Woman of the waste up there.
> Behind a hedge, or the bare
> Bough of a tree!

> No novelty are you,
> O Lady of all my time,
> Veering unbid into my view
> Whether I near Death's mew,
> Or Life's top cyme!

Since the moon is a "furtive feminine shape" and "reluctantly" reveals itself "nude of cloud," the moon's pattern is elusive, hidden, belatedly revealed. It leads the mind and heart into their expansions ("Life's top cyme") and then undermines those expansions, mewing them up in death. With such an image, Hardy can give a rich tragic weight to the slightest moments. An enthralled lover journeys home in "First Sight of Her and After": "the pattern grows / Of moonshades on the way."

In her 1926 review of *Human Shows,* Marianne Moore commented: "The sense of masonry with shadows on it, of Gothic ogives and mullions, enriches what would without it, perhaps, still be poetry, but how insistent are these imagined interiors and exteriors." Moore was probably thinking of the "mullioned windows" in "One Who Married above Him" and the "mullioned pane" in "At Shag's Heath" which preside at the conclusion of two tragic relationships. Most impressively, "In Sherborne Abbey" links the moon's irradiation with the "insistent" Gothic pattern:

> The moon has passed to the panes of the south-aisle wall,
> And brought the mullioned shades and shines to fall
> On the cheeks of a woman in a pew there. . . .
> Forms round them loom, recumbent like their own,
> Yet differing; for they are chiselled in frigid stone.

But the living and dead forms are not so different after all. The living forms which emerge out of the dark into the patterned moonlight will assume their engraved fate:

> a cloud comes over the moon:
> The print of the panes upon them enfeebles, as fallen in a swoon,
> Until they are left in darkness unbroke and profound,
> As likewise are left their chill and chiselled neighbours around.

Hardy had used such images much earlier. In "The Church-Builder" "The Church flings forth a battled shade / Over the moon-blanched sward" and the suicide will soon "cross the patterned floor" to perform his act. A woman returns to the obsolete scene of what was once her "culminant crest of life" and as she broods in the church, the "chancel" of the first stanza becomes

the "check-floored chancel" of the second and then the "fateful chancel"
and finally "this hoary chancel, / Where all's the same."

The irradiation of a pattern, the growth of a realization and a fate, is
associated by Hardy with an interesting kind of lighting effect. One thinks
of those *Gestalt* designs where the patterns fade in and out, the white and
dark patterns alternately dominating. In Hardy the moon enacts the emergence of the darker pattern out of the lighter one, just as the outlines we
never saw during the day we now see at night. Another analogy for Hardy's
lighting effect is that of looking through a negative placed against the light
and then looking at the negative placed opposite yourself and the light: the
in-depth figures of the first view with all their rich detail become the stark
flat chalky figures of the second view. Edmund Gosse said that in "Neutral
Tones" Hardy shows a characteristic habit of "taking poetical negatives of
small scenes," and I seem to sense in these negatives the eerie workings of
an inner and outer illumination: the illumination both waxes (we see it for
the first time) and wanes (what we see has the pale obsolescence of a skeleton
of a corpse). This waxing-waning effect can be easily explained: the image
we now see waxing clearly illumined is the image of the past which still binds
us within its shell or the image of a life now straightened and waning. Thus
a fated woman emerges "from shade to the moonlight ray." A missed opportunity becomes a man's fate as "The midnight whitened." In "The Har-
bour Bridge" the bridge's "lines of rope and spar / Trace themselves black
as char"; through them we see the "cut black-paper portraits" of people and
hear a couple impose on themselves a pattern of crossed fidelity—at which
point the poem concludes:

> They go different ways.
> And the west dims, and yellow lamplights shine:
> And soon above, like lamps more opaline,
> White stars ghost forth, that care not for men's wives,
>     Or any other lives.

In "The Wind's Prophecy" Hardy is about to exchange his girlfriend, Tryphena, for Emma. The light images either symbolize the old love pattern
coming to an end or the new love pattern beginning its fateful course. As
Hardy journeys to Cornwall, the gray lights of the cloudy day deepen into
the white spectral lights of the night:

> gulls glint out like silver flecks
> Against a cloud that speaks of wrecks. . . .
> A distant verge morosely gray

> Appears, while clots of flying foam
> Break from its muddy monochrome. . . .
> And every chasm and every steep
> Blackens as wakes each pharos-shine.

"The Revisitation" is a complex and beautiful medley of lighting, meditation, and a revisit to the past:

> With my faint eyes on the feeble square of wan-lit window frame,
> A quick conviction sprung within me, grew, and grew

—that he can relive a twenty-year-old scene of love. As he walks to the old trysting spot, "the spry white scuts of conies flashed before me" on "the open drouthy downland" and "the peewits, just as all those years back" revealed "their pale pinions like a fitful phosphorescence / Up against the cope of cloud."

> And so, living long and longer
> In a past that lived no more, my eyes discerned there, suddenly,
> That a figure broke the skyline.

It is indeed "Agnette" and, in the morning, the harsh "upedging sun" exposes the wanness of the vision, "that which like a spectre shook me." The pattern of obsolescence is all too visible in Agnette herself—"That which Time's transforming chisel / Had been tooling night and day." Agnette leaves and the narrator watches her form "smaller grow and smaller." In "A Cathedral Facade at Midnight," Hardy applies the waning and waxing light to an historical theme:

> The lunar look skimmed scantly toe, breast, arm
> Then edged on slowly slightly,
> To shoulder, hand, face; till each austere form
> Was blanched its whole length brightly
> Of prophet, king, queen, cardinal in state. . . .
> And the stiff images stood irradiate.

Irradiated, the obsolescence of the images is exposed—as though the moon had cooperated with "the sure, unhasting, steady stress / Of Reason's movement, making meaningless / The coded creeds of old-time godliness."

Finally, Hardy's patterns cast a distinctive kind of shade. The pattern ages so slowly and imperceptibly that the mind cannot follow the process. Yet when the pattern's final destiny is revealed, the process seems, to our minds, to occur with spectral speed. We realize that since the first unconscious inceptions of the pattern and its obsolescent conclusion reality has changed subtly, slowly, and in hidden ways; and now the tortoise of reality has suddenly overtaken and passed us. Thus the growth of a pattern in Hardy's poetry is often accompanied by a shadow which moves with an imperceptible slowness and then suddenly extends itself, its import fully revealed. "Shades far extend / Like lives soon to end." Death is "imminent" when "evening shades are stretching out." The sun throws "a shade to where / Time travelled at that minute. . . . Little saw we in it" but the shade extends in the direction of her who would soon die. Shadows attend a chapel-organist's suicidal impulse (the patterned "light" of the "lowering sun peering in at the window-pane" throws "shades from the boys of the chore / In the gallery, right upon me")—and at the end of the poem: "the sun lowers and goes; shades deepen; the lights are turned up." A woman sings the same early love song "when in afteryears / The shades stretched out, / And paths were faint." We have already cited the growing "pattern of moonshades" in "First Sight of Her and After." We seem to miss the intermediate stages of our fate-bound lives just as Hardy misses the summer in "Before and after Summer": in February he sees a radiant pattern in the "shafts of sleet . . . a half-transparent blind / Riddled by rays from sun behind." He hopes for summer only to find himself in winter again: "Shadows of the October pine / Reach into this room of mine." When did the "happy suns" of summer occur? "I, alas, perceived not when." "No prelude did I there perceive / To a drama at all, / Or foreshadow what fortune might weave / From beginnings so small." Hardy's most skillful example of his literal physical foreshadowing is probably "A Man Was Drawing near to Me":

> I'd no concern at anything,
> No sense of coming pull-heart play;
> Yet, under the silent outspreading
>     Of even's wing
>     Where Otterham lay,
> A man was riding up my way. . . .
> There was no light at all inland,
> Only the seaward pharos-fire,
> Nothing to let me understand. . . .
> There was a rumble at the door,
> A draught disturbed the drapery,
> And but a minute passed before,
>     With gaze that bore
>     My destiny,
> The man revealed himself to me.

The future destiny lurks in the "silent outspreading" and "pharos-fire"; it arrives slowly and suddenly springs. We might apply the suggestive remark which John Livingston Lowes made about Hardy's novels: "We move with Hardy at life's crucial moments through a taciturn, brooding, crepuscular world, in which dread things awaited come to pass, as if the waiting and the coming were, through some unconscious power that works through each, one thing."

Hardy's most suggestive synthesis of the elements we have traced—branching patterns, engraved imprints, spectral illuminations, subtle shades —is perhaps "Lying Awake," first published the year before Hardy died.

> You, Morningtide Star, now are steady-eyed, over the east,
>     I know it as if I saw you;
> You, Beeches, engrave on the sky your twigs, even the least;
>     Had I paper and pencil I'd draw you.
> You, Meadow, are white with your counterpane cover of dew,
>     I see it as if I were there;
> You, Churchyard, are lightening faint from the shade of the yew,
>     The names creeping out everywhere.

The last line is surprising because it suddenly shifts the perspective from the speaker, presumably musing from his bed ("I know it as if I saw you") to people underground ("The names creeping out everywhere"). Indeed, the emergence of the names seems, like the workings of the speaker's mind, almost a contemplative activity by these graves. The shift of perspective makes us wonder: to whom does "Lying Awake" refer? Are the living observer and the living dead after all, in some sense, the same? This eerie suggestion is supported by the change from the natural light of the star in the first stanza to the negative light cast by the shade of the yew in the last stanza. "Lying Awake" seems to be an activity, partly conscious, partly organic, which includes the "steady-eyed" stars, the beeches which actively seem to engrave the sky, the meadow slumbering under its own counterpane and the speaker whose meditation seems rooted in an obscure continuity with nature. The final "lightening faint" emergence of shadow-light is a fitting accompaniment to our shock at the life of these "names" and, more deeply, at the intimation of that obscure depth where human awareness and nature evolve organically into the consummate engravements of a white tombstone.

One of the specific ways of seeing Hardy's development as a poet is by tracing the way he evolved a deeper understanding of the pattern image.

Approximately sixty of the examples we have cited are from volumes of poetry Hardy published after the death of his wife in 1912—though a few of these may have been composed earlier. Only about six of our examples come from the earlier volumes of poetry. On a few occasions in his novels Hardy used the image to signify the external patterns of nature or fate which the detached narrator sees: "Each and all were alike in this one respect, that they followed a solitary trail like the inwoven threads which form a banner, and all were equally unconscious of the significant whole which they collectively showed forth" (*Desperate Remedies,* 1871); "their lonely courses formed no detached design at all, but were part of the pattern in the great web of human beings then weaving in both hemispheres" (*The Woodlanders,* 1887). By virtue of his convention of narrative omniscience, Hardy himself as artist is not involved in these webs. In the cosmological poems, many of which Hardy wrote toward the end of his novelist career and published in 1901, this natural pattern becomes the "world-webs" woven by the blind "World-weaver," the "coils" of "right enmeshed with wrong" which Mother Nature has "wrought unwittingly." But Mother Nature's prophet, Hardy the didactic poet, does not yet work unwittingly within these world webs. In *The Dynasts* (1904–8) Hardy greatly expands the image and throughout the epic shows "the human race . . . as one great network of tissue . . . like a spider's web." The Immanent Will is a cosmic artist who "works unconsciously, as heretofore, / Eternal artistries in Circumstance . . . patterns wrought by rapt aesthetic rote." The "sum" of the "fibrils, veins, / Will-tissues, nerves, and pulses of the Cause, / That heave throughout the Earth's compositure" is "like the lobule of a Brain / Evolving always what it wots not of" ("Fore Scene"). Again, however, Hardy who pares his fingernails behind the scene "wots" what he is up to with epic omniscience. Nevertheless he is more intrigued with the point of view of the onlooker. Looking at the planet earth, we see the Will's "brain-like network . . . interpenetrating, entangling, and thrusting hither and thither the human forms (1.6.3)." As our cinematographic view focuses more closely ("The point of view then sinks downwards through space"), the cosmic pattern gives way to concrete scenes of "the peoples, distressed by events which they did not cause . . . writhing, crawling, heaving, and vibrating in their various cities" ("Fore Scene"). Beholding these scenes we forget the pattern which becomes evident again only when our lens "zooms" away. It is fascinating to see Hardy then translate this pattern motion into the private world of his lyrics. So far, in the novels, the cosmological poems, and *The Dynasts,* Hardy has been the detached narrator or poet pointing to patterns in the outside world. In the poems which follow *The Dynasts*—especially in the poems which Hardy wrote after his wife's death when he realized the tragic pattern of his own married life—he internalizes the image of a pattern. The paradox of the Immanent Will, evolving what it wots not of, becomes the paradox of Hardy's own awareness caught within the patterns of its own making. The patterned motions which the epic poet of *The Dynasts* saw at work in the world, the lyric poet now sees at work in the observing eye and mind themselves.

In 1911 Hardy composed "The Abbey Mason" about the founder of the perpendicular style of Gothic architecture. Ezra Pound called the poem Hardy's personal "aesthetic." The abbey mason's "diagram-lines" are completed by the rain: "He closelier looked; then looked again; / The chalk-scratched draught-board faced the rain, / Whose icicled drops deformed the lines / Innumerous of his lame designs, / So that they streamed in small white threads / From the upper segments to the heads / Of arcs below, uniting them / Each by a stalactitic stem." Thus, waiting "upon Nature for his cue," he achieved a new style with its "Petrified lacework—lightly lined / On ancient massiveness behind." A few months after he wrote "The Abbey Mason," Hardy wrote "The Convergence of the Twain": the Immanent Will has welded together the "paths coincident" of the iceberg and the Titanic which now "Cold currents thrid, and turn to rhythmic tidal lyres." Does Hardy yet see the connection between the aesthetic patterns of "The Abbey Mason" and the patterns of fate in "The Convergence of the Twain"? After 1912 he discovers the connection and dramatizes the "intimate welding" of aesthetic pattern and world pattern. And this common pattern begins to be felt very clearly not only in images of moon and branch but in patterns of meditative structure, patterns of language, and patterns of rhythm.

In spite of their complexity, might it still be said that Hardy's concern with tragic patterns is obsessive and restrictive? For myself, I experience exhilaration in following these patterns, partly because of their beauty and economy, partly because of the intimations of a larger life outside any one pattern of experience. Hardy makes us aware of the obsolescing patterns of our own consciousness. There is a final irony in this poetic gift, like that which Hardy saw in the case of the abbey mason: "dank death had wormed / The brain wherein the style had grown" but the abbey mason's new art "starred the land . . . Till every edifice in the isle / Was patterned to no other style."

JAN B. GORDON

# Origins, History, and the Reconstitution of Family: Tess's Journey

*Tess of the D'Urbervilles* commences as if it were an extension of the dialogue that abruptly concluded Wordsworth's *The Excursion*. But instead of the broken metaphysical conversation between the Solitary and the Wanderer, those two personages who stalk the romantic landscape, the reader overhears an exchange between the tipsy Jack Durbeyfield and the village parson. The elder Durbeyfield is told that, contrary to the sense of discontinuity that he now experiences, partially as an aftermath to the evening's mead and partially as a function of his family's poverty, he is the missing link of a once noble familial chain that is now in its decadence. Parson Tringham is the first of many people in the novel who associate theology with the claims of the past, for he is an amateur historian who has supposedly discovered the origin of Durbeyfield ancestry in the vaults of the village church. Ironically, he uses "buried" knowledge to, in effect, inform poor Jack Durbeyfield that, at least in terms of lineage, he is temporarily "buried."

Hardy's novel, then, begins with an absence of continuity, some blank page in family chronology. And it is the need to fill that void that spurs Durbeyfield to dispatch his daughter, Tess, to reclaim kinship with the distant cousin, Alec d'Urberville. The reconstitution of the family is the sole method by which man might live his history. And Tess's sad journey in this novel is always directed towards community disguised as history or tradition; she moves from the relative isolation of the rural (Durbeyfield) to the ano-

From *ELH* 43, no. 3 (1976). © 1976 by The Johns Hopkins University Press.

nymity of the urban (d'Urber-ville) even in her assumption of the new name. But if her pilgrimage begins with a quest for family history and a desire to transform the decadence of discontinuity into historical continuity, it sadly concludes with the oppression of Tess at the hands of her own past. Although numerous commentators upon Tess's plight have cited her own sexual repression or intensive socialization as the basis for her fall from innocence, a confusion about the relationship between origins, history, and community may be at the heart of all her choices. She discovers that the ties of history are largely fictional constructions made by men to explain their behavior rather than those invisible links that yoke present to past.

Perhaps this accounts for the remarkable variation upon a Victorian theme that is represented in Tess's tearful departure from the Durbeyfield household in order to claim kinship. If the great age of nineteenth century fiction is characterized by the figure of the orphan who is adopted by surrogate parents—the Heathcliffs, Pips, and Dorotheas who exhibit the "ontological displacement" which J. Hillis Miller has observed—it may well end with alternatives like that of Tess who at least partially wills her own discontinuity from an immediate family in order to reconstitute a different one. The orphan itself is a remarkable emblem for an age that spent so much of its intellectual energy looking for an *Origin of the Species,* a Key to All Mythologies, or an *Oxford English Dictionary* and then establishing some lineage of descent. Surely, there is a psychopathology of disconnection that relates Darwin's quest for origins and succession to Newman's interest in the "true" apostolic succession, to all of those deathbed scenes in Victorian fiction where wills are opened and the fiction of familial succession is established or maintained. Like so many of her forebears then, Tess seeks a regression of her family's origins. What is important in this journey to "beginnings" is the manner in which the search for history-as-continuity is related to the reconstitution of the family.

There is evidence that Tess alone can accomplish the "d'Urberville connection" because, unlike those earlier orphans of Victorian fiction, she is a transitional figure. Although she exhibits some modern sensibilities, Tess remains a child of the anachronism that is Wessex. She combines the past and the present even in her language:

> Mrs. Durbeyfield habitually spoke the dialect; her daughter who had passed the Sixth Standard in the National School under a London-trained mistress, spoke two languages; the dialect at home, more or less: ordinary English abroad and to persons of quality.
>
> (chap. 3)

Tess, by generation as well as by sensibility, is a transitional figure, which makes her highly adaptable and hence adoptable for her role as a missing historical link. She interiorizes the traits that are separately exhibited by the participants of the dialogue with which the novel commences, uniting her father's attachment to sensual indulgence with Parson Tringham's fascination for the names and places of the past. She alternates between her father's loss of a sense of time (he is habitually tardy in returning from Rolliver's Inn) and the Parson's conviction that history alone is the component of community. Like her father, she is lulled into the stupor of forgetfulness during the night ride when Prince, the horse, is killed. But like the Parson, she wants to be a believer in history and ancestry, only to be betrayed by the fiction of a continuous history upon arriving at Trantridge:

> This embodiment of a d'Urberville and a namesake differed even more from what Tess had expected than the house and grounds had differed. She had dreamed of an aged and dignified face, the sublimation of all the d'Urberville lineaments, furrowed with incarnate memories representing in hieroglyphic the century of her family's and England's history. But she screwed herself up to the work at hand, since she could not get out of it.
>
> (chap. 5)

This alternation between historical attachment and emotional betrayal is, writ large, the theme of *Tess of the D'Urbervilles*. As the natural world endlessly pursues its seasonal rhythms in Hardy's novel, so the narrator follows Tess's career in the vocabulary of "Phases" and the characters are immersed in an oscillation involving cycles of departures and return: from Marlott, Trantridge, and even Talbothays Dairy.

Such is part of the dialectic of transition. Tess's status as an intersection between two modes of existence is not too different from the inns and taverns which are on the verge of being absorbed by larger chains of breweries. Like the institutions which are a part of her "world," Tess exists somewhere between independence and the dependence that will make her part of a larger, more successful "family." Little wonder that an exteriorization of this split in Tess's being is represented, respectively, in the two men of her life: the sensual, satanically red-haired Alec d'Urberville who is interested not at all in the past when we first met him; and the pious Angel Clare for whom the past means virtually everything. It is precisely in their relationship to history that the two men shape Tess's own vision of the relative importance of personal and communal history. For Tess, an unwanted pregnancy means that she has a "past," but in the context of her father's wishes, she has ironically fulfilled her destined role as the link that unites *family* and *history*. For old Jack Durbeyfield they are clearly one and the same; he desires to overcome the threat of historical absence by grafting his own decadence onto a stronger family tree and thereby synchronizing historical continuity and family growth. Although the critical emphasis has fallen heavily upon interpreting Tess's obsession with her past sins as a legacy of the Victorian feminine psyche, it is just as true that she *acquires* her father's conviction that the destinies of family and history are intertwined—and then acts on it.

Her pilgrimage is nothing less than the attempt to undo the fiction that she has learned by killing off her past, both literally and figuratively. Having learned from her confession that the revelation of one's private history is not effective in wiping clean the slate of public history, Tess must kill the one being who symbolizes the fruitless attempt to reclaim the past, Alec d'Urberville. But Alec is also part of the two sides of Tess's being, and his death, as we shall see, results in the strange deterioration of her own physical condition; it is almost as if theirs was a murder-suicide pact. If the wedding night confession associates Tess with her saintly namesake, Teresa, her murder of Alec d'Urberville suggests that the other side of denial is the violence of criminal action. Martyrdom and impulsive action; confession and murder; the lost memory of events versus the almost omniscient presence of the past— all are part of the hopeless division that is *Tess of the D'Urbervilles*. But that division in human sensibility is first suggested in the opening confrontation between Historical Man and the Ahistorical Tippler who allows himself to be seduced by the myth of origins.

Tess's initial visit back to what she assumes to be her past is one of those Victorian "arrangements," perhaps fully understood only by a generation whose Queen occasionally married off her offspring to a first cousin in order to establish an Imperial Family. Although such is not technically incest, there is the suggestion that the intended union of Alec d'Urberville with Tess skirts taboo in "Sir" John's farewell address to his daughter:

> "Good-bye, me maid," said Sir John, rising his head from his breast as he suspended his nap, induced by a slight excess this morning in honour of the occasion. "Well, I hope my young friend will like such a comely sample of his own blood. And tell'n Tess, that being sunk, quite, from our former grandeur, I'll sell him the titles—yes, sell it—and at no onreasonable figure."
>
> (chap. 7)

Claude Lévi-Strauss has developed an elaborate explanation for the almost universal taboo against incest in primitive societies by noting the fear of what he calls "an absence of difference." The horizontal union of members of the same "family" (tribe) serves to overcome the sense of difference between members by creating a crisis of identity that either produces violence or initiates the sacred. It always involves a transformation of history, represented for the French anthropologist in the movement from diachronic to synchronic. The union of two members of the same family dissolves their separate identities (necessary to preserve order) and does away with the sense of difference. In its violation of exogamy, incest resembles "Indian giving," that which should be shared with the other in marriage is kept for the self. The narcissism involved in incest is hence an interesting paradigm for all the failed connections in the novel. The taboo gives a negative definition to the forbidden object, inspiring religio-erotic awe. Facing ontological discontinuity, the gap or absence in time which separates the Durbeyfields from the myth of their origins, Tess overcomes the threat of extinction by claiming the kinship that obliterates the sense of difference. In the process, however, she loses her own sense of a distinctive, definable "self"; whereas she had formerly been the link between present and past, she now assumes a diaphanous pose. Unable to regard Alec as either relative or lover, Tess is imprisoned by indecision. At Alec's request to treat her as a lover

> She drew a quick pettish breath of objection, writhing uneasily on her seat, looked far ahead, and murmured, "I don't know—I wish—how can I say yes or no when—"
>
> (chap. 11)

Tess becomes, in a sense, pure vehicularity; in the attempt to overcome the threat of ontological discontinuity, she loses her own will and becomes purely an agent. Increasingly, Hardy's descriptions of Tess's "world" are punctuated by an emphasis upon absence: the hollow red mouth; the heavy baggage of departure which nonetheless seems "without burden"; and the ensuing loss of personality as she senses herself absorbed by a hostile landscape.

What had been combined in Tess the transitional figure is tragically separated following her liaison with Alec. Surely, there is a relationship between the sense of historical disconnection which it is Tess's mission to bridge and her own sense of personal displacement:

> An immeasurable social chasm was to divide our heroine's personality thereafter from that previous self of hers who stepped from her mother's door to try her fortune at Trantridge poultry-farm.
>
> (chap. 11)

Just as her family comes to believe in the fiction that they really possess two names—Durbeyfield and the more noble d'Urberville—so the heroine of Hardy's novel becomes aware of the existence of two Tesses, one preceding and one following her relationship with Alec. Hardy would seem to be implying that the fixation upon any myth of origins results in a schizoid sensibility, and that there is a direct relationship between a "crisis" of history and the threat to personal authenticity. Her seduction occurs not only as the result of equating history with community, but physically takes place in a stretch of forest known as The Chase, "the oldest wood in England" (chap. 11). Tess's continual burden in Hardy's novel is to retrace those events which lead to her social deterioration in just the same way that her father had wished to restore the family to its rightful place in history. Such a dynamic is clearly regressive, even as it moves toward the goal of *restoration*, be it of Tess's purity or the bogus purity of an unadulterated family name. Tess comes to wish that she had never been born and dreams of tombs and burial sites, an archaeology similar to that exhibited by those vaults wherein the d'Urberville family records were uncovered by Parson Tringham. Little wonder that in her wanderings up and down the roads of Wessex with baggage and cart, she comes to resemble her peripatetic father's more sinuous pilgrimages. Once convinced of the necessity of pursuing a fictional history, Tess of the d'Urbervilles comes to live her past both as a metaphor and in fact. And to be one's past is to have a curious relationship with both the natural and the personal worlds.

The displacement of self is initially accompanied by a loss of *prospect*, and the two events are associated as collateral systems:

> Verily another girl than the simple one she had been at home was
> she now, bowed by thought, stood still here, and turned to look
> behind her. She could not bear to look forward into the Vale.
>
> (chap. 12)

Although this backwards glance is an understandable concomitant of shame, it also carries with it the implicit assumption that Tess is an object of pursuit. It is a way of placing herself at the center of the gaze of the "other," even while trying to flee, as if one could be simultaneously both subject and object of her existential space. At its heart such a desire is clearly part of the attempt to recapture the lost self by imagining it to be the sole object of interest in a particular community. Even as she wanders about the landscape, unable to look ahead into the future, Tess becomes further victimized because her private path inevitably intersects the public language, gossip. Both are equally circuitous:

> The event of Tess Durbeyfield's return from the manor of her
> bogus kinsfolk was rumored abroad, if rumor be not too large a
> word for a space of a square mile.
>
> (chap. 13)

Gossip is one of the ways in which Tess continues to be shaped by history,
for it is the language of the past, alternately exaggerated and then condensed
at the whim of the speaker. It provides yet another excuse for community in
the world where there is little, and is part of the public conspiracy to invade
private spaces. Gossip is the pretense to recover originality even as it adds
layer upon layer to interpretation and moves the hearer ever farther from
genuine origins. And it tends to operate in Hardy's novel much as do the
other ill-fated attempts at recovery. From overhearing some of the gossip
that accompanies Tess's return to Marlott, the reader knows it to be fictional.
Her former schoolfellows and acquaintances believe her to be married to a
dashing, wealthy man who has gone away on business. The language of the
past is as counterfeit as are the D'Urbervilles of Trantridge. And yet, Tess
must leave church after imagining she is the object of whispers. Hardy seems
to be suggesting that, like those historical records uncovered by Parson
Tringham, gossip produces the ultimate egoism, for it too is another false
attempt to make connections where none exists:

> She might have seen that what had bowed her head so pro-
> foundly—the thought of the world's concern at her situation—
> was founded on an illusion. She was not an existence, an expe-
> rience, a passion, a structure of sensations, to anybody but her-
> self. To all humankind besides Tess was only a passing thought.
>
> (chap. 14)

Hence the loss of a future, symbolized in the refusal to gaze ahead, is abetted
by the intensive concentration upon self that is always a feature of self-pity.
And this process by which the self is gradually imprisoned only reenforces
the failure to make connections. As the novel gains momentum, Tess becomes
a self-regulating treadmill.

Even the most traditional of ways in which we make connections—by
letter—often goes astray in *Tess of the D'Urbervilles*. The novel is scarcely
under way when Prince is run down by the night mail coach, producing yet
another gap, another absence in the way in which people potentially reach
one another. And the famous letter to Angel Clare that just misses its intended object because it accidentally slips beneath the carpet is, of course,
another futile effort to establish a connection between present and past that

instead leaves a large gap in human communication. When Tess, almost penniless, attempts to write her estranged husband in Brazil, she must address the epistle to Clare's parents for forwarding. One of the more peculiar features of Hardy's novel is the extent to which it assumes the dimensions of an epistolary novel. There are letters from Joan Durbeyfield that conceal as much as they disclose; there are sincere *cris de coeur* from Tess; and financial statements from Clare's parents. Like the language of gossip, these letters tend to float about the countryside often arriving either too late or not at all. Just as the people wander about the landscape alternately uprooted only to resettle temporarily, so their language seems baseless as a mode of communication, instead having value primarily as utterances of real or imagined desperation. Such is part of a consistent pattern in Hardy's mature novels: discontinuity in space and time is always heightened by the attempt to remedy it, whether that attempt be in the form of a private language (letter), public language (gossip), or historical record (the canon of ancient families). All represent the universal struggle to achieve community by establishing a fiction of origins, and just as surely all these modes fail to the extent that they only heighten the discontinuous. The recurrence of coincidence which so many readers of Hardy's novels have noticed may well be not the deterministic workings of fate, but rather the physical enactment of consciously willed attempts to fill in or otherwise explain the discontinuous. Coincidence is, after all, one way of talking about the identity of continuity. There is evidence that, just as the fiction of origins is largely counterfeit, so the alleged discontinuities exist more in the mind of the perceiver than in reality. As Tess leaves Marlott a second time, following the death of her child, she is less an historical figure than she thinks: "In a few days the children would engage in the games as merrily as ever, without the sense of any *gap* left by her departure" (chap. 16). The sense of absence and its corollary, the wish to bridge the discontinuous, is not a part of the child's space. The necessity of history would appear to be largely an adult demand.

Following Tess's seduction she strives to "undo" her past, as if one could somehow discount history. She wishes to grow not by the accretion of new experiences, but rather through denial—the withdrawal from new spaces. And the rhythm of Hardy's novel undergoes a decided change. For now, instead of "claiming kin" (chap. 15), she wishes to obliterate all evidence of relation—a decision which includes the negation of her own history: "To escape the past and all that appertained thereto was to annihilate it, and to do that she would have to get away" (chap. 15). There is an apparently conscious attempt to reverse the direction of her life's journey. Yet, in spite of her wish to flee the gossip and the imagined gaze of her community by starting out in a direction "almost opposite that of her first adventuring" (chap. 16), Tess really moves not far at all. As in her wedding-night dream, the farther she attempts to roam, the closer she finds herself tied to her own past. Just as the elders' gossip presents Tess with a self-reflexive language insofar as it has no definable source, so her travels become similarly labyrinthine, as she turns back upon previously well-trodden paths:

> Yet such is human inconsistency that one of the interests of the new place to her was the accidental virtue of its lying near her forefather's country. . . . The dairy called Talbothays, for which she as bound, stood not remotely from some of the former estates of the d'Urbervilles, near the great family vaults of her grand-dames and their powerful husbands. She would be able to look at them, and think that d'Urberville, like Babylon, had fallen, but that the individual innocence of a humble descendant could lapse as silently. All the while she wondered if any strange good thing might come from her being in her ancestral land; and some spirit within her rose automatically as the sap in the twigs.
>
> (chap. 15)

She remains just as fixated upon her past as she had been when earlier agreeing to her father's suggestion that she become an emissary of history. And although her life has the appearance of a new origin, Hardy is quick to tell us, ironically, that "It is Tess Durbeyfield, otherwise d'Urberville, somewhat changed—the same, but not the same; at the present stage of her existence living as a stranger and an alien here, though it was no strange land that she was in" (chap. 14). The life at Talbothays Dairy is not dissimilar from that scene of her previous affair. Cows have replaced the chickens of Trantridge Farm, and Tess still has the charmed touch to get them to deliver, albeit milk rather than eggs. Little wonder that Tess seems so willing to repeat the errors of her relationship with Alec d'Urberville; to be a captive of history is to be doubly a prisoner.

Angel Clare comes from a situation like that of Tess, but his response to his family's demands is very different. The reader is but barely into Hardy's account of Angel's lineage when we confront the gap of discontinuity, although it is horizontal, occurring between members of the same family, rather than vertically between families:

> Mr. Clare the elder, whose first wife had died and left him a daughter, married a second late in life. This lady had somewhat unexpectedly brought him three sons, so that between Angel, the

youngest, and his father, The Vicar, there seemed to be almost a missing generation.

(chap. 18)

Even though he has a father, the spacing of the family means that Angel Clare is, at least symbolically, an orphan. Rather than obeying his father's request for a "family connection" by entering the university as a preparation for taking Orders, as did his brothers, Angel turns his back upon his family:

> He spent years and years in desultory studies, undertakings and meditations; he began to evince considerable indifference to social forms and observances. The material distinctions of rank and wealth he increasingly despised. Even the "good old family" (to use a favorite phrase of a late local worthy) had no aroma for him.
>
> (chap. 18)

When it comes time for Angel to think about marriage, his parents first insist upon knowing whether the intended comes from a "good family," a value that their son consciously denies in his refusal to consider Mercy Chant, the daughter of a neighbor. What is clear about Angel's departure from his parents' plans is his steadfastness in reconstituting a new family that is far more authentic than that formed by Tess when she first left Marlott. Although of considerably greater natural intelligence than the other farm folk at Talbothays Dairy, he takes a real delight in their companionship, even going so far as to share quarters with them at Dairyman Crick's. The "new family" differs from Angel's natural family insofar as it is not a conglomerate of likenesses or a place where identity is demanded. Nor is the dairy a geography for forced kinship, but rather it is a space where differences are encouraged.

> His host and his host's household, his men and his maids, as they became intimately known to Clare, began to differentiate themselves as in a chemical process. . . . The typical and unvarying Hodge ceased to exist. He had been disintegrated into a number of varied fellow-creatures—beings of many minds beings infinite in difference; some happy, many serene, a few depressed, one here and there bright even to genius, some stupid, others wanton, others austere.
>
> (chap. 18)

But even as he "grows away from old associations" (chap. 18) to rearrange a new family among the rustics at Talbothays Dairy, Angel Clare continues to believe in history not experientially, but as an abstract value important to the acquisition of other knowledge. Whereas Alec had no use for history at all, Angel strives to instruct Tess, if for no other reason than to make her more presentable to his father. Although he is unwilling to accept his father's conviction in the historical inevitability of canon law, Angel Clare quickly wishes to become Tess's history tutor. And just as surely, Tess wishes to discount lineage in favor of a conviction in the uniqueness of each individual:

> "Because what's the use of learning that I am one of a long row only—finding out that there is set down in some old book somebody just like me, and to know that I shall only act her part; making me sad, that's all. The best is not to remember that your nature and your past doings have been just like thousands' and thousands' and that your coming life and doings'll be like thousands' and thousands'."

> (chap. 19)

Her argument with recorded history even extends to Tess's reluctance to have the wedding banns published for fear that such will resurrect the past. The truth of the matter is that both Tess and Angel Clare have an ambivalent relationship with history. Although both wish to escape the demands of their respective families as a way of escaping the past, Tess and her lover are simultaneously unable to achieve a world without time. Although she professes to wish for a "perpetual betrothal" and Angel Clare rebels against the idea of a traditional family with the words, "How is *family* to avail the wife of a man who has to rough it as I have, and shall have to" (chap. 26), both quickly succumb to marriage. Ostensibly an institution for solemnizing the exchange of vows, their family quickly becomes a part of history. The inn where Tess and Angel spend their wedding night is part of the ancient d'Urberville estate, and the pictures of her fictional ancestors form a veritable gallery of guilt that looks down upon the newlyweds. Even as she attempts to start her life over again, Tess remains firmly affixed to her past:

> They drove by the level road along the valley to a distance of a few miles, and reaching Wellbridge, turned away from the village to the left, and over the great Elizabethan bridge which gives the place its name. Immediately behind it stood the house wherein they had engaged lodgings, whose exterior features are so well known to all travellers through the Froom Valley; once portion of a fine manorial residence, and the property and seat of a d'Urberville, but since its partial demolition a farmhouse.

"Welcome to one of your ancestral mansions!" said Clare as he handed her down.

(chap. 34)

The pilgrimage that has become a labyrinth has returned us to another "faked marriage" at another farmyard in the seemingly endless attempt to synchronize history and family. As if to accentuate the failure of the couple to begin anew by casting off history and family, Tess, against her mother's advice, becomes a historian by insisting upon confessing her past beneath the imaginary portraits of her ancestors.

Whereas time had seemed suspended at Dairyman Crick's during the long summer of romance, the emergence of history is apparent in the relative haste with which autumn comes upon Wellbridge. Tess's confession is, of course, part of the apparent human necessity to equate the possession of a past or a history with the boundaries of personal identity. Tess does what she has done twice previously—she begins anew by turning her attention back to her own personal history. The exchange of vows—with its intended attention upon the future—has been transformed into a joint confession with its burden of the past. As was the case with her first attempt to join a decadent "family" into a pre-existent historical base, Tess assumes that history is one of the vehicles of purification, that she will be a "pure" woman after this verbal immersion in the stream of her past. What actually occurs is quite the reverse: her confession only heightens the discontinuity, as Angel Clare comes to conceive of not one, but two Tesses. Following the prolonged silence that concluded her narrative, Angel comes to think of his beloved as a separate person from the one whom he had married:

> "I thought, Angel, that you loved me—me, my very self! If it is I you do love, O how can it be that you love and speak so? It frightens me! Having begun to love you, I love you for ever—in all changes, in all disgraces, because you are yourself. I ask no more. Then how can you, O my own husband, stop loving me?"
> "I repeat, the woman I have been loving is not you."
> "But who?"
> "Another woman in your shape."
> She perceived in his words the realization of her own apprehensive foreboding in former times. He looked upon her as a species of imposter; a guilty woman in the guise of an innocent one.

(chap. 35)

Tess believes, erroneously, that the personal history related in her confession provides her with the continuity of an historical self that demands the same allegiance that history has always demanded from Tess herself. But the myth of a fall, necessary to so many public as well as private histories, establishes two kingdoms whether it be the saved and the damned or the pure and the impure. Hence, to insist upon history, as Tess does, is to use the idea of continuity to conversely establish a gap in one's being. There occurs a split between a former and a present self, made more acute by the very transitional nature of Tess's position in her own family. Having always been an agent, either to fetch her straying father from the enchantments of a nearby tavern or to bring her strayed family into an alliance with the mythology of nobility, Tess comes to believe in her own lack of will: "Tess was now carried along upon the wings of the hours, without the sense of a will (chap. 22). This deterioration of self reaches its limit in death, but prior to that, Teresa Durbeyfield exhibits almost classical symptoms of the split personality.

R. D. Laing has suggested that discontinuity in the self is often a later stage in the ever-growing detachment of the self from the physical world. What Laing has called the "schizoid sensibility" is therefore often related to paranoia; we retreat from some imagined threat from the outside world by engaging in some internal detachment wherein one "self" (termed "false self" by Laing) becomes the defensive fortress for a more genuine or "true self." Tess's romance with Angel Clare is surely noteworthy insofar as she elevates her lover beyond the physical in order to negate the physical. In this perverse transcendence, but one which befits her puritan origins, Tess insists upon making Angel Clare part of the Divine kingdom:

> However, when she found herself alone in her room for a few minutes—the last day this on which she was ever to enter it— she knelt down and prayed. She tried to pray to God, but it was her husband who really had her supplication. Her idolatry of this man was such that she herself almost feared it to be ill-omened.
>
> (chap. 33)

Throughout their courtship her one desire has been "to call him her lord" (chap. 33). In making desire a function of distance—to borrow one of the themes of J. Hillis Miller's book on Hardy—she creates a gap between herself and the physical world. Her personality takes upon itself the contours of the "tease," as she alternately tempts and then withdraws from Angel Clare. This alternation in Tess's being has, of course, always been present, just as it was in the opening dialogue between the drunk and the historian that framed *Tess of the D'Urbervilles:*

A spiritual forgetfulness co-existed with an intellectual remembrance. She walked in brightness, but she knew that in the background those shapes of darkness were always spread.

(chap. 31)

Following her confession Angel Clare comes to see Tess as two distinct people
precisely because that is the particular manifestation of her own lack of will.
Neither Angel Clare nor Tess is able to relate to the other's being-in-the-
world, but only to the discontinuities of the self provided by a perverse
theology or a perverse vision of history that separates even as it promises to
integrate. In Tess's case, her particular mode of distancing herself, the convenient confusion of the Lord's word with Angel's mutterings, has an added
consequence: it makes her more vulnerable to the return of Alec d'Urberville
who has now similarly detached himself from the world of physical desire
in order to claim kinship with the divine. In replacing the cape of the rake
with the mantle of the Lord, he has exchanged places with Angel Clare both
in the Reverend Clare's family and with Tess.

The greater one's reliance upon a literal history or a real past, the greater
seems to be the detachment from "self." Tess, feeling herself the victim of
male aggression, shaves off her eye brows and assumes a sort of Joan of Arc
haircut. In a classic illustration of introjection, she identifies with the aggressor in order to bring about the cessation of personal violence. Although
"he seemed to be her double" (chap. 34), such identification may represent
detachment from self as much as it does the imagined unity of the love bond.
In the process, of course, she becomes precisely the "impostor" which she
had earlier feared to be one of Angel's opinions. Her retreat from the physical
world is hastened by the repeated intrusions of legend into nature. She is no
longer capable of hearing the crowing of a cock without thinking of its
significance as an omen. It is a way of replacing the present with the collective
beliefs of the past, just as surely as marrying on New Year's Eve and replacing
resolutions with confessions. Tess's space comes to be literally filled with
symbolic events: a coach seen on the wedding day; milk turning sour without
apparent cause; and waylaid cider. The natural world ceases to exist as a
cluster of more or less random events in and for itself. It comes to have
relevance only insofar as it relates to the past and can be interpreted in the
light of either personal history (Tess's guilt) or communal history (legend).
Tess comes increasingly to live her past entirely, and Hardy would seem to
be implying that such a desire is very close to death itself. In this dynamic,
as was true in the instance of Tess's identification with her aggressor, everything becomes its opposite: marriage days are divorce days; attempts to

communicate only heighten distance; and even language itself becomes an exercise in ventriloquy or meta-language: "she found herself conjecturing on the matter as a third person might have done" (chap. 37). Tess comes to see non-being as the most plausible mode of being and almost welcomes Clare's nocturnal attempt to place her in the coffin of her ancestors. It is a premonition of her end, an ironic fulfillment of Parson Tringham's announcement of extinction with which the novel opened. The "family of the past" and reliance upon it means, in effect, that one joins them in death. Upon returning to his own home Angel Clare is asked a question that focuses the convergence of family and the quest for origins.

> "We have not exactly quarreled," he said. "But we have had a difference—"
> "Angel—is she a young woman whose history will bear investigation?"

This question comes from the same mother who had earlier been so interested in what kind of family Tess came from despite her son's disclaimers of the importance of family. Now, his answer might best be an ironic, "too much investigation."

Early in the novel, shortly after her non-affair with Alec d'Urberville, Tess had briefly thought of a line from Southey, in reference to a maid "in love with her own ruin" (chap. 13). The phenomenology of the ruin presents even the most casual reader with some deeper insight into Tess's plight. Ruins tend to have historical significance to the extent that they represent the intersection of the natural world with the historical world. An edifice that no longer is in possession of its living, day-to-day function comes to exist as artifice or artifact as it is reclaimed by nature: haunted houses lapsing into decay or instruments demoting a lapsed civilization overgrown by weeds. What all those legends and old wives' tales had been in the realm of language, the ruin is in the expanse of nature: an object which functions imaginatively or symbolically in inverse proportion to its practical function. As Tess comes to live her past, she comes to exist more as a monument and less as a person. As well as being symptomatic of the "petrification" that afflicts martyrs, this existence as some "stoned" relic comes to pervade the way in which Tess views the world. Objects lose the presence of the physical much as Tess loses so much of her physical charm and come to function, rather, as historical *emblems:*

> She could not bear to let them go. Angel had put them into her hand, had obtained them bright and new from his bank for her;

his touch had consecrated them to souvenirs of himself—they
appeared to have had as yet no other history than such as was
created by his and her own experiences—and to disperse them
was like giving away relics. But she had to do it, and one by one
they left her hands.

(chap. 41)

This represents a subtle, albeit important shift in the way in which people
conceive of history. Gradually, Tess Durbeyfield must learn that history is
not something one joins or reclaims. It does not exist as some point behind
time which lies across the breach of discontinuity. Rather history is lived
time, created by mutual experiences. The ruin is not an emblem of dead time,
but involves instead the conception of history as shared experience and participates in that "interval" that Bataille has termed "the sacred." Only lit-
eralists like Parson Tringham or old Jack Durbeyfield see history in
metaphors of absence or extinction. As Ian Gregor has suggested, history,
from a different perspective, is the temporality of community. In *Tess of the
D'Urbervilles,* the ruin is an empty family in ancestral burial vaults at the
beginning of things, but the collective center that is Stonehenge during Tess's
last hours. Both are part of the past, part of the way in which people organize
and give purpose to their lives. Both are places where the myth if not the
fact of former families dwells on. But Hardy also suggests that it is only
those who imagine history as a metaphor that are capable of surviving the
crisis of a more literal history. Angel Clare, unlike Tess, is not ambivalent in
his desire to "escape from his past existence" (chap. 49) and surely Brazil
represents a genuine effort in this direction. But most important to his escape
from the prison of history is the recognition that history exists more as a
mode by which people imaginatively conceive of the world than as a record
of past deeds:

The historical interest of her family—that masterful line of d'Urbervilles—whom he had despised as a spent force, touched his
sentiments now. Why had he not known the difference between
the political value and the imaginative value of these things? In
the latter aspect her d'Urberville descent was a fact of great dimensions; worthless of economics, it was a most useful ingredient
to the dreamer, to the moralizer on declines and falls. It was a
fact that would soon be forgotten—that bit of distinction in poor
Tess's blood and name, and oblivion would fall upon her hered-

itary link with the marble monuments and leaded skeletons at Kingsbere. So does Time ruthlessly destroy his own romances.

(chap. 49)

It is not only that the "fact" of history dies, perhaps forever in the nineteenth century, but that those who believe and act upon the facticity of history die. Both the Reverend Clare's family and the Durbeyfield family share a similar structure—elder(s) separate from either a younger child or younger children by some temporal gap that makes the family seem as if it were two families. Those adjacent to the temporal discontinuity are alienated narratively, if not literally from the rest of the family. In both cases the transitional alien departs from his (her) own family in order that he might constitute a different one: Angel Clare leaves his family for one of a milder faith among the rustics at Talbothays and Tess leaves her family for the presumed economic security that she believes to stem from true origins. In both cases their places are taken by a surrogate:

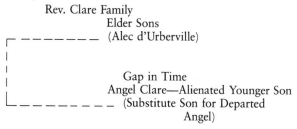

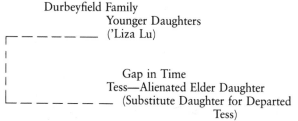

The symmetry of family structures is paralleled by a symmetry of action in *Tess of the D'Urbervilles*. Alec d'Urberville, the sensualist, re-emerges in the novel as the (temporarily) redeemed son. He assumes in the Reverend Clare's imagination the place formerly occupied by the departed "real" son, Angel Clare. And he is just as easily tempted to renounce his faith, and with it, the faith of his adopted father, as Angel Clare had been when he left the Reverend Clare's family. Alec d'Urberville and Angel Clare are also similar in that they both see Tess as representing values antithetical to those symbolized by the elder Clare and his wife: family, history, faith. But during his brief career as a redeemed man Alec is an extension of Parson Tringham, for he combines the authority of historical lineage with the authority of theological man. And both types of authority are shown to be equally counterfeit: he is no more a saved man than he is a member of an ancient noble family. But in one of her last encounters with this man of her past, Tess sees him in an arena which hints at the hold which family, history, and faith have over her. Tess is surprised by d'Urberville in the church of her fictitious ancestors:

> She musingly turned to withdraw, passing near an altar-tomb, the oldest of them all, on which was a recumbent figure. In the dusk she had not noticed it before, and would hardly have noticed it now but for an odd fancy that the effigy moved. As soon as she drew close to it she discovered all in a moment that the figure was a living person; and the shock to her sense of not having been alone was so violent that she was quite overcome, and sank down nigh to fainting, not, however, till she had recognized Alec d'Urberville in the form.
>    He leapt off the slab and supported her.
>    "I saw you come in," he said smiling, "and got up there not to interrupt her meditations. A family gathering, is it not, with these old fellows under here? Listen."
>
> (chap. 52)

In *Tess of the D'Urbervilles,* family, history, and faith have an easy alliance, and one that plays directly into poor Tess's mode of distancing herself from the natural world. In one of her last letters she writes Angel Clare in desperation to return in order that she might be "save[d] . . . from what threatens me" (chap. 53)—notably, Alec d'Urberville. Detached from the admission of genuine physical desire and any real involvement in the physical world, she can relate to her husband only in the vocabulary of salvation. Her murder of those values which have wreaked such havoc in her life is the other side of Tess's martyrdom. As her relationship with Alec has always been tinged with guilt, so she objectifies that guilt of her somewhat mechanical stabbing of him. And, as her union with Angel Clare has always been pervaded by a false transcendence, so her personal submission before the divine master of her life abuts in its logical limit—the wasting away that creates a suicide out of a ruin. Death to the other or death to oneself are alternatives in the same way that the criminal and the saint complement one another as *figurae* in the life and art of the Nineties.

This obsession with the wrong kind of history in *Tess of the D'Urbervilles* manifests itself, as it does in Hardy's *Jude the Obscure,* as a "false family"—a *menage à trois* that is founded upon the pretense of rescue. Both Alec d'Urberville and Angel Clare find themselves "husbands" of the same woman because the imaginary obligation to save her is the sole mode of access. Angel's return from Brazil creates a pornographic situation: heightened voyeurism and its premise, a detachment of being; submission of the "victim" to a theological pose that masks physical desire; and an exaggerated sense of urgency. This is yet another alternative family that does not survive because its obsession with history-as-origin limits any teleology.

Although the meeting with Alec d'Urberville in the ancient church is one kind of bizarre "family reunion" in a double sense, the anticipated marriage of Angel Clare with 'Liza-Lu, one of Tess's surviving sisters, is another. Angel Clare, who has come to recognize that the history of man is not dead people or dead facts but the history of man's imagination, has embarked upon a new kind of family that has a special meaning in the context of nineteenth-century politics. In 1869, under the urging of Gladstone, a bill was passed in Parliament as an extension of the Divorce Bill of 1857 that legalized marriage to a deceased wife's sister. It was part of the general liberalization of marriage and divorce laws in the mid- and late-nineteenth century from the tradition of canon law that Arnold, among others, saw as evidence of the bankruptcy of dissent. In marrying a mere child, Clare clearly hopes to escape involvement with one so close to the pains that stem from the gap of historical discontinuity. In the fulfillment of Tess's dying wish to teach 'Liza Lu and to "bring her up for your own self" (chap. 58), Angel Clare is placing his faith in the present and future self rather than in some bogus historical self. It is not that he turns his back upon history, but rather that history has become the handmaiden of social relationships rather than the goddess of ruins. In their triangulated relationship, Tess, Alec, and Angel had all sought to escape their real family in order to seek a better union with the authority of an origin: history, God, or the earth, respectively. But in the "new" marriage of Angel Clare and 'Liza-Lu, there is no difference between past and future, the old family and the new family:

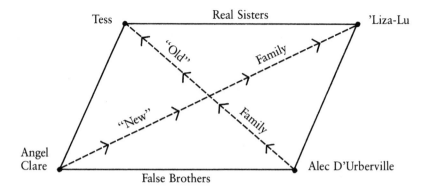

This new world upon which Angel and 'Liza gaze at the conclusion of *Tess of the D'Urbervilles* is urban, set in Wintoncester. The old farm families, like Joan Durbeyfield's, have been dispossessed, and the ancient Gothic buildings now serve a distinctively modern function, part of the legal bureaucracy which announces Tess's execution. If there is an "ache" to this "modernism," there is also the suggestion that the crisis of history to which Alec and Tess have sacrificed themselves can only be surmounted by men like Angel Clare who recognize that history has a mythological dimension that makes it more applicable as a mode of ordering the future family than as a vehicle for achieving the authority of a definable origin. One escapes the extinction of family of which the Parson had warned in the novel's first chapter by conceiving of the transitive aspect of origins which implies continuity—as does Angel when he announces his return to Tess's landlady with the words, "tell her that a *relative* is anxious to see her" (chap. 55). They are the same words that Tess herself had used when seeking out her "relative." Tess's point of origin, however, carried with it only its intransitive aspect; that is, history, for her, has no object but its continual clarification. *Tess of the D'Urbervilles* commences with the infusion of the fear of absence or extinction mandated by a crisis of history, but concludes with the renewal that stems from a suspicion that history is ever-present. It is a form of succession as well as a beginning of deterioration.

The absorption in origins is associated by Hardy with incest—that loss of a "sense of difference" that is, initially, self-reflexive, but ultimately violent and ruinous. The crisis of history is always related to a crisis of self. By contrast, history conceived of transitively is part of the dynamics of inheritance and carries with it the expansion of family into something like "community." But the city of Wintoncester is not an unqualified gain: without a sense of the immediacy of origins or with the realization that our dark beginnings are imaginative rather than real, there is no longer a viable "sacred" to the past. The last chapter is almost pagan in its secularity. In marrying 'Liza-Lu, Angel Clare will have achieved identity "with a difference," and is therefore using, rather than being used by, history.

The strange publication history of Hardy's novel suggests that its author felt some of the same pressures as do his characters. Faced with the "gap" of a missing section of the novel, omitted from chapter ten of *Tess of the D'Urbervilles* during its initial serial publication as a concession to Victorian morality, Thomas Hardy revisited his narrative, writing several prefaces between 1891 and the publication of the Wessex Edition in 1912. He sought, by his own admission, to collect the "detached episodes" and to restore the novel to its "original manuscript" ("Preface" to the Wessex Edition of 1912). The origin was clearly an authority from which his bowdlerized tale had fallen, and he even went so far as to amend the controversial sub-title, "A Pure Woman," to the original title of the novel. To be confronted with the absence involved by the discontinuous is to become prey to the demands of restoration, whether one be Tess searching for her "true" history or Hardy locating his original novel. Contrary to being a blank page, history is that process by which novelists, apparently, as well as characters, transform the dead past into the living present.

ROSS C. MURFIN

# New Words: Swinburne
# and the Poetry of Thomas Hardy

In Hardy's first poems, whether in "Revulsion" or "Hap," "Amabel" or "At a Lunar Eclipse," human lives seem to be of utterly negligible import or significance when weighed against the overpowering, crushing indifference of "Nature" or "Love," "Time" or the "Flashing Firmament." These are poems, finally, not about resolution and independence, certainly not about the alpine power of the human mind that dwells apart in its tranquility, but, rather, about human powerlessness. What power these poems contain and convey as poems, therefore, must reside in jarring paradoxes, in self-exploding structures, in dialectics of tone and content, in unresolvable thoughts and feelings. That is to say, the power of these poems lies in the utterly frustrated anger of a speaker like the jilted young woman of "She to Him" (1866), who, though aware that her whole life will be adequately summed up someday when her former lover sighs "Poor jade," nonetheless thinks it worth a little energy to lament and protest this life of ruin which "Sportsman Time," who "rears his brood to kill," will inevitably bring to pass. It is this poetic voice—a voice that can only affirm through denial—it is this poetic structure—a structure founded upon the opposition of wishes and facts, acts of defiance and acts of surrender—it is this tone or mood—latent with both acquiescence *and* anger—that gives Hardy's early poems the pathos of Swinburne's earliest *Poems and Ballads*, poems which ask countless times,

From *Swinburne, Hardy, Lawrence, and the Burden of Belief.* © 1978 by The University of Chicago. The University of Chicago Press, 1978.

Is it worth a tear, is it worth an hour,
  To think of things that are well outworn?
Of fruitless husk and fugitive flower,
  The dream foregone and the deed forborne?
              ("The Triumph of Time," ll. 9–12)

Sometimes subtle, sometimes even dramatic changes in Hardy's world-view, and in those poetic structures which embody a poet's sensibility, can be found in those verses that were composed in or after the year 1870. Hardy, following Swinburne's lead, later tried to explain away transitions by claiming that the excruciatingly painful lines written earlier in his career advance a "series of feelings or fancies . . . in widely differing moods" through "dramatic or impersonative" pieces, highly "imaginative writings" that convey "mere impressions of the moment, and not convictions or arguments." In other words, Hardy, like Swinburne, apparently tried to put his past behind him by suggesting that his most agonized agnosticisms, his most maimed, incomplete, and in some way unsuccessful poems of dissent, were monodramas.

In Hardy's case, the gradual disappearance from his early poetry of the themes of loss and acquiescence may well have been the result of certain biographical catalysts. In 1870, Hardy fell passionately in love with Emma Lavinia Gifford, the woman he married in 1874, and it was also during this period (1871–74) that he realized his ambition to become a published author. Beginning with *Desperate Remedies* (1871) and following up with *Under the Greenwood Tree* (1872), *A Pair of Blue Eyes* (1873), and *Far from the Madding Crowd* (1874), Hardy grew in writing ability almost as rapidly as in popularity and wealth. He planted, he watered, and Something (as Clough would have put it) gaveth increase.

Literary influences must have been at least as responsible as biographical facts for the transition in which Hardy moves out of a period of agonized, anti-romantic protest into a new period of post-romantic affirmation. To deny the influence of this clear and well-marked literary trend, or pattern of transition, upon Hardy's worldview and aesthetic would be particularly myopic in light of the fact that a similar pattern can be found in the work of Tennyson, Carlyle, Arnold, and Swinburne, work that Hardy read intimately and often, work that antedated his own poetry and fiction by anywhere from two (Swinburne) to thirty (Tennyson) years.

One of the immediately obvious transitions observable in the poetry of (or after) 1870 is a greater emphasis on "Chance" than on "Fate." To be sure, this "Chance"—or "Circumstance"—of the later poems often has such a deterministic ring as to seem *almost* synonymous with "Fate," but the tone of the poetry written after 1870 seems to indicate that the change in vocabulary is, indeed, symptomatic of real transition. In "Ditty," a poem Hardy composed in 1870 (the very year he met Emma Gifford), the speaker, like dozens of others since the disappointed lover of "Amabel" (1865), admits that "bond-servants of Chance / We are all," and that

> To feel I might have kissed—
> Loved as true—
> Otherwhere, nor Mine have missed
> My whole life through
>
> . . . . . . . . . .
> Is a smart severe.
>                     (ll. 28–33)

What makes this poem so different from those earlier, agonized love-laments, such as "Revulsion," is the tone of the somewhat clumsy final stanza. Gone is the bitter, early Swinburnian rhetoric of complaint, gone is young Teufelsdröckh's will to cease loving or to cease living, gone, too, is that tendency of Hardy's earlier poems to disintegrate, in the final stanza, into disjointed images, contradictory claims, unanswered questions. In its place is a positive exclamation that comes close to declaring a new willingness to make the best of, perhaps even to celebrate, the accidental gifts of "unknowing" chance:

> I but found her in that, going
> On my errant path unknowing,
> I did not out-skirt the spot
> That no spot on earth excels,
> —Where she dwells!
>                     (ll. 41–45)

The speaker admits throughout his ditty that it is tempting to look upon the woman he has met by accident as the divine answer to prayer, as a portion of the loveliness which she has made more lovely. The temptation, strong as it is, is fairly well resisted by the speaker (who is inseparable from the poet). He exorcises the romantic exaggeration by forcing it into quotation marks and attributing it not to himself but, rather, to the outside world. Speaking of nature on a springtime day, he says that

> Upon that fabric fair
> "Here is she!"

> Seems written everywhere
> Unto me.

To be sure, we instantly attribute nature's one-line romantic poem to the observer, but when he so openly admits his own projection ("*Seems* written . . . / Unto me") and never allows it to become more than a projection (as did the speaker of "Neutral Tones") he proves himself the ultimate master of his fancy.

The poet of "Ditty," then, would resist not only the romantic notion that great romances are the rarefied designs of "Love" (the speaker of "At a Bridal" had been deluded by precisely that pathetic hope), but also the belief that the *inamorata* is some kind of metaphysical find, a route to transcendental bliss. When the poet comes to accept the fact that his lady "is nought, / Even as I, beyond the dells / Where she dwells," he is not just saying that he and his mate, like Wordsworth's Lucy, have dwelt among untrodden ways. He also means that their union is not one of phantoms—of men and women but spirits too. It is, rather, the marriage of beings who don't exist beyond the physical "dells" in which they dwell, not only the provincial environment by which they have been limited and determined, but also the temporal bodies which they can neither leave in life nor survive in death.

The tendency to accept the limitations of a physical reality and "Chance" too indifferent and erratic to be personified as God or Fate is even more noticeable in another "Wessex" poem that was composed after the initial 1865–67 group. "The Temporary the All" (almost certainly composed during the early seventies) systematically ridicules transcendence-seeking idealism and states what Hardy gradually came to see as the facts about nature's indifference—not malign indifference or seeming indifference but real, dumb indifference. The phonetics and metrics of the poem, which imitate rather successfully Old English kennings, are unique in the Hardy canon, but the narrative structure of "The Temporary the All" is one which, to varying degrees, gives form to Hardy's poetry and fiction from the lyrics of 1870 onwards. A dreamer—a romantic persona distanced from the post-romantic philosophy and aesthetic of his or her omniscient "author"—is taught the danger of unrealistic fancies (faith in romantic love, nature's divine presence, social apocalypse) by the temporal process. In the meantime, the progressive, point-by-point stanza (or chapter) structure of the poem (or novel) teaches the very same lesson to the reader as he or she moves through a different time continuum, that is, the temporal process of reading.

In "The Temporary the All," the speaker recalls a time when "Change and Chancefulness . . . / Set me . . . near to one unchosen" (ll. 1–2). Once

"Fused . . . in friendship" with the unchosen associate, however, the speaker soon looked beyond their union to the establishment of an Ideal Friendship with some perfectly kindred (and perfectly hypothetical) soul. He remembers the day when he "self-communed,"

> "Cherish him can I while the true one forthcome—
> Come the rich fulfiller of my prevision."
>
> (ll. 5–6)

The former romantic recalls that, when a woman entered his life by "chance," she seemed "unformed to be all-eclipsing" but an acceptable diversion "'till arise my forefelt / Wonder of women'" (ll. 10–12). Next, a series of shabby "tenements" fell far short of that Wordsworthian, "visioned hermitage" where he had longed to go with perfect friend and ideal lover in order to "transcend" life through some "high handiwork" that, he had hoped, "'will . . . Truth and Light outshow'" (ll. 13–18). Chance, ultimately, brought the fulfillment of not one dream, and in the last stanza the experienced speaker (who speaks of the past and present, not the future; whose words are not enclosed in quotation marks; whose present experience frames his past innocence) can finally communicate, uninterrupted by the dreaming voices of his past, the fact that "Mistress, friend, place, aims to be bettered straightway" have never been bettered. Those experiences which drifted into life atomistically, on the winds of "Change and chancefulness," were "never transcended" (l. 24). The "intermissive aim" has become, in his present view, the only reasonable ambition for the artist on an "earth-track" (l. 19, l. 23). The "temporary" has come to be seen as identical with the "All"—in the speaker's mind, in Hardy's mind (these two, after all, seem to become one), and in the reader's understanding.

The poetic form of "The Temporary the All" is a structure of resolution exactly like those linear, synthetic structures of Swinburne's *Songs before Sunrise* and not all that different from that larger, more complex pattern of "The Two Voices," the poem in which Tennyson had emerged from his own agnostic agony by hearing out warring voices of faith and disbelief and then by achieving that liberating resolve to celebrate the simple mysteries of the here and now, symbolized at the end of the work by the image of an ordinary family on Sunday morning. In Hardy's poem of what Lawrence would later refer to as "Coming Through," the thesis (the romantic dream of divine states of existence) and the antithetical voice (the mundane fact about the barrenness of the quotidian) are resolved. They are synthesized by the post-romantic structure into that emergent philosophy that is "beyond church" and says that the mundane is all we have or need of the divine, that the temporary *is* the all of life.

With that affirmation, of course, the static, unchanging, romantic ideals that once seemed worthy of man's dreams gradually come to be the subjects of irony, occasionally even ridicule, in Hardy's mature verse. Like the young dreamer whose various dreams of transcendence are exploded, step by step, as time passes in "The Temporary the All," "The Ivy Wife," a vine seeking to grow into indivisible union with various dark and handsome trees, eventually finds and shows her quest for romantic unity to be a destructive quest as she moves in time from stanza to stanza, from beech to ash, being poisoned by the one, strangling the other. (Swinburne had already described romantic love through the metaphor of a strangling, poisoning serpent in "Laus Veneris," and both Swinburne's and Hardy's lyrics are imperiled by Shelley's "Alastor," a despairing romantic poem which nearly renders those post-romantic efforts redundant. In the precursor's poem "those that love" are compared to the "parasit[ic] plants" which like "restless serpents . . . twine their tendrils" about the "trunks" and "boughs" of grey-grown "beech" and "oak" [ll. 431–45].)

"The Ivy Wife" is an embarrassingly silly exercise in dogmatic poetry. What makes it interesting is not its aesthetic achievement but, rather, the fact that it is collected in *Wessex Poems* and thus juxtaposed with earlier lyrics in which sympathetic speakers long for perfect union with a beloved. (In "She to Him IV" [1866], a lover wishes in vain to be "fused" to another "by ecstasy.") The date of composition of "The Ivy Wife" is known to be some—perhaps many—years later than 1866, and the attitude of the poem toward romantic fusion is anything but that of intense longing.

For Hardy, evidently, the reverie has faded. The early romantic dream songs of poets such as Blake are now transposed into a minor key by Hardy (as they were by Shelley and Swinburne before him). In *Paradise Lost* Milton described an innocent Adam and Eve "le[ading] the vine / To wed her Elm; she spous'd about him twines / Her marriageable arms" (V, ll. 215–17). Blake had fashioned these lines into an image of romantic love:

> Love and harmony combine,
> And around our souls intwine,
> While thy branches mix with mine,
> And our roots together join.
> ("Song," from *Poetical Sketches*)

But Hardy suggests, through his own entwining "Ivy Wife," that lovers who would always be joining and mixing with another soul, always striving for perfect and harmonious unity with a beloved, are latter-day Satanic over-reachers. Through their ascendant twinings they will eventually destroy their beloveds and, at the same time, be brought down by them (poisoned by impurities or weighted down by mere physical reality). Hardy's serpentine vine precipitates just such a double catastrophe when, clutching too close and reaching too high, she sets in motion a latter-day version of the Fall. "In my triumph," the Ivy-Wife says, as she recalls reaching from an ash for the heavens beyond,

> I lost sight
> Of afterhaps. Soon he,
> Being bark-bound, flagged, snapped, fell outright,
> And in his fall felled me!
>
> (ll. 21–24)

Hardy seems to suggest that, like Satan, ascent-prone romantics bring down not only their intended victims but, in so doing, are themselves bruised, crushed, down-trodden, the agents of their own plunging doom.

In place of a romantic ideal of love as perfect unity, in place of the bitter complaint against life in a world where the old, romantic ideal is no longer tenable, the poems composed in or after 1870 resynthesize and redefine love as it occurs in two emergent, post-romantic forms. One of these definitions can be found in poems like "The Husband's View" or "The Dark-Eyed Gentleman," where love is stripped of all destructive or at least corrosive spiritual pretenses and is described as sexuality-without-shame. This tendency to define and to learn to accept love in what Hardy saw as its most unromantic, elemental form was one of the facets of his art that most influenced D. H. Lawrence. In "The Dark-Eyed Gentleman," a lusty woman of the earth sings out:

> I pitched my day's leazing in Crimmercrock Lane,
> To tie up my garter and jog on again,
> When a dear dark-eyed gentleman passed there and said,
> In a way that made all o' me colour rose-red,
>           "What do I see—
>           O pretty knee!"
> And he came and tied up my garter for me.
>
> . . . . . . . . . . . . . . . . . .
> Yet now I've beside me a fine lissom lad,
> And my slip's nigh forgot, and my days are not sad;
>           . . . No sorrow brings he

And thankful I be
That his daddy once tied up my garter for me!
(ll. 1–7, 15–16, 19–21)

The other type of human love defined by Hardy's post-1870 poetry is that of brotherhood or, as he so often called it, borrowing directly from Swinburne, "loving-kindness." This alternate mode of loving will be discussed at some length later in the chapter, for its importance to the post-romantic social ideals of humility, responsibility, and self-sacrifice is immense. Suffice it to say at this point that "The Burghers" offers a choice example of loving-kindness as it interacts with its counterpart, unabashed sexuality, bodily expression. This perfectly progressive and illustrative poem describes the initial, nearly homicidal rage felt by a husband who learns of his wife's passionate affair with a lover, the "sad thoughts" that follow the demise of his too-high expectations, the "drowse" of indifference the husband feels as his initial, self-righteous outrage passes, and finally the eventual decision to act out of kindness toward the lovers by freeing them from the prison both of social convention and of jealousy spawned of irrational idealism. (A veritable embodiment of Beyond-Church "Charity," a humanely revised God, this husband even decides to bestow upon the penniless adulterers their "daily bread.") The pattern of "The Burghers" becomes, for Hardy, a kind of paradigm of loving-kindness, one which he improvises upon several times in the course of his poetic and novelistic career, perhaps most persuasively, if not most purely, in *Jude the Obscure*.

It was Carlyle, of course, who had contributed the seminal definitions of these two, post-romantic reductions of the supposedly ethereal romantic vision of love. In his treatise *On Heroes and Hero-Worship*, he had turned to Novalis (as Hardy would later turn) to find a new, revised, and reduced definition of heaven. There he comes upon, and relates, a heretical revision of an old Biblical passage. " 'There is but one Temple in the Universe,' says the devout Novalis, 'and that temple is the Body of Man. ... We touch Heaven when we lay our hands on a human body.' " "*We* are the miracle of miracles," Carlyle hastens to add in this proto-Lawrentian passage, and in *On Heroes and Hero-Worship*, as in all his other works, he goes on to outline yet another plain and simple, post-romantic ideal of love—that of caring, helpfulness, shared troubles, and divided labors—the goal of human kindness which Teufelsdröckh is groping to define when he begins, in the "Everlasting Yea" chapter of *Sartor Resartus*, to look upon his "fellowman with an infinite Love, an infinite Pity."

Sexual energy or loving-kindness, each in its own way, replaces romantic love as a desired relationship in the poems Hardy wrote after 1870, especially between 1870 and 1890. This is not to say, of course, that the concept of romantic love disappears but rather that it, like the pathetic fallacy, like the enervated, solipsistic speaking voice of the early poems, becomes a kind of straw man which the poet frames, carefully controls, and continually cuts down in favor of his newly evolved definitions and devices. The reason I have preferred the term "post-romantic" to an equally ambiguous but usable term such as "modern" is precisely because of the constant presence of generalized romantic concepts in Hardy's works, as in Swinburne's, and the extreme degree to which his mature poems and fictions are rhetorical, imagistic, and structural metamorphoses of romanticism as he conceived it. In *Poems of the Past and Present* (1901), Hardy includes a poem entitled "I Said to Love," which neither he nor J. O. Bailey includes in their respective lists of poems composed during the 1860s, a poem which, by virtue of its extreme similarity to "He Abjures Love" (1883), must have been composed sometime during the early 1880s. In this lyric, the speaker is clearly addressing that destructive, strangling, absurd dream of romantic love which had often seemed as desirable as elusive to the yearning, youthful, Swinburnian poet of the 1860s. Once again, Hardy uses quotation marks and shifts in tense, this time to safely distance himself from that attractive old deity who had once promised "a heaven beneath the sun" (stanza 1), that holy One who had, in fact, become a sadistic god to whom adoring masochists prayed for inflicted agonies (stanza 2):

> I said to Love,
> "It is not now as in old days
> When men adored Thee and thy ways
>     All else above;
> Named thee the Boy, the Bright, the One
> Who spread a heaven beneath the sun,"
>     I said to Love.
>
> I said to him,
> "We now know more of thee than then;
> We were but weak in judgment when,
>     With hearts abrim,
> We clamoured thee that thou would'st please
> Inflict on us thine agonies,"
>     I said to him.
>
>                         (ll. 1–14)

The presence of Swinburne's early poetry in Hardy is still occasionally detectable, but the role of that presence is now utterly different. Hardy is now able to confront and deny what he believes to be the romantic faith or expectation directly, as opposed to the nervous confrontation implied by his earlier, agonized mimicry of Swinburne's poems of protest. Swinburne, therefore, can now become a stand-in for his own spiritual and poetic adolescence, a youth "weak in judgment" who "clamoured" for "inflict[ed] . . . agonies." Hardy thus represses his own moment of crisis, first by transferring it to the youthful Swinburne of *Poems and Ballads,* then by locking that Swinburne within the finality of quotation marks and surrounding him with the mature rhetoric of the beyond-all-that.

In another poem of the same vintage, Hardy reiterates his address to those distorting, destructive fancies which led young innocents, "weak in judgment . . . , / With hearts abrim," to see "Love," in the "old days," as something more than sex, kindness, or a combination of the two. In "He Abjures Love" (1883), the speaker abandons the rose-colored vision which precedes "Love's . . . fever-stricken . . . disquietings" and accepts a world of "common," "gray," "faulty . . . things beholden." "No more will now rate I," the speaker declares,

> The common rare,
> The midnight drizzle dew,
> The gray hour golden,
> The wind a yearning cry,
> The faulty fair,
> Things dreamt, of comelier hue
> Than things beholden.
>
> (ll. 31–41)

To be fair, both "He Abjures Love" and "I Said to Love" confess, subtly, some sadness in abandoning "things dreamt." The former asks, "after love what comes?" and answers, "A few sad hours"; the latter claims mankind is becoming too cynical, "too old in apathy," to worry that the race may be diminished with the passing of the "kindling coupling-vow" of a "cherubic" vision. More important, however, these lyrics demonstrate the fact that Hardy's attitude toward romantic love underwent a significant, if not quite dramatic, change between those early years of crisis, in which his various voices cry out in agony that real lovers, "of earth's poor average kind," are "blank" and "common" to each man who has a dream-vision of a beloved ("At Waking," 1869), and those later, transitional years in which he resolves to quit rating "Things dreamt, of comelier hue / Than things beholden" (1883).

As is the case with the very similar transitions from agony to acceptance in the Swinburne canon, moreover, Hardy's changing attitudes towards self or love or nature or society or time are accompanied by parallel transitions in his attitudes toward all the others. Nature, for instance, is no longer even dreamed of as a realm of Intellectual Love or Beauty or moral order but, rather, is accepted as a meaningless cycle neither benevolent nor malign to man. (John Stuart Mill had recently argued that "conformity to nature has no connection with right and wrong.") In one of the poems collected in *Wessex Poems* but composed well after the 1865–67 group, the poet admits that he would still like to believe that nature is really the "sweetness, / Radiance that"

> I thought thee
> When I early sought thee,
> Omen scouting,

that he wouldn't mind believing again that "Love alone had wrought thee— / Wrought thee for my pleasure," nay, even for his poetry:

> Planned thee as a measure
> For expounding
> And resounding
> Glad things that men treasure.

The trouble is, time will not allow a man to reenter his youth or its faiths; there is no going home again to the romantic world of the poet's infancy, and emergence, we learn from "Time" as the poem unfolds in time, is as inevitable as it is desirable:

> But such readorning
> Time forbids with scorning—
> Makes me see things
> Cease to be things
> They were in my morning.
> ("To Outer Nature," ll. 1–20)

Once this realization, this inner change, has been brought about, the need to cry out in protest to nature for her failures (one of the catalysts of Swinburne's and Hardy's earliest poems) disappears. It is replaced by that conviction expressed in "The Lacking Sense" which had been expressed only a few years earlier in Swinburne's "Hertha" and *Erechtheus*, namely, that a man should "Deal" unconscious, amoral nature "no scorn, no note of malediction" but should "Assist her where thy creaturely dependence gives thee room, / For thou art of her womb" (ll. 26–28). The speaker of the poem, who is addressing "Time," the somehow articulate child of Mother Nature, to find out why His mother always "wounds the lives she loves," is told that the great world weaver is "blind," that "sightless are those orbs of hers" that bring to man "fearful unfulfilments." What the poem seems to suggest, below and beyond the fictional dialogue it purveys, is not so much that Milton was wrong because God is even blinder than he was but, rather, that Milton and his romantic progeny were *terribly* wrong because their blindness to nature's own blindness gave us a vision that deprived us of all sight, making us ask restless, foolish questions like the ones the still-untutored questioner of this poem's first stanza poses: Is Nature an "angel fallen from grace"? How do we explain her "fallings from her fair beginnings"? "Why weaves she not her world-webs to according lutes and tabors"? These, after all, are the very questions Hardy believes Milton, Wordsworth, and Shelley asked, respectively, and Hardy's poem answers them by implying that nature was never angelic but, rather, that we were seduced into a fall from the truth about nature by Milton; that the reason Wordsworthian children, as they mature, suffer "fallings from us, vanishings" of their vision is that their own utterly insubstantial fancy is falling and vanishing; and that if the "world weaver's" artwork seems a bit unrefined it is because poets such as Shelley (here is a horribly reductive misreading of "The Witch of Atlas") insisted upon making their own spritely imaginations the *sine qua non* of their definitions of divine creativity. Thus they blinded our orbs to the possibility that to believe in such a creator is to expect too much; thus they precipitated our fall into despair by encouraging us to do what the Satanic Byron of Carlyle's heretical criticism did, namely, to "strain after the unlimited."

In a poem collected with "The Lacking Sense" in *Poems of the Past and the Present* and roughly dated 1883 by the autobiography, Hardy uses the rather baffling, but perfectly Swinburnian technique of personifying nature in order to have her deny that she is an ordered or communicative or moral entity desiring or deserving of the celebration, the cursing, and (in either case) the allegorization and personification which she has so long elicited from mankind. No realm of moons like "Night queens," no harborer of "stars . . . sublime," this Herthian mother of mountains and men deplores the "mountings of mind-sight," the recently elevated "range of " man's "vision," which now allow him to see so far and dream so high that he inevitably finds only "blemish / Throughout my domain," that is, throughout the only reality man will ever know. The unfortunate belief, at once romantic and melioristic to stay within Swinburne's terminology, that "Every best thing . . . to best purpose / Her powers preordain" brings such bitter disappointments and even such social violence that Hardy's speaker hopes, in the final stanza of her poem, to

> grow, then, but mildews and mandrakes,
> And slimy distortions,
> Let nevermore things good and lovely
> To me appertain.
> ("The Mother Mourns," ll. 75–76, 85–88)

Hardy's new, reduced expectations about nature do not prevent him from using that convention of pathetic fallacy which marked his first poems almost as heavily as it filled Swinburne's early work with intense, brooding inner and outer landscapes. The difference lies in the way in which Hardy *uses* the pathetic fallacy. Just as he begins to use romantic love as a straw man to knock down in favor of new definitions of love in his post-1870 poetry, he uses the pathetic fallacy in his later work as a symptom of that romantic faith in the unity of self and nature which his own poetry denies. In "The Milkmaid" and "The Seasons of Her Year" (entitled "The Pathetic Fallacy" in the manuscript), Hardy uses his structure of progressive, point-by-point poetic didacticism to show that there is absolutely no spiritual connection or correspondence between inner life and external nature except that which is fancied by dreamers (or poets) oblivious to the reality of the perfectly mute and morally blank natural world. In the only slightly more bearable third poem of the group, "The King's Experiment," he creates yet another meaningless, unconscious, indifferent, yet somehow garrulous Dame Nature to ridicule a romantic lover who, because of his own temporary happiness, somehow feels at one with the One:

> "Why warbles he that skies are fair
> And coombs alight," she cried, "and fallows gay,
> When I have placed no sunshine in the air
> Or glow on earth today?"
>
> (ll. 5–8)

In poems like "The King's Experiment," Hardy uses what he believed to be a peculiarly romantic tradition (of "seeing everywhere the image of [one's] own mood") to challenge some of the foibles of that romantic vision of nature communicated by the tradition. Alone in a country setting, the speaker of "Nature's Questioning" hears nature sounding a little like Mycerinus, for it is "lipping" such Arnoldian questions as: "Has some Vast Imbecility, / Mighty to build and blend, / But impotent to tend, / Framed us?" "Or come we of an Automaton / Unconscious of our pains?" Or are we scourged by "some high Plan . . . / As yet not understood?" As the poem progresses, of course, we become aware that the "Questioning" is the poet's, not "Nature's," the final stanza reminding us that

> the winds, and rains,
>   And Earth's old glooms and pains
>   Are still the same, and Life and Death are neighbors nigh.

Just as Hardy surrounded a youthful, romantic identity with a more mature and stoical voice in "The Temporary the All," here he places one vision of nature (that of "Field, flock, and lonely tree" which "All seem to gaze at me . . . / Their faces dulled, constrained, and worn") within another (that of "winds, and rains . . . and Life and Death"). Thus he allows the latter to show up the former for what it is, namely, a projection of the disappointment the speaker feels when, having gone "Omen scouting" in the natural world for "Glad things that men" may "treasure" ("To Outer Nature"), he finds only a chance-ridden realm where "Good" and "gloom" and "Plan" and "pains . . . are neighbors nigh" ("Nature's Questioning," ll. 21–28). By the time the speaker "responds," in the poem's final stanza, to the "questions" which "Nature" asks by mumbling, "No answerer I," we are all too aware of the involution of reality which the romantic effects: it is Nature that has no answers, and it is the poet who is "dulled" and "worn" by his own metaphysical questions.

Far from being a system of images which in some way corresponds to man's individual and collective consciousness, nature for Hardy becomes a dumb, organic system that merely ferments individualized units of life and then, upon their extinction as individual beings, unconsciously and amorally disintegrates and reincorporates them into its own great compost heap. Speaking of "Shelley's Skylark" (1887?), Hardy defines his departure from the "faint penumbra" of the influential predecessor by celebrating not those elevating powers which were symbolized by the bird of Shelley's lyric but, rather, the fact that "Somewhere afield here something lies / In Earth's oblivious eyeless trust," a bird "That moved a poet to prophecies— / A pinch of unseen, unguarded dust" (ll. 1–4). Thus, for Hardy, the unseen bird of Shelley's "ecstatic" vision can only be doubly unseen (hence the pun, "unseen, unguarded"); a quest for it would be utterly impossible (even the quest for the body of the literal bird unseen by Shelley is a quest fit for "fairies"). All that Hardy can hope to "find" in his latter-day hymn is the fact that "the lark that Shelley heard" sang and "lived" just "like another bird" and "perished," a "ball of feather and bone."

As Walter F. Cannon has argued in an essay on nineteenth-century paleontology, "Poetry had to revise its habits. 'Thou wast not born for death, immortal bird,' was true, to Keats's knowledge; it is simply silly to a modern student. Nightingales will be fossils a million years from now." Like Teufelsdröckh's later view of nature as a mysterious, unconscious, and amoral life-eroding, life-creating cycle that quickly covers and metamorphoses human battlefields and monuments, and like Swinburne's similar conception of the natural realm in *Songs before Sunrise* and *Erechtheus*, Hardy's vision of nature after 1870 comes to be that of an indifferent organic system of recycling energies. In "Voices from Things Growing in a Country Churchyard," the flowers all declare whose bodies they incorporate, and in "The Dead Drummer" (1899), later entitled "Drummer Hodge," Hardy anticipates poets like Brooke, Owen, Thomas, and Rosenberg, by saying that "portion" of the field where the young man fell "Will Hodge forever be; / His homely Northern breast and brain / Grow up a Southern tree" (ll. 14–16). (For poets of the later era, of course, the English flesh transformed the tropical "Southern tree" into an English yew.)

In another short Hardy poem, entitled "Transformations," the poet's sole concern is with this theme of the dead who remain forever within the chance-ridden realm of living nature. In the final stanza of "Transformations," the poet simultaneously echoes not only ancient folk ballads but also Swinburne's "Anactoria," FitzGerald's *Rubáiyát,* and T. H. Huxley's assertion in "The Physical Basis of Life" (1868–69) that, in the context of the ever-continuing cycle of natural life, "so far as form is concerned, plants and animals are not separable," since a man who lives by nature's store will soon be fertilizing its continued organic production. Hardy, like Huxley, states that the material essences of the dead become incorporated in the eternal fibrous life of nature. By so doing, he cleverly revises the Easter morning (and thus preempts the Judgment Day) scenario: tomb-site utterances like "He is not here, but is risen" now become preludes to mere arboreal inspection:

> So, they are not underground,
> But as veins and nerves abound
> In the growths of upper air,
> And they feel the sun and rain,
> And the energy again
> That made them what they were!
>
> (ll. 13–18)

A man can never transcend, avoid, or reverse the process that time, chance, and nature determine for him. Hardy knew all too well, with Moschus, that men, "so strong and tall and wise," once they "be dead," lie and "sleep . . . both sound and long a sleep that is without waking" ("Lament for Bion," ll. 100–104). Once the skylark or the soldier has fallen, the substances of that brief life "will for ever be" subject to nature's unpredictable, indifferent cyclic powers. In Shelley's "Adonais," the shapes and fragrances of symbolic flowers are ultimately transformed, after frost, into the fiery radiance of eternal stellar light, but, as the belated and stoical "Rain on a Grave" reminds us, once Hardy's first wife has perished, her only hope for an immortal existence lies in the springtime fact that

> Soon will be growing
>   Green blades from her mound,
> And daisies be showing
>   Like stars on the ground,
> Till she form part of them—
> Ay—the sweet heart of them,
> Loved beyond measure
> With a child's pleasure
>   All her life's round.
>                           (1913, ll. 28–35)

It is more accurate to refer to Hardy's mature work as a poetry of strength, endurance, and stoical acceptance than as a poetry of optimism or of celebration, for Hardy's works, although they anticipate the last pages of *Go Down, Moses* (a veritable paean to recycled organic material), by no means attain the triumphant tone of Faulkner's prose. Nevertheless, it is clear that in the Phoenix-like descent and, in descent, rebirth, the poetry has rid itself of, and emerged from, that agonized and defeated tone characteristic of the earliest, anti-romantic laments, poems paralyzed between the fraudulence of past faiths and the horror of life without them. As Hardy stoically writes in "The Impercipient," one of his post-1870 *Wessex Poems*, "O, doth a bird deprived of wings / Go earth-bound wilfully!" (Swinburne had characterized his own maturation as having his "wings clipped," and in "A Match," his heretical ode to the God of Love, he had sought to "Pluck out" love's "flying feather.")

Hardy has gained a perspective on the past in part by framing its pain in his mature poetry. He surrounds the crises, the troubled progress, of a more youthful life and art with the knowledge possessed in the present, with a progressive and didactic structure that deflates weak dreams into stoical assertions. By doing so, he distances himself from, analyzes, and uses his own past (much as Swinburne did in "Prelude" and in *Erechtheus*) to methodically demonstrate the pathos, the conflicts, and sometimes even the tragedy brought about by all romantic overreaching. By doing so, he also manages to illustrate the value of not expecting too much from life and of seeing other men as delicate, perishable beings whose sufferings, while they cannot be transcended, can be shared.

MARGARET MAHAR

# Hardy's Poetry of Renunciation

With his final novel, *Jude the Obscure*, Thomas Hardy made his escape from narrative form. That it was an escape can be felt by comparing the novels to the lyric poetry, particularly those poems written after 1897. Hardy wrote over nine hundred lyrics throughout his career, and it seems likely that the poetry always provided a needed outlet, but the turn of the century can be taken as the date of his ultimate escape from the burden of the Aristotelian plot. What had been the luxury and freedom of the nineteenth-century novel, its sheer length, had become for Hardy a prison term, an interval to be filled. Even the opening chapters of *Jude the Obscure* suggest the author's desire to short-circuit the linearity of narrative sequence when he refers to his hero as "the predestinate Jude" and writes: "Jude was the sort of man who was born to ache a good deal before the fall of the curtain upon his unnecessary life should signify that all was well with him again." The bulk of the narrative can at best postpone that tragic end as the narrator is compelled to tell the whole long story once again.

It is a story Hardy has told many times before of men and women who unwittingly duplicate their own tragic failures and the tragic failures of their predecessors. J. Hillis Miller has marked the degree of parallelism of events and characters in Hardy's novels as well as the distance which separates desire and aim. It is the lack of rational causal links between past and present which determines that in Hardy's narratives, the present cannot fulfill the past, but merely repeat it. Insofar as the parallel lines which become the basic

From *ELH* 45, no. 2 (1978). © 1978 by The Johns Hopkins University Press.

configuration of Hardy's plots do converge, such convergence is typically a fatal coincidence. Hardy's characters are rarely able to find a rational link to connect the tragic errors of the past with present action, and so any temporal distance between parallel situations rarely produces progress. Finally, as the doublings of Hardy's plots prove increasingly fruitless, the difference between the beginning and end of a narrative becomes increasingly insignificant. Jude begins as a quest hero, yet the plot parodies the linearity of quest as Jude shuttles from Marygreen to Christminster to Marygreen to Christminster again. A story which begins with Jude's marriage to Arabella and Sue's marriage to Phillotson detours to describe divorce and the precarious union between Jude and Sue before returning to the remarriage of Sue and Phillotson, Arabella and Jude in an ending which is only a broken mirror image of the beginning.

Yet a significant difference and distance between beginning and end is precisely the basis of an Aristotelian plot, which Frank Kermode describes as founded on the principle of a double-take. The classical plot thrives on telling difference within identity as the end both curves back to the beginning and generates meaning out of the space between beginning and end, a space which Hardy found increasingly sterile as he attempted to fill—or fulfill—the demands of narrative form. As Jude's story becomes a succession of failures distinguished only by the places in which Jude fails—"At Marygreen," "At Christminster," "At Melchester," "At Shaston"—the temporal sequence of narrative collapses into the single fact of the end, known from the outset, that Jude would suffer. When I speak of the collapse of narrative form, I mean only "narrative form" as Hardy defined it, and a "collapse" only as measured against that definition. Hardy's strict theory of narrative form is emphasized in his own account of how he abandoned the novel "with all the less reluctance . . . in that the novel was . . . gradually losing all artistic form, with a beginning, middle, and end, and becoming a spasmodic inventory of items which had nothing to do with art." Hardy felt that the novel's "realism" must be rationalism, that the novel should pay homage to detail, to differences of place and time, as the variety within unity of an Aristotelian whole. Yet finally the cruel details which will distinguish Jude's suffering in each episode are not telling details which can justify or support the plot, but instead are overwhelmed by the monolithic fatality of the whole.

Clearly, Hardy's theory of narrative form as necessarily organic must be distinguished from his own practice. Jude the Obscure, and perhaps less obviously all of Hardy's novels, are self-conscious regarding their inability to rationalize the cause and effect of tragedy or join past and present within a credible organic whole. The success of Hardy's own most brilliant and ruthlessly honest plots produces a satirical version of the Aristotelian plot, as in the end Kermode's double-take becomes black humor—"Donne because we are too menny." Nevertheless, it is precisely this difference, between what Hardy felt the novel should be and what it became, in his own hands, which may have driven him in horror from the form.

In the lyric poem, Hardy found his freedom. Edward Said has suggested that when Hardy rejected the novel in favor of "a purposeful compressed lyric" he renounced the burden of repetitious narrative which must "if it is to be mimetic as well as productive . . . repeat as well as record the 'fathering-forth,' 'the over and overings' (the phrases are Gerard Manley Hopkins's) of human life." In Said's brief description, however, that turn from novel to lyric sounds almost bitter and a retreat: "That poetry depicts an impasse among things human, spiritual, divine, and inert, an impasse that is aesthetically useful to Hardy because it isolates things from one another and, mocking the sterility of time, proceeds to reassemble them in order to let them be destroyed. Time-bound narrative here cedes its spacious character and its familial coherence to crabbed, often destructive convergences in which time and purpose are emasculated at the moment of coincidence. One thinks in particular of Hardy's majestically ironic poem 'The Convergence of the Twain.'" Hardy's lyrics are purposeful in their compression, but even on the page they rarely look "crabbed." It is the novels which are crowded, dense with the relevant details of coincidences which close in on the characters; the lyrics renounce the effort at sustained explanation of cause and effect. In those lyrics, "time and purpose" are not so much aggressively and self-destructively "emasculated" as more wisely undercut or evaded. By abandoning the novel, Hardy freed himself from that type of pretended explanation and sustained and organic representation which he associated with the novel form. The formal constraints of his poems are just that, purely formal constraints, the logical necessities of rhyme and meter which are the invention of the artist and need not pretend to, nor bow to, the temporal succession and teleology of Aristotelian form. Hardy's lyrics make an art of the collapse of the novel, and the distance and difference between beginning and end, so important to Aristotelian plot, is abdicated in favor of the identity of rhyme.

The ease and apparent simplicity of the process is displayed within a very simple poem—"How She Went to Ireland."

> DORA'S gone to Ireland
>   Through the sleet and snow:
> Promptly she has gone there

> In a ship, although
> Why she's gone to Ireland
> Dora does not know.
>
> That was where, yea, Ireland,
>     Dora wished to be:
> When she felt, in lone times,
>     Shoots of misery,
> Often there, in Ireland
>     Dora wished to be.
>
> Hence she's gone to Ireland,
>     Since she meant to go.
> Through the drift and darkness
>     Onward labouring, though
> That she's gone to Ireland
>     Dora does not know.

The poem poses a conundrum: Dora's gone to Ireland, but "why" she went, even "that" she went "Dora does not know." Presumably Dora went to Ireland in a coffin. The poem, however, does not assert this meaning and the question of "how she went to Ireland" does not really matter. The poem's negative meaning, its unreason, lies in the blank space between desire and fulfillment. Dora's wish is fulfilled in some terribly left-handed way, such skewed symmetry is the fashion of the world, and whether death or some other equally non-rational force is the "explanation" of the poem is unimportant. What is significant is the degree of unreason which can be carried, so gracefully, within rhyme. The final "Dora does not know" echoes "Since she meant to go" and the echo seems nearly an answer to the poem's problem. Hardy's poems, like his novels, pose structural paradoxes, historical paradoxes, that can't be bridged or answered, but the effect of the form is to disclose and then dissolve the problem. Hardy's poems are not puzzles, holding a secret meaning. In his most typical lyrics past and present face each other in balanced stanzas and the explanation for the change lies in the white space between. Alliteration, refrain, meter, rhyme—each is a repetitive device which turns the poem in on an ever-vanishing center, a crux of meaning which disappears in the innocence of rhyme. With absolute and terrifying innocence rhyme voices the identity of accident: "wished to be" / "misery," "meant to go" / "does not know." Rhyme seems after all to provide reason; if Ireland is repeated often enough it seems logical that Dora should end there.

Of course the innocence of rhyme is, for Hardy, no innocence at all. Alliteration, refrain, meter, rhyme, those devices which so blatantly admit to accidental or purely formal identity, all the more blatantly assert the sterility of that distance, the lack of meaningful connection or contrast between the beginning and end of the rhyme—or time. Rhyme may have a lulling effect, but the unreason between lines is all the more horrifying when discovered. Nevertheless, precisely because the rhyme is not witty, because it does not attempt a purposeful connection, it succeeds. The juxtaposition of rhyme does not, I think, create an ironic effect in Hardy's poetry. For irony suggests that distance provides a further, second meaning and in these poems the notion of meaningful distance is mocked as merely the space on the page which the poet chooses not to use, the white space between rhyming stanzas or lines. In *Jude the Obscure* form may function as defense as the length of the narrative defers a predestined end, but the lyrics triumph by the boldest evasion. The effect of the rhyme is to enclose, encircle, and by the continuous negativity of the circle, to free. This is the triumph of the "Poems of 1912–13," poems written after the death of Hardy's first wife, Emma.

The marriage had been unhappy, and the "Poems of 1912–13" are poems of grief and regret, but they are love poems as well. The loss of the wife revives memories of the girl Hardy had met on Beeny Cliff, and he is haunted by both the fullness and the emptiness of the past. Death emphasizes the distance between early love and later division, for now "All's past amends / Unchangeable" ("The Going"). In this opening poem of the cycle the poet seems bewildered by his sudden and unexpected grief, asking why the wife who died departed so "quickly . . . / And calmly, as if indifferent quite," and why that unloved, unloving wife haunts him now:

> Why do you make me leave the house
> And think for a breath it is you I see
> At the end of the alley of bending boughs
> Where so often at dusk you used to be;
> > Till in darkening dankness
> > The yawning blankness
> Of the perspective sickens me!

The final three lines of the stanza seem an emblem for the crisis of dualism in Hardy's life and art. "Perspective" holds the clue to the dualism and identity of past and present viewpoint in Hardy's poems. As J. Hillis Miller has observed "the formal structure of Hardy's fiction is generated by the juxtaposition of the retrospective view of the narrator . . . and the narrow mystified view of the protagonist" while "in the lyric poetry these two perspectives are joined in a single mind." In this poem the speaker who sees a "yawning blankness" is both the young lover and the disillusioned husband. The perspectives of past and present are joined in a single consciousness, yet such joining does not reconcile past with present. The speaker as old man knows no more than the speaker as young man. Each knows desire as thwarted.

The two points of view are separate and yet dizzyingly interchangeable. "Perspective" is such a terribly self-reflexive concept that it is impossible to say whether the present is seen from the viewpoint of the past or the past from the viewpoint of the present, though that the situation is polar, with a gap between them, is clear. The speaker sees only blankness—where the link of a memory should be. The cause of that blankness, however, shifts with a shift of perspective, and the final lines of the stanza can be read backwards or forwards. Quite simply, is this a poem of grief or regret—grief that the loved one is gone, or regret, that there is so little to grieve? The "me" of the final line may be the bereaved lover who projects his sense of loss on the present scene; or it may be the very emptiness of the past which creates the husband's sense of loss in the present. The terms of the perspective are interchangeable for in each case the object is the same—"yawning blankness." That this object is also the subject is the partial truth of perspectivism, for in a perspectival framework it may be that one can only see oneself. The poles of past and present are then dissolved to "blankness" and in that blankness both the dualism and unity of past and present is expressed.

"After a Journey," a central poem in the cycle, eases the paradox:

> Summer gave us sweets, but autumn wrought division?
> Things were not lastly as firstly well
> With us twain, you tell?
> But all's closed now, despite Time's derision.

The poet stands after and before both summer and autumn, in a winter perspective. Time's divisions can be seen, but despite that change no further change seems possible. The sense of closure, encircling the inexplicable gap between desire and regret, is imaged in the final poem of the series, "Where the Picnic Was":

> Now a cold wind blows
> And the grass is gray,
> But the spot still shows
> As a burnt circle—aye,
> And stick-ends, charred,

> Still strew the sward
> Whereon I stand,
> Last relic of the band
> Who came that day!

The voice of this poem is the voice of a man beyond hurt, a man who has at last earned the right to become a ghost. Past, present, and future are one to him, desire and regret, expectation and memory, are one. He is no longer even pretending to make the future reconcile or redeem the past; the circle encloses an emptiness, an irreconcilable and open space. The unity of the circle is not rational, but this is not to say that the difference between summer and autumn, beginning and end, is meaningless. The paradox is maintained rather than collapsed by a circle with an empty center. It is simply that no effort is made to fill or bridge that empty space. For the poet of winter perspective it becomes a breathing space, and the difference and meaning between past and present is allowed to escape in that space.

In some very important way Hardy's poems release rather than condense meaning. This is perhaps why the variety and complexity of Hardy's poetic forms have frustrated so many of his readers. Samuel Hynes is frankly dismayed: "It should be apparent (and one is surprised that it wasn't apparent to Hardy) that elaborate, irregular stanzas lay claim, by their very irregularity, to some special importance, and delay the movement. One asks, 'Why did he make that line shorter, and that line longer?' The answer, in Hardy's case, is usually that there *is* no apparent reason, and even the best of his most elaborate 'inventions' seem quite accidental, as though the receptacle had been constructed first, and then an idea had been dropped into it (one can't help recalling Mrs. Hardy's remark about 'verse skeletons')." Hynes goes on to argue that "For Hardy . . . the inseparability of form and content, which we set so much store by, simply did not exist" and concludes: "Hardy did . . . use a great many verse forms, but this abundance . . . was a sign of a fundamental disability in Hardy: he could not create a form which would transfer its excellences from one poem to another. . . . Of the best of Hardy's poems, scarcely two are in the same metrical form; Hardy went on to the end of his life trying again." Form and meaning are not joined in Hardy's poems, but this is not a sign of a "fundamental disability." Hardy offers a devastating example of his ability to join form and meaning in *Jude the Obscure,* and his technical mastery as a prosodist suggests that he might, if he wished, have effected a similar union in the poems. He was not, however, in search of a form to fit his meaning—instead he proliferated forms which dispel meanings.

These forms, as Kenneth Marsden has noted, usually look very tidy on the page. He suggests that the "formal strictness and musicality" of the verse acts as a bulwark against disorder, and that Hardy's use of formal repetition, particularly rhyme-linked stanzas and the refrain, represents an effort to halt the flux of time. Yet the suggestion of "musicality," frequent in discussions of Hardy's form, contradicts the image of the poem on the page, static and regular, resisting time. As Marsden himself notes later, Hardy's is a form "half lyric, half meditative, in which the voice seems both to defy and obey the underlying structure." It is when reading the poems aloud that one finds the discontinuity, an unexpected irregularity, which may actually halt the movement of the poem, making the reader stumble. The opening stanzas of "In Front of the Landscape" illustrate the challenge:

> PLUNGING and labouring on in a tide of visions,
>     Dolorous and dear,
> Forward I pushed my way as amid waste waters
>     Stretching around,
> Through whose eddies there glimmered the customed landscape
>     Yonder and near
> Blotted to feeble mist. And the coomb and the upland
>     Coppice-crowned
> Ancient chalk pit, milestone, rills in the grass-flat
>     Stroked by the light,
> Seemed but a ghost-like gauze, and no substantial
>     Meadow or mound.

On first reading, this poem is, like many of Hardy's best poems, difficult to read aloud, impossible to sight-read. It is only with practice, that the reader finds the poem's true rhythm. For the same "cunning irregularity" which may seem to halt the movement of the poem may also, as Donald Davie has observed, drive the poem forward: "Though symmetry is maintained . . . it is so masked by the rhythmical variation that, instead of checking back to register how this stanza reproduces the earlier ones, we are propelled forward to see what will happen in the last. And thus we experience an unfolding from first to last, not a folding back three times over." As in the case of rhyme, it is the assumption of identity which is the joke, here a joke on the reader, making him stumble, and if discontinuities also push him eagerly forward, the final "double-take" is only aesthetic. The poem offers no answer to its puzzle, the joke of beginnings and endings is never explained. Hardy's poetry is often elaborately formal, but that formality is slight and a sham. The poems are quite self-consciously not monuments which by representing a life or an epoch stand as bulwarks against the ongoingness of time; the lyrics do not aspire to the novel's bulk. Their strength lies elsewhere, in their renunciation, a refusal of realism, which is for Hardy a refusal of both illusion and disillusion.

This is the economy of renunciation at work in "During Wind and Rain":

> They sing their dearest songs—
> He, she, all of them—yea,
> Treble and tenor and bass,
>   And one to play;
> With the candles mooning each face. . . .
>   Ah, no; the years O!
> How the sick leaves reel down in throngs!
>
> They clear the creeping moss—
> Elders and juniors—aye,
> Making the pathways neat
>   And the gardens gay;
> And they build a shady seat. . . .
>   Ah, no; the years, the years;
> See, the white storm-birds wing across!
>
> They are blithely breakfasting all—
> Men and maidens—yea,
> Under the summer tree,
>   With a glimpse of the bay,
> While pet fowl come to the knee. . . .
>   Ah, no; the years O!
> And the rotten rose is ript from the wall!
>
> They change to a high new house,
> He, she, all of them,—aye,
> Clocks and carpets and chairs
>   On the lawn all day,
> And brightest things that are theirs. . . .
>   Ah, no; the years, the years;
> Down their carved names the rain-drop ploughs.

Again, the form is a circle which describes a blank within. The poem follows the cycle of the seasons from winter through fall. Each season is given its stanza and the space between is filled only by the refrain: "Ah, no;

the years O! / How the sick leaves reel down in throngs! . . . Ah, no; the years, the years; / Down their carved names the rain-drop ploughs." The final line of each stanza offers a rhythmical variation on the last, but, as always in Hardy's poetry, that irregularity is slight and inexplicable. The detail of difference is poignant, yet it neither ties the stanzas together nor quite distinguishes the seasons of loss. The final effect and intention of the refrain is to create only the loosening sound of wind and rain, a sweeping, unreasoning continuity which gathers beginning, middle and end into its hollow, asserting the oneness of all natural loss. Shelley ended his "Ode to the West Wind" by asking "If winter comes, can Spring be far behind?" and Hardy's poem answers yes—both behind and ahead. Hardy affirms the cyclical state of things as they are, and that affirmation is neither quite acquiescence nor a springboard to transcendence. His mind is occupied elsewhere and the "yes" is a yes which defines, encircles, and discloses—so as to free the poet from the burden of explanation. Shelley is writing a poem of revolution and he leaps backward and then forward, breaking the cycle, making loss significant as a human difference between past and present, and so a prophecy of a final human gain. Hardy does not strain to find prophecy in time. With a wise passivity he simply follows the cycle of the seasons, refusing to be tempted by the unreasoning continuity of a circle or a sun. It is a circle he knows as the endless dance of desire, in which the origin may seem different, but the end is always the same—a defeat which obliterates the difference between days.

Hardy refuses to be tempted by the promise which seems to distinguish each season. The singularity of each scene—"With the candles mooning each face," "the garden gay . . . a shady seat," "a glimpse of the bay, / While pet fowl come to the knee"—these are the moments of a linear narrative dissolved in the continuous present of wind and rain. The charm of "Clocks and carpets and chairs" all the "brightest things that were theirs" is evoked and renounced. The glittering concrete, those hard and fast things that belong to the sun, to the representational world, these are the things named as lost, these are the bright images which Hardy's poems renounce. Samuel Hynes offers the shrewdest comment on "During Wind and Rain" when he speaks of its "imagistic bareness": "The scenes are rarely realized in any detail, and few readers, I should think, actually visualize the rain and the darkness; archetypal imagery bypasses this step to comprehension. The emotion-producing detail is there—the falling leaf or the night wind—but the specific surroundings are largely ignored. The imagery produces tone rather than picture." Visual detail and specific context are given over to the anonymous rhythm and tone of things passing away, the cry of leaves "which concerns no one at all."

"Clocks and carpets and chairs" are also the furnishings of a novel, and it is that "spasmodic inventory of items" which Hardy has renounced. "All the brightest things that were theirs" are the objects of a particular desire at a particular point in time. For Hardy a list of such items proved merely "spasmodic . . . without beginning, middle or end;" the dance of desire came to seem a to-and-fro shuffle "as we ply spasmodically our pleasuring" ("We Are Getting to the End"). The objects of desire blur in a meaningless series, and the subjects of desire, the characters of a novel, are also distinguished as alike—"He, she, all of them—aye." Here the list of characters is made present and affirmed, in order to be denied. The "ayes" and "yeas" which punctuate the poem have the effect of definite exclusion, as in the final line of Hardy's penultimate poem: "Yes. We are getting to the end of dreams!" ("We Are Getting to the End").

Hardy's poems do not pretend to the discrete representationality of a novel set in Wessex in a certain past. In the novels the past time was definite, marking a distance between the narrator and his characters, but for the poet of winter perspective, "all's closed now" and the tense is often a continuous present, or as in "During Wind and Rain," a contradictory but simultaneous present tense in which "They sing their dearest songs" as "Down their carved names the rain-drop ploughs." Even in their relation to each other, the poems pretend to no telling difference between earlier and later. As Hynes notes: "With the exception of *Satires of Circumstances,* each volume contains dated poems ranging over several decades (*Winter Words* spans sixty-one years); the internal organization rarely has any chronological order, except in obvious groups like the 'Poems of Pilgrimage,' the 'Poems of 1912–13,' and the war poems." In the poems there is no consciousness like Jude's which believes in linear time. Hardy could "find" a poem he had written years earlier and publish it—presumably it was as "true" as it ever was.

This is also the evasive gain of "During Wind and Rain." For in that poem, detail does not collapse into the wreckage of historical fact, but instead dissolves into the anonymity—which is, after all, soothing—of the sound of wind and rain. It is rather like the sound of waters in "Under the Waterfall":

> WHENEVER I plunge my arm, like this,
> In a basin of water, I never miss
> The sweet sharp sense of a fugitive day

Fetched back from its thickening shroud of gray.
   Hence the only prime
   And real love-rhyme
   That I know by heart,
   And that leaves no smart,
Is the purl of a little valley fall
About three spans wide and two spans tall
Over a table of solid rock,
And into a scoop of the self-same block.

  . . . . . . . . . . . . . . . . . .

. . . under the fall, in a crease of stone,
Though where precisely none ever has known,
Jammed darkly, nothing to show how prized,
And by now with its smoothness opalized,
   Is a drinking glass;
   For, down that pass
   My lover and I
   Walked under a sky
Of blue with a leaf-wove awning of green
In the burn of August, to paint the scene.

The rhyme of the water does not attempt to distinguish meanings. A chaste
and circular rhyme, it is "real" because it is an exact repetition, but "leaves
no smart" because the pain of separation, the difference between what was
and what is, is elided, or, like the chalice, to "smoothness opalized" by the
continuous rhythms of the water.

   The details which do distinguish past from present are compressed in
the third stanza:

   And we placed our basket of fruit and wine
   By the runlet's rim, where we sat to dine;
   And when we had drunk from the glass together,
   Arched by the oak-copse from the weather,
   I held the vessel to rinse in the fall,
   Where it slipped, and sank, and was past recall.

These are the too distinct memories which bring pain, and the virtue of the
poem's central simile is that it does not attempt to recover such a direct
image of the past, but measures instead the distance between wash-bowl and
waterfall: "The basin seems the pool, and its edge / The hard smooth face

of the brook-side ledge, / And the leafy pattern of china ware / The hanging plants that were bathing there." This is the juxtaposition of Coleridge's "Fancy," attempting neither synthesis nor dissolution and recreation of the image. Instead, the image is pointed to—as lying at some distance. Not only is the wash-bowl an incongruous image to stand for the pool of a waterfall, but the link between the two is a negative link. Plunging his arms into the wash basin, the speaker is reminded of the futile attempt to recover the chalice at the bottom of the waterfall. The chalice is "past recall" both in the past and in the present, and it is that loss, that absence, which joins wash-bowl and waterfall. The missing chalice is the missing link, and this is the delight of the poem, the basis for the poet's delight in his true love rhyme. For if he still possessed the chalice it would spoil the memory, standing as a too concrete, too meaningful representative of the past which has only a troubling significance and no rightful place in the present—another item for the junk-heap of history. Instead, "'in a crease of the stone, / Though where precisely none has known / . . . its presence adds to the rhyme of love / Persistently sung by the fall above. / No lip has touched it since his and mine / In turns therefrom sipped lovers' wine.'" The chalice remains the same, an inviolate, undemanding memory at the heart of the cascade's rhyme—which never needs to be explained.

Hardy's art is made of parallels, and in his poetry simile and metaphor are the dominant figures. The closer relations suggested by metonymy and synecdoche are rare, and even his metaphors do not pretend to bridge. Shelley provides the ideal definition of "vitally metaphorical language" in *A Defense of Poetry*: "[it] marks the before unapprehended relations of things and perpetuates their apprehension, until the words which represent them become, through time, signs for portions or classes of thought instead of pictures of integral thoughts." Shelley's own poetic practice betrays the theory. His long lines become litanies, stretching toward their object, never achieving that object, instead scanning, constantly reinterpreting and so extending that space of "generous superstition" in between. By the sheer speed of his line Shelley's language often seems almost to overtake his intention, but victory is at best fiery. Less dramatic, Hardy's shorter line and stanza is no less generous. One metaphor will suffice for he knows already that the distance between desire and its object is unbridgeable—it has been traveled so many times before. Shelley half-believes himself a monist; Hardy, always a dualist, knows that the only continuity is circular, the only unity underlying this unreasonable "relation between things" is the hole at the centre of the circle. This diminished space is not, however, an indication of diminished desire.

The space is open—a possibility which will be tried no longer, but which remains open and which precludes the bitterness of collapse. For Hardy monism would be bitterness, not hope.

Just as Hardy's rhymes and stanzas create a breathing space between past and present, his metaphors allow relief from both the "thing itself," what he refers to as the object's "true name," and our memory of it, the "false name" we call it by. Hardy's images are self-consciously erring representatives of that which is absent. The reflection of the moon in "Rushy-pond," "cork-screwed . . . like a wriggling worm," an image for "her very wraith, as scanned" is a familiar example of Hardy's most indirect mode of representation ("At Rushy Pond"). As in "Under the Waterfall" the pain and failure of attempting to recover the past is avoided. The shadow of the moon—now waned—stands for the shadow of the woman—now past "the bloomage of her prime." Any more direct mode of presentation, an image which mirrored her face, would be either an idealization, and so, more than the cork-screwed moon, a lie against the past, or honest, and so bitterly inadequate to the memory of the present. She cast a shadow when she left, and it is that shadow—the moment of her leaving—which is lengthened. The extremes of what she was and what she has become are avoided. What is alike in the past and in the present is that things are passing away.

If *Jude the Obscure* was written from the perspective of the end, much of this poetry is written from a further perspective, beyond the end. This is not eternity but a time rather like Emily Dickinson's midnight, that moment when a fly buzzes, and both life and death are held at bay. "The Love Letters," a short poem from *Winter Words,* illustrates the mode:

> I met him quite by accident
> In a bye-path that he'd frequent.
> And, as he neared, the sunset glow
> Warmed up the smile of pleasantry
> Upon his too thin face, while he
> Held a square packet up to me,
>     Of what, I did not know.
>
> "Well," said he then: "they are my old letters.
> Perhaps she—rather felt them fetters. . . .
> You see, I am in a slow decline,
> And she's broken off with me. Quite right
> To send them back, and true foresight;
> I'd got too fond of her! To-night
>     I burn them—stuff of mine!"

He laughed in the sun—an ache in his laughter—
And went. I heard of his death soon after.

The story comes "by accident" and we catch only the echo of the ending. It is already sunset when the poem begins, the tale is nearly over, and there is no need to recount the way to the end. Here there is no piling of fact on fact—no attempt to postpone collapse by consecutive labor. From a winter perspective there is no need to postpone the ending, for there is no need to justify the ending in terms of a beginning. And there is no failure of justification when the end comes. What happened is beyond hope and regret. His laugh in the sun, "an ache in his laughter," is sufficient to suggest the memory of the difference between beginning and end, a suggestion of a memory sufficient to hold the poem's center.

The images of Hardy's poems point neither backwards to their object, nor forward to an idea of the object. They postpone the effort of interpretation, noting the curious but unsatisfactory similarity between the object and the idea, and focusing on the further shadow cast by the idea, the memory of desire, the only link between origin and aim. So when "Love Watches a Window" opens, the object of desire has already disappeared:

"HERE in the window beaming across
Is he—the lineaments like him so!—
The saint whose name I do not know,
With the holy robe and the cheek aglow.
Here will I kneel as if worshipping God
When all the time I am worshipping you,
   Whose Love I was—
You that with me will nevermore tread anew
   The paradise-paths we trod!"

She came to that prominent pew each day,
And sat there. Zealously she came
And watched her Love—looking just the same
From the rubied eastern tracery-frame—
The man who had quite forsaken her
And followed another, it was thought—
   Be't as it may,
Thinner, more thin, was the lady's figure wrought
   By some ache, year on year.

Well now she's dead, and dead is he
From whom her heart once drew delight,

> Whose face glowed daily, lover-bright,
> High in the glass before her sight.
> And still the face is seen as clear
> In the rubied eastern window-gleam
> 　　As formerly;
> But not seen now is a passioned woman's dream
> 　　Glowing beside it there.

The lover has gone, and only the idea remains—"With the holy robe and the cheek aglow." In *Jude the Obscure* foreshortening seemed a harsh denial; here it is a graceful movement. The lack of full representation seems generous. The full story of her lover's wanderings need not be told: "Be 't as it may." "For now she's dead and dead is he," but the ending is not a blunt stop. The story is condensed to an emblem, the face seen clear "in the rubied eastern window-gleam," but it is also lengthened and diffused in the shadow of that emblem, "a passioned woman's dream / Glowing beside it there."

Hardy once praised a painting of the "*shadow* of the crucifixion instead of the crucifixion itself," as an example of making "the old faith . . . seem again arresting . . . by turning it in reverse positions." Hardy's poetry is also at one remove from both the original faith and the emblem of that faith, and can, when it wishes, measure it "in reverse" from ending to beginning. Hardy has given up the search for the object of belief which would be its own beginning and end. "A Sign-Seeker" is a relatively early poem about a man searching for such a sign sufficient unto itself, a fulfilled emblem standing as guarantee of both antecedent being and life after death. He scans natural and human world for "radiant hints of times to be— / Of heart to heart returning after dust to dust," and concludes:

> Such scope is granted not to lives like mine . . .
> 　　I have lain in dead men's beds, have walked
> 　　The tombs of those with whom I had talked,
> Called many a gone and goodly one to shape a sign,
> And panted for response. But none replies;
> 　　No warnings loom, nor whisperings
> 　　To open out my limitings,
> And Nescience mutely muses: When a man falls he lies.

Hardy is not renouncing his belief in antecedent being—he is affirming his dualism. No truth will free him from his temporal perspective, no whisperings will "open out the limitings" of a circle in which beginning and end are always one and always separate. Yet the suggestion that the response he

seeks might be a "warning," and the rhyme of "whisperings" with "limitings" almost implies that if the Word did come it might be too sufficient,
the perfect rhyme of "dust to dust," the collapse of "limitings" to a final
limit, the collapse of time to an ending that cast no shadows: "When a man
falls he lies."

"A Nightmare, and the Next Thing" suggests the danger:

> ON this decline of Christmas Day
> The empty street is fogged and blurred:
> The house-fronts all seem backwise turned
> As if the outer world were spurned:
> Voices and songs within are heard,
> Whence red rays gleam when fires are stirred,
> Upon this nightmare Christmas Day.
> The lamps, just lit, begin to outloom
> Like dandelion-globes in the gloom
> The stonework, shop-signs, doors, look bald;
> Curious crude details seem installed.
> And show themselves in their degrees
> As they were personalities
> Never discerned when the street was bustling
> With vehicles, and farmers hustling.
> Three clammy casuals wend their way
> To the Union House. I hear one say:
> "Jimmy, this is a treat! Hay-hay!"
>
> Six laughing mouths, six rows of teeth,
> Six radiant pairs of eyes beneath
> Six yellow hats, looking out at the back
> Of a wagonnette on its slowed-down track
> Up the steep street to some gay dance,
> Suddenly interrupt my glance,
>
> They do not see a gray nightmare
> Astride the day, or anywhere.

Hardy was in his late eighties when he wrote this poem. The "decline of
Christmas day" is "fogged and blurred" for a man who has seen so many
Christmases pass away. There is a lack of contrast in the scene. Accustomed
meanings turn their face to the wall: "The house-fronts all seemed backwise
turned . . . The stonework, shop-signs, doors look bald" and what appears
against the grayness are "curious crude details" which "show themselves in

their degrees / As they were personalities." The multiple and disparate details which distinguish past and present Christmases blur and from the chaos of continuity emerges the singular and universal truth of "six laughing mouths, six rows of teeth, / Six radiant pairs of eyes beneath." In his commentary on this poem J. O. Bailey suggests that "the nightmare" is a foreboding of death and the "next thing" is death itself. Certainly the third stanza seems a moment of revelation, the "next thing," but whether it is a revelation of death or life is difficult to say. Meaning has become too specific. The "over-determined poles" of birth and death are one in the identity of literal meaning. The balance which allows the poet his winter perspective on the contradictions of past and present has been disturbed. Here the object of belief is made present. Whisperings have become too explicit. This is the unity of the thing itself, in which idea and the object are one, and no metaphor can distance it as the memory of an object never quite achieved. The poet's eye is held by that image and in the final two lines of the poem he saves himself by a shift of perspective. The poet detaches himself from his own vision and frees himself by becoming one with those who do not see the gray nightmare—or the too literal meaning that emerges from the blur of that fantasy. Similarly, at the end of "God's Funeral" Hardy evades both the "gloom" and the "gleam" by joining the procession of mourners: "Thus dazed and puzzled 'twixt the gleam and gloom / Mechanically I followed with the rest." "Dazed and puzzled" is a feint: Hardy knows exactly what he has to fear from both gleam and gloom, the illusion and disillusion of those who "grew self-deceived, / . . . And what we had imagined we believed," those who attempted to naturalize or rationalize the imagination, striving to make the imagination's desire demonstrable as true belief.

For Hardy, it is wiser not to try to con the relations between things in search of "the eternal, the infinite, the one." This is the decision implicit through much of Hardy's poetry, made explicit in the final poem of *Winter Words*, "He Resolves to Say No More."

> O MY soul, keep the rest unknown!
> It is too like a sound of moan
> When the charnel-eyed
> Pale Horse has nighed:
> Yea, none shall gather what I hide!
>
> Why load men's minds with more to bear
> That bear already ails to spare?
> From now alway

Till my last day
What I discern I will not say.

Let Time roll backward if it will
(Magians who drive the midnight quill
With brain aglow
Can see it so,)
What I have learnt no man shall know.

And if my vision ranged beyond
The blinkered sight of souls in bond,
—By truth made free—
I'll let all be,
And show to no man what I see.

"—By truth made free—" is perhaps the most blasphemous line in Hardy's poetry. If he allowed himself bitterness the line would be bitter, for he scorns the hidden knowledge of a martyred prophet. Hardy's experiential, non-prophetic wisdom teaches that the truth would not free—it would collapse. The passive wisdom of "I'll let all be" is the affirmation of Hardy's own one true belief, a belief in dualism, that doubling of perspective, rhyme, and metaphor, an irreconcilable doubling in time which his poetry does not wish to overcome. "All's closed now," there's no need.

ELAINE SHOWALTER

# The Unmanning of the Mayor of Casterbridge

To the feminist critic, Hardy presents an irresistible paradox. He is one of the few Victorian male novelists who wrote in what may be called a female tradition; at the beginning of his career, Hardy was greeted with the same uncertainty that had been engendered by the pseudonymous publication of *Jane Eyre* and *Adam Bede*: was the author man or woman? *Far from the Madding Crowd*, serialised in the *Cornhill* in 1874, was widely attributed to George Eliot, and Leslie Stephen wrote reassuringly to Hardy about the comparisons: "As for the supposed affinity to George Eliot, it consists, I think, simply in this that you have both treated rustics of the farming class in a humorous manner—Mrs. Poyser would be home I think, in Weatherbury—but you need not be afraid of such criticisms. You are original and can stand on your own legs."

It hardly needs to be said that Stephen's assessment of Hardy's originality was correct; but on the other hand, the relationship to Eliot went beyond similarities in content to similarities in psychological portraits, especially of women. Hardy's remarkable heroines, even in the earlier novels, evoked comparisons with Charlotte Brontë, Jane Austen, and George Eliot, indicating a recognition (as Havelock Ellis pointed out in his 1883 review essay) that "the most serious work in modern English fiction . . . has been done by women." Later, Hardy's heroines spoke even more directly to women readers; after the publication of *Tess of the D'Urbervilles*, for ex-

From *Critical Approaches to the Fiction of Thomas Hardy* edited by Dale Kramer. © 1979 by Elaine Showalter. Macmillan, 1979.

ample, Hardy received letters from wives who had not dared to tell their husbands about their premarital experience; sometimes these women requested meetings which he turned down on his barrister's advice. Twentieth-century criticism has often focused on the heroines of the novels; judging from the annual *Dissertation Abstracts* (Ann Arbor, Michigan) this perennial favourite of dissertation topics has received new incentive from the women's movement. Recent feminist criticism, most notably the distinguished essays of Mary Jacobus on Tess and Sue, has done much to unfold the complexities of Hardy's imaginative response to the "woman question" of the 1890s. Hardy knew and respected many of the minor women novelists of his day: Katherine Macquoid, Rhoda Broughton, Mary Braddon, Sarah Grand, Mona Caird, Evelyn Sharp, Charlotte Mew. He actually collaborated on a short story with the novelist Florence Henniker, and possibly revised the work of other female protégées; his knowledge of the themes of feminist writing in the 1880s and 1890s was extensive.

Yet other aspects of Hardy's work reveal a much more distanced and divided attitude towards women, a sense of an irreconcilable split between male and female values and possibilities. If some Victorian women recognised themselves in his heroines, others were shocked and indignant. In 1890, Hardy's friend Edmund Gosse wrote: "The unpopularity of Mr. Hardy's novels among women is a curious phenomenon. If he had no male admirers, he could almost cease to exist. . . . Even educated women approach him with hesitation and prejudice." Hardy hoped that *Tess of the D'Urbervilles* would redeem him; he wrote to Edmund Yates in 1891 that "many of my novels have suffered so much from misrepresentation as being attacks on womankind." He took heart from letters from mothers who were "putting 'Tess' into their daughters' hands to safeguard their future," and from "women of society" who said his courage had "done the whole sex a service." Gosse, however, read the hostile and uncomprehending reviews of such women as Margaret Oliphant as evidence of a continuing division between feminist critics, who were "shrivelled spinsters," and the "serious male public." There were indeed real and important ideological differences between Hardy and even advanced women of the 1890s, differences which Gosse wished to reduce to questions of sexual prudery. Hardy's emphasis on the biological determinism of childbearing, rather than on the economic determinants of female dependency, put him more in the camp of Grant Allan than in the women's party. In 1892 he declined membership in the Women's Progressive Society because he had not "as yet been converted to a belief in the desirability of the Society's first object"—women's suffrage. By 1906 his conversion had taken place; but his support of the suffrage campaign was based on his hope (as he wrote to Millicent Garrett Fawcett) that "the tendency of the women's vote will be to break up the present pernicious conventions in respect of manners, customs, religion, illegitimacy, the stereotyped household (that it must be the unit of society), the father of a woman's child (that it is anybody's business but the woman's own except in cases of disease or insanity)."

Looking at the novels of the 1890s, and at Hardy's treatment of his heroines as they encounter pernicious conventions, A. O. J. Cockshut has concluded that there were unbridgeable gaps between Hardy's position and that of *fin-de-siècle* feminism:

> Hardy decisively rejects the whole feminist argument of the preceding generation, which was the soil for the growth of the idea of the "New Woman" à la Havelock Ellis and Grant Allen; and this is his final word on the matter. The feminists saw the natural disabilities as trivial compared with those caused by bad traditions and false theories. Hardy reversed this, and he did so feelingly. The phrase "inexorable laws of nature" was no cliché for him. It represented the slowly-garnered fruits of his deepest meditations on life. It was an epitome of what found full imaginative expression in memorable descriptions, like that of Egdon Heath. The attempt to turn Hardy into a feminist is altogether vain.

But the traditional attention to Hardy's heroines has obscured other themes of equal significance to a feminist critique. Through the heroes of his novels and short stories, Hardy also investigated the Victorian codes of manliness, the man's experience of marriage, the problem of paternity. For the heroes of the tragic novels—Michael Henchard, Jude Fawley, Angel Clare—maturity involves a kind of assimilation of female suffering, an identification with a woman which is also an effort to come to terms with their own deepest selves. In Hardy's career too there is a consistent element of self-expression through women; he uses them as narrators, as secretaries, as collaborators, and finally, in the (auto) biography he wrote in the persona of his second wife, as screens or ghosts of himself. Hardy not only commented upon, and in a sense, infiltrated, feminine fictions; he also understood the feminine self as the estranged and essential complement of the male self. In *The Mayor of Casterbridge* (1886), Hardy gives the fullest nineteenth-century portrait of a man's inner life—his rebellion and his suffering, his loneliness and jealousy, his paranoia and despair, his uncontrollable unconscious. Henchard's efforts, first to deny and divorce his passional self, and ultimately to accept and educate it, involve him in a pilgrimage of "unmanning" which is a movement towards both self-discovery and tragic vulnerability. It is in the analysis of this New Man, rather than in the evaluation of Hardy's New Women, that the case for Hardy's feminist sympathies may be argued.

*The Mayor of Casterbridge* begins with a scene that dramatises the analysis of female subjugation as a function of capitalism which Engels had recently set out in *The Origins of the Family, Private Property and the State* (1884): the auction of Michael Henchard's wife Susan at the fair at Weydon-Priors. Henchard's drunken declaration that Susan is his "goods" is matched by her simple acceptance of a new "owner," and her belief that in paying five guineas in cash for her Richard Newson has legitimised their relationship. Hardy never intended the wife-sale to seem natural or even probable, although he assembled in his Commonplace Book factual accounts of such occurrences from the *Dorset County Chronicle* and the *Brighton Gazette*. The auction is clearly an extraordinary event, which violates the moral sense of the Casterbridge community when it is discovered twenty years later. But there is a sense in which Hardy recognised the psychological temptation of such a sale, the male longing to exercise his property rights over women, to free himself from their burden with virile decision, to simplify his own conflicts by reducing them to "the ruin of good men by bad wives" (chap. 1).

This element in the novel could never have been articulated by Hardy's Victorian readers, but it has been most spiritedly expressed in our century by Irving Howe:

> To shake loose from one's wife; to discard that drooping rag of
> a woman, with her mute complaints and maddening passivity; to
> escape not by a slinking abandonment but through the public sale
> of her body to a stranger, as horses are sold at a fair; and thus
> to wrest, through sheer amoral willfulness, a second chance out
> of life—it is with this stroke, so insidiously attractive to male
> fantasy, that *The Mayor of Casterbridge* begins.

The scene, Howe goes on, speaks to "the depths of common fantasy, it summons blocked desires and transforms us into secret sharers. No matter what judgments one may make of Henchard's conduct, it is hard, after the first chapter, simply to abandon him; for through his boldness we have been drawn into complicity with the forbidden."

Howe brings an enthusiasm and an authority to his exposition of Henchard's motives that sweeps us along, although we need to be aware both that he invents a prehistory for the novel that Hardy withholds, and that in speaking of "our" common fantasies, he quietly transforms the novel into a male document. A woman's experience of this scene must be very different;

indeed, there were many sensation novels of the 1870s and 1880s which presented the sale of women into marriage from the point of view of the bought wife. In Howe's reading, Hardy's novel becomes a kind of sensation-fiction, playing on the suppressed longings of its male audience, evoking sympathy for Henchard because of his crime, and not in spite of it.

In this exclusive concentration on the sale of the wife, however, Howe, like most of Hardy's critics, overlooks the simultaneous event which more profoundly determines Henchard's fate: the sale of the child. Paternity is a central subject of the book, far more important than conjugal love. Perhaps one reason why the sale of the child has been so consistently ignored by generations of Hardy critics is that the child is female. For Henchard to sell his son would be so drastic a violation of patriarchal culture that it would wrench the entire novel out of shape; but the sale of a daughter—in this case only a "tiny girl"—seems almost natural. There may even be a suggestion that this too is an act insidiously attractive to male fantasy, the rejection of the wife who has only borne female offspring.

It is the combined, premeditated sale of wife and child which launches Henchard into his second chance. Orphaned, divorced, without mother or sisters, wife or daughter, he has effectively severed all his bonds with the community of women, and reenters society alone—the new Adam, reborn, self-created, unencumbered, journeying southward without pause until he reaches Casterbridge. Henchard commits his life entirely to the male community, defining his human relationships by the male codes of money, paternity, honour, and legal contract. By his act Henchard sells out or divorces his own "feminine" self, his own need for passion, tenderness, and loyalty. The return of Susan and Elizabeth-Jane which precipitates the main phase of the novel is indeed a return of the repressed, which forces Henchard gradually to confront the tragic inadequacy of his codes, the arid limits of patriarchal power. The fantasy that women hold men back, drag them down, drain their energy, divert their strength, is nowhere so bleakly rebuked as in Hardy's tale of the "man of character." Stripped of his mayor's chain, his master's authority, his father's rights, Henchard is in a sense unmanned; but it is in moving from romantic male individualism to a more complete humanity that he becomes capable of tragic experience. Thus sex-role patterns and tragic patterns in the novel connect.

According to Christine Winfield's study of the manuscript of *The Mayor of Casterbridge*, Hardy made extensive revisions in chapter 1. The most striking detail of the early drafts was that the Henchard family was originally composed of two daughters, the elder of whom was old enough to try to dissuade Susan from going along with the sale: " 'Don't mother!' whispered

the girl who sat on the woman's side. 'Father don't know what he's saying.'"
On being sold to the sailor Newson, however, Susan takes the younger girl
("her favourite one") with her; Henchard keeps the other. Hardy apparently
took this detail from the notice of a wife-sale in the *Brighton Gazette* for
25 May 1826: "We understand they were country people, and that the
woman has had two children by her husband, one of whom he consents to
keep, and the other he throws in as a makeweight to the bargain."

Hardy quickly discarded this cruel opening, and in the final text he
emphasises the presence and the sale of a single infant daughter. From the
beginning, she and her mother form an intimate unit, as close to each other
as Henchard and his wife are separate. Susan speaks not to her husband,
but to her baby, who babbles in reply; her face becomes alive when she talks
to the girl. In a psychoanalytic study of Hardy, Charles K. Hofling has taken
this bond between mother and daughter as the source of Henchard's jealous
estrangement, but all the signs in the text point to Henchard's dissociation
from the family as his own choice. The personalities of husband and wife
are evidenced in all the nuances of this scene, one which they will both
obsessively recall and relive. Hardy takes pains to show us Henchard's rigid
unapproachability, his body language eloquent of rejection. In Henchard's
very footsteps there is a "dogged and cynical indifference personal to himself"; he avoids Susan's eyes and possible conversation by "reading, or pretending to read" a ballad sheet, which he must hold awkwardly with the
hand thrust through the strap of his basket (chap. 1). The scene is in marked
contrast to Mrs Gaskell's opening in *Mary Barton*, for example, where fathers and brothers help to carry the infants; Hardy plays consciously against
the reader's expectation of affectionate closeness. When Susan and Elizabeth-
Jane retrace the journey many years later, they are holding hands, "the act
of simple affection" (chap. 3).

Henchard's refusal of his family antedates the passionate declaration of
the auction, and it is important to note that such a sale has been premeditated
or at least discussed between husband and wife. There are several references
to previous threats: "On a previous occasion when he had declared during
a fuddle that he would dispose of her as he had done, she had replied that
she would not hear him say that many times more before it happened, in
the resigned tones of a fatalist" (chap. 2). When Newson asks whether Susan
is willing to go with him, Henchard answers for her: "She is willing, provided
she can have the child. She said so only the other day when I talked o't!"
(chap. 1). After the sale, Henchard tries to evade the full responsibility for
his act by blaming it on an evening's drunkenness, a temporary breakdown
in reason and control; he even blames his lost wife's "simplicity" for allowing

him to go through with the act: "Seize her, why didn't she know better than bring me into this disgrace! . . . She wasn't queer if I was. 'Tis like Susan to show such idiotic simplicity" (chap. 2; ellipsis mine). His anger and humiliation, none the less, cannot undo the fact that the bargain that was struck, and the "goods" that were divided (Susan takes the girl, Henchard the tools) had been long contemplated. When it is too late, Henchard chiefly regrets his over-hasty division of property: "She'd no business to take the maid— 'tis my maid; and if it were the doing again she shouldn't have her!" (chap. 1).

In later scenes, Hardy gives Henchard more elaborated motives for the sale: contempt for Susan's ignorance and naiveté; and, as Henchard recalls on his first pilgrimage to Weydon-Priors, twenty-five years after the fair, his "cursed pride and mortification at being poor" (chap. 44). Financial success, in the mythology of Victorian manliness, requires the subjugation of competing passions. If it is marriage that has threatened the youthful Henchard with "the extinction of his energies" (chap. 1), a chaste life will rekindle them. Henchard's public auction and his private oath of temperance are thus consecutive stages of the same rite of passage. Henchard's oath is both an atonement for his drunken surrender to his fantasies, and a bargain with success. In Rudyard Kipling's *The Man Who Would Be King* (1899), a similar "contrack" is made, whereby Peachey Carnehan and Daniel Dravot swear to abjure liquor and women. When Dravot breaks his promise, they are exiled from their kingdom; so too will Henchard be expelled from Casterbridge when he breaks his vows. Save for the romance with Lucetta, in which he appears to play a passive role, Henchard is chaste during his long separation from his wife; he enjoys the local legend he has created of himself as the "celebrated abstaining worthy" (chap. 5); the man whose "haughty indifference to the society of womankind, his silent avoidance of converse with the sex" (chap. 13) is well known. His prominence in Casterbridge is produced by the commercialised energies of sexual sublimation, and he boasts to Farfrae that "being by nature something of a woman-hater, I have found it no hardship to keep mostly at a distance from the sex" (chap. 12). There is nothing in Henchard's consciousness which corresponds to the aching melancholy of Hardy's poem "He Abjures Love" (1883):

> At last I put off love,
>     For twice ten years
> The daysman of my thought,
>     And hope, and doing.

Indeed, in marrying Susan for the second time, Henchard forfeits something of his personal magic, and begins to lose power in the eyes of the towns-people; it is whispered that he has been "captured and enervated by the genteel widow" (chap. 13).

Henchard's emotional life is difficult to define; in the first half of the novel, Hardy gives us few direct glimpses of his psyche, and soberly refrains from the kind of romantic symbolism employed as psychological notation by the Brontës and by Dickens—dreams, doubles, hallucinatory illnesses. But the very absence of emotion, the "void" which Hardy mentions, suggests that Henchard has divorced himself from feeling, and that it is feeling itself which obstinately retreats from him as he doggedly pursues it. When J. Hillis Miller describes Henchard as a man "driven by a passionate desire for full possession of some other person" and calls the novel "a nightmare of frus-trated desire," he misleadingly suggests that the nature and intensity of Hen-chard's need is sexual. It is an absence of feeling which Henchard looks to others to supply, a craving unfocused loneliness rather than a desire towards another person. Henchard does not seek possession in the sense that he desires the confidences of others; such reciprocity as he requires, he coerces. What he wants is a "greedy exclusiveness" (chap. 41), a title; and this feeling is stimulated by male competition.

Given Henchard's misogyny, we cannot be surprised to see that his deepest feelings are reserved for another man, a surrogate brother with whom he quickly contracts a business relationship that has the emotional overtones of a marriage. Henchard thinks of giving Farfrae a third share in his business to compel him to stay; he urges that they should share a house and meals. Elizabeth-Jane is the frequent observer of the manly friendship between Henchard and Farfrae, which she idealises:

> She looked from the window and saw Henchard and Farfrae in the hay-yard talking, with that impetuous cordiality on the May-or's part, and genial modesty on the younger man's, that was now so generally observable in their intercourse. Friendship be-tween man and man; what a rugged strength there was in it, as evinced by these two.
>
> (chap. 15)

Yet Elizabeth-Jane is also an "accurate observer" who sees that Henchard's "tigerish affection . . . now and then resulted in a tendency to domineer" (chap. 14). It is a tigerish affection that does not respect that other's sepa-rateness, that sets its own terms of love and hate. Farfrae's passivity in this relationship is feminine at first, when he is constrained by his economic dependence on Henchard. There is nothing homosexual in their intimacy;

but there is certainly on Henchard's side an open, and, he later feels, incautious embrace of homosocial friendship, an insistent male bonding. Success, for Henchard, precludes relationships with women; male camaraderie and, later, contests of manliness must take their place. He precipitately confides in Farfrae, telling him all the secrets of his past, at a point when he is determined to withhold this information from Elizabeth-Jane: "I am not going to let her know the truth" (chap. 12). Despite Henchard's sincerity, the one-sidedness of the exchange, his indifference to Farfrae's feelings if he can have his company, leads the younger man to experience their closeness as artificial, and to resist "the pressure of mechanized friendship" (chap. 16).

The community of Casterbridge itself has affinities with its Mayor when it is first infiltrated by Farfrae and the women. Like Henchard, it pulls itself in, refuses contact with its surroundings. "It is huddled all together," remarks Elizabeth-Jane when she sees it for the first time. The narrator goes on: "Its squareness was, indeed, the characteristic which most struck the eye in this antiquated borough ... at that time, recent as it was, untouched by the faintest sprinkle of modernism. It was compact as a box of dominoes. It had no suburbs—in the ordinary sense. Country and town met at a mathematical line" (chap. 4; ellipsis mine). The "rectangular frame" of the town recalls Hardy's descriptions of the perpendicularity of Henchard's face; entering Casterbridge Susan and Elizabeth-Jane encounter the "stockade of gnarled trees," the town wall, part of its "ancient defences," the "grizzled church" whose bell tolls the curfew with a "peremptory clang" (chap. 4). All these details suggest Henchard, who is barricaded, authoritarian, coercive. He has become, as Christopher Coney tells the women, "a pillar of the town" (chap. 5).

Deeply defended against intimacy and converse with women, Henchard is vulnerable only when he has been symbolically unmanned by a fit of illness and depression; his susceptibility to these emotional cycles (the more integrated Farfrae is immune to them) is evidence of his divided consciousness. His romance with Lucetta takes place during such an episode: "In my illness I sank into one of those gloomy fits I sometimes suffer from, on account o' the loneliness of my domestic life, when the world seems to have the blackness of hell, and, like Job, I could curse the day that gave me birth" (chap. 12). Again, when Henchard is living with Jopp, and becomes ill, Elizabeth-Jane is able to penetrate his solitude, and reach his affections. At these moments, his proud independence is overwhelmed by the woman's warmth; he is forced into an emotionally receptive passivity. Yet affection given in such circumstances humiliates him; he needs to demand or even coerce affection in order to feel manly and esteemed.

In health, Henchard determines the conditions of his relationships to women with minimal attention to their feelings. His remarriage to Susan is the product of "strict mechanical rightness" (chap. 13); his effort to substantiate the union, to give it the appearance of some deeper emotion, is typical of his withholding of self:

> Lest she should pine for deeper affection than he could give he made a point of showing some semblance of it in external action. Among other things he had the iron railings, that had smiled sadly in dull rust for the last eighty years, painted a bright green, and the heavily-barred, small-paned Georgian sash windows enlivened with three coats of white. He was as kind to her as a man, mayor, and churchwarden could possibly be.
>
> (chap. 14)

To Susan, his kindness is an official function, and although he promises her that he will earn his forgiveness by his future works, Henchard's behaviour to women continues to be manipulative and proprietary. He deceives Elizabeth-Jane in the uncomfortable masquerade of the second courtship; he has not sufficient respect for Susan to follow her instructions on the letter about her daughter's true parentage. When he wants Lucetta to marry him, he threatens to blackmail her; when he wants to get rid of Elizabeth-Jane he makes her a small allowance. He trades in women, with dictatorial letters to Farfrae, and lies to Newson, with an ego that is alive only to its own excited claims.

Having established Henchard's character in this way, Hardy introduces an overlapping series of incidents in the second half of the novel which reverses and negates the pattern of manly power and self-possession. These incidents become inexorable stages in Henchard's unmanning, forcing him to acknowledge his own human dependency and to discover his own suppressed or estranged capacity to love. The first of these episodes is the reappearance of the furmity-woman at Petty Sessions, and her public denunciation of Henchard. Placed centrally in the novel (in chap. 28), this encounter seems at first reading to have the arbitrary and fatal timing of myth; the furmity-woman simply appears in Casterbridge to commit her "nuisance" and to be arraigned. But the scene in fact follows Henchard's merciless coercion of Lucetta into a marriage she no longer desires. This violation, carried out from rivalry with Farfrae rather than disappointed love, repeats his older act of aggression against human feeling. Thus the declaration of the furmity-woman, the public humbling of Henchard by a woman, seems appropriate. It is for drunk and disorderly behaviour, for disrespect

to the church and for profanity that she is accused; and her revelation of
Henchard's greater disorder is an effective challenge to the authority of patriarchal law. Hardy's narrative underlines the scene explicitly as forming the
"edge or turn in the incline of Henchard's fortunes. On that day—almost at
that minute—he passed the ridge of prosperity and honour, and began to
descend rapidly on the other side. It was strange how soon he sank in esteem.
Socially he had received a startling fillip downwards; and, having already
lost commercial buoyancy from rash transactions, the velocity of his descent
in both aspects became accelerated every hour" (chap. 31). The emphasis at
this point is very much on Henchard's fortunes and his bankruptcy; although
the furmity-woman's story spreads so fast that within twenty-four hours
everyone in Casterbridge knows what happened at Weydon-Priors fair, the
one person from whom Henchard has most assiduously kept the secret—
Elizabeth-Jane—unaccountably fails to confront him with it. Indeed, Hardy
seems to have forgotten to show her reaction; when she seeks him out it is
only to forgive his harshness to her. Retribution for the auction thus comes
as a public rather than a private shaming; and Henchard responds publicly
with his dignified withdrawal as magistrate, and later, his generous perfor-
mance in bankruptcy.

The next phase of Henchard's unmanning moves into the private sphere.
Hearing of Lucetta's marriage to Farfrae, he puts his former threat of blackmail into action, tormenting her by reading her letters to her husband. Henchard cannot actually bring himself to reveal her name, to cold-bloodedly
destroy her happiness; but Lucetta, investing him with a more implacable
will than he possesses, determines to dissuade him, and so arranges a secret
morning meeting at the Roman amphitheatre, which is far more successful
than even she had dared to hope:

> Her figure in the midst of the huge enclosure, the unusual plain-
> ness of her dress, her attitude of hope and appeal, so strongly
> revived in his soul the memory of another ill-used woman who
> had stood there and thus in bygone days, had now passed away
> into her rest, that he was unmanned, and his breast smote him
> for having attempted reprisals on one of a sex so weak.
>
> (chap. 35)

"Unmanning" here carries the significance of enervation, of a failure of nerve
and resolve; and also the intimation of sympathy with the woman's position.
The scene is carefully constructed to repeat the earlier meeting in the arena,
when the wronged Susan came to Henchard in all her weakness; Henchard's
"old feeling of supercilious pity for womankind in general was intensified by

this suppliant appearing here as the double of the first" (chap. 35). But Hardy does not allow us such simple sentiments; he intensifies the ironic complexities that make this meeting different. There is certainly a sense in which Lucetta is both touchingly reckless of her reputation, and weak in her womanhood; these elements will come together in the fatal outcome of the skimmington ride, when her wrecked honour and her miscarriage provide the emotional and physical shocks that kill her. While the Victorian belief in the delicacy of pregnant women, and also the statistical realities of the maternal death rate, are behind this incident (no contemporary reader of *The Mayor of Casterbridge* found it difficult to believe), Hardy obviously intends it symbolically as a demonstration of female vulnerability.

But, in another sense, Henchard is still deceiving himself about women's weakness, and flattering himself about men's strength; his "supercilious pity" for womankind is obtuse and misplaced. Lucetta's pathetic appearance, her plea of loss of attractiveness, is deliberately and desperately calculated to win his pity and to pacify his competitiveness. She is employing "the only practicable weapon left her as a woman" in this meeting with her enemy. She makes her toilette with the intention of making herself look plain; having missed a night's sleep, and being pregnant ("a natural reason for her slightly drawn look") she manages to look prematurely aged. Skilled at self-production and self-promotion, Lucetta thus turns her hand successfully to this negative strategy, with the result that Henchard ceases to find her desirable, and "no longer envied Farfrae his bargain." She has transformed herself into a drooping rag; and Henchard is again eager to get away. Lucetta's cleverest stroke is to remove the stimulus to Henchard's sense of rivalry by telling him that "neither my husband nor any other man will regard me with interest long" (chap. 35). Although he is defeated by a woman, Henchard's understanding of women is still constituted by a kind of patriarchal innocence; he is ashamed of himself but for all the wrong reasons.

It is out of this unmanning, out of his disturbed self-esteem which has been deprived of an enemy, that Henchard tries to reassert his legitimate authority, and rebuild his diminished stature, by invading the welcoming ceremonies for the Royal Personage. Defiantly clad in "the fretted and weather-beaten garments of bygone years," Henchard indeed stands out upon the occasion, and makes himself as prominent and distinctive as Farfrae, who wears "the official gold chain with great square links, like that round the Royal unicorn" (chap. 37). The scene is the necessary preamble to the fight between the two men; Henchard's flag-waving salute to Royalty is really a challenge to Farfrae, the lion against the unicorn. He puts himself in the young mayor's path precisely in order to be snubbed and driven back, to be inflamed so that he can take his revenge in "the heat of action." The wrestling-match with Farfrae is the central male contest of the novel—rivalries over business and women resolved by hand-to-hand combat. But in mastering Farfrae, even with one hand tied behind his back, Henchard is again paradoxically unmanned, shamed, and enervated. The sense of Farfrae's indifference to him, the younger man's resistance to even this ultimate and violent coercion of passion, robs Henchard of the thrill of his victory. Again, it is the apparently weaker antagonist who prevails; and in the emotional crisis, roles are reversed so that Farfrae is the winner. As for Henchard,

> The scenes of his first acquaintance with Farfrae rushed back upon him—that time when the curious mixture of romance and thrift in the young man's composition so commanded his heart that Farfrae could play upon him as on an instrument. So thoroughly subdued was he that he remained on the sacks in a crouching attitude, unusual for a man, and for such a man. Its womanliness sat tragically on the figure of so stern a piece of virility.
>
> (chap. 38)

The rugged friendship between man and man, so impressive when seen from a distance by Elizabeth-Jane, comes down to this regressive, almost foetal, scene in the loft. Henchard has finally crossed over psychically and strategically to the long-repressed "feminine" side of himself—has declared love for the first time to another person, and accepted the meaning of that victory of the weak over the strong. Thus, as Dale Kramer points out, "In relation to the pattern of tragedy, the 'feminine' Henchard is by his own definition a weakened man." But again, Henchard's surrender opens him for the first time to an understanding of human need measured in terms of feeling rather than property. In his hasty and desperate lie to Newson, Henchard reveals finally how dependent he has become on ties of love.

Thus the effigy which Henchard sees floating in Ten Hatches Hole, whence he has fled in suicidal despair after the encounter with Newson, is in fact the symbolic shell of a discarded male self, like a chrysalis. It is the completion of his unmanning—a casting-off of the attitudes, the empty garments, the façades of dominance and authority, now perceived by the quiet eye of Elizabeth-Jane to be no more than "a bundle of old clothes" (chap. 12). Returning home, Henchard is at last able to give up the tattered and defiant garments of his "primal days," to put on clean linen. Dedicating himself to the love and protection of Elizabeth-Jane, he is humanly reborn.

The final section of the novel fulfils the implications of Henchard's un-

manning in a series of scenes which are reversals of scenes in the first part
of the book. It is Elizabeth-Jane who assumes ascendancy: "In going and
coming, in buying and selling, her word was law" (chap. 42). He makes her
tea with "housewifely care" (chap. 41). As the "netted lion," Henchard is
forced into psychological indirection, to feminine psychological manoeuvres,
because he does not dare to risk a confrontation: "He would often weigh
and consider for hours together the meaning of such and such a deed or
phrase of hers, when a blunt settling question would formerly have been his
first instinct" (chap. 42). It is a humbling, and yet educative and ennobling
apprenticeship in human sensitivity, a dependence, Hardy writes, into which
he had "declined (or, in another sense, to which he had advanced)."

In his final self-imposed exile, Henchard carries with him mementoes
of Elizabeth-Jane: "gloves, shoes, a scrap of her handwriting, . . . a curl of
her hair" (chap. 44; ellipsis mine). Retracing his past, he has chosen to
burden himself with reminders of womanhood, and to plot his journey in
relation to a female centre. Even the circle he traces around the "centripetal
influence" of his stepdaughter contrasts with the defended squareness of the
Casterbridge he has left behind, the straight grain of masculine direction.
Henchard's final pilgrimage, to Elizabeth-Jane's wedding, is, detail by detail,
a reliving of the journey made by the women at the beginning of the novel.
He enters the town for the last time as they entered at the first; the poor
relation, the suppliant, the outsider. "As a Samson shorn" he timidly presents
himself at the kitchen door, and from the empty back parlour awaits Elizabeth-Jane's arrival. As Susan and Elizabeth-Jane watched him preside over
the meeting of the Council, so he now must watch his stepdaughter preside
over her wedding party. As Susan was overpowered by the sight of her former
husband's glory, and wished only "to go—pass away—die" (chap. 5), so is
Henchard shamed and overwhelmed by Elizabeth-Jane's moral ascendancy.
What is threatened and forgotten in the first instance comes to pass in the
second—the rejected guest departs, and neither Elizabeth-Jane nor the reader
sees him more.

In a sense which Hardy fully allows, the moral as well as the temporal
victory of the novel is Elizabeth-Jane's. It is she to whom the concluding
paragraphs are given, with their message of domestic serenity, their Victorian
feminine wisdom of "making limited opportunities endurable," albeit in "a
general drama of pain" (chap. 45). Casterbridge, under the combined lead-
ership of Elizabeth-Jane and Farfrae, is a gentled community, its old rough
ways made civil, its rough edges softened. We might read the story of Henchard as a tragic taming of the heroic will, the bending and breaking of his
savage male defiance in contest with a stoic female endurance. In such a

reading, Henchard becomes a second Heathcliff, who is also overcome by the domestic power of a daughter figure; like Heathcliff, Henchard is subdued first to the placidites of the grange, then to the grave.

Yet this romantic and nostalgic reading would underestimate Hardy's generosity of imagination. Virginia Woolf, one of Hardy's earliest feminist critics, attributed the "tragic power" of his characters to "a force within them which cannot be defined, a force of love or of hate, a force which in the men is the cause of rebellion against life, and in the women implies an illimitable capacity for suffering." In Henchard the forces of male rebellion and female suffering ultimately conjoin; and in this unmanning Hardy achieves a tragic power unequalled in Victorian fiction. It may indeed be true that Hardy could not be accounted a feminist in the political terms of the 1880s, or the 1970s; but in *The Mayor of Casterbridge* the feminist critic can see Hardy's swerving from the bluff virility of the Rabelais Club, and the misogyny of Gosse, towards his own insistent and original exploration of human motivation. The skills which Henchard struggles finally to learn, skills of observation, attention, sensitivity, and compassion, are also those of the novelist; and they are feminine perhaps, if one contrasts them to the skills of the architect or the statesman. But it is because Hardy dares so fully to acknowledge this side of his own art, to pursue the feminine spirit in his man of character, that his hero, like the great heroines he would create in the 1890s, is more Shakespearean than Victorian.

RAMÓN SALDÍVAR

# Jude the Obscure: *Reading and the Spirit of the Law*

*The letter killeth, but the spirit giveth life.*
—2 Corinthians

Concern for the nature and response of an author's audience is, in some respects, one of the original tasks of literary criticism. Over the past decade, however, attempts to incorporate rhetorical, linguistic, and cognitive theories into literary criticism have led to the development of a hefty bibliography on the nature of the reader's role in the communication network of author, text, and reader. These reader-oriented studies stress, from their various perspectives, that the reader, as much as any character, contributes to the shaping of the novel's fictive world through his interpretive actions.

The value of this recent emphasis on the reader's role in fiction and of "reception history" in general could very well be tested by a text such as the author's "Postscript" to *Jude the Obscure*. There, the reading public is accused of "curing" the novelist of all desire to write prose fiction. In this case Hardy would seem to have us question the reader's role in the *destruction* of texts, for in no uncertain terms, it is the reader, in his incapacity to read, who is the problem. Since we cannot read his meaning properly, even when there has been no "mincing of words" in its enunciation, complains Hardy, he will spare himself and the reader by simply ceasing to write novels.

Yet readers often find this and Hardy's later comment that he expected *Jude the Obscure* to be read as "a moral work" somewhat disingenuous. We can hardly imagine, after the reception of *Tess* and after his attempt to cancel his contract with Harper & Brothers for *Jude,* that Hardy would not have

From *ELH* 50, no. 3 (1983). © 1983 by The Johns Hopkins University Press.

anticipated the "shocked criticisms" that the publication of the novel evoked. In fact, when Hardy announces in the "Preface to the First Edition" that the novel will "deal unaffectedly with the fret and fever, derision and disaster, that may press in the wake of the strongest passion known to humanity," and then denies that "there is anything in the handling to which exception can be taken," he raises the very real possibility that the novel will be misread.

And it was misread. Angry reviewers and a solemn bishop saw in it, among other things, a cynical attack on the sacrament and institution of marriage. In a letter of November 1895 to Edmund Gosse, Hardy continued to express his concern for the proper reading of his novel by indicating that *Jude* was not merely "a manifesto on 'the marriage question'" (although, of course, it involves it)," but was more the story of the tragic result of two marriages because of "a doom or curse of hereditary temperament peculiar to the family of the parties." The fact is, of course, as critics have convincingly argued, that the novel *is* concerned with the marriage laws in more than just a casual way. And Hardy himself points out that the plot of *Jude* is "geometrically constructed" around the marital realignments of the four principal characters. They repeatedly change their relationships through their alternately prospective and retrospective visions of one another and of the options society and nature allow them.

Poised between a desire for natural freedom and the need for a stabilizing social order, Hardy's characters try to act within their "geometrically constructed" system of marital and symbolic associations to accommodate their desires and needs. Hardy is clear about this. He tells us that *Jude the Obscure* dramatizes the sociological effect of the Victorian failure to reconcile the antithetical realms of culture and nature: "The marriage laws [are] used . . . to show that, in Diderot's words, the civil law should be only the enunciation of the law of nature" ("Postscript"). But the difficulty of reading *Jude* properly may well stem from the fact that the novel is more than a realistic analysis of the historical condition of marriage in late Victorian England. I would like to suggest that the ambiguous status of the act of reading in the author's prefatory statements is only an indicator of a more radical investigation concerning reading and interpretation. By considering the interplay between "natural" and "civil" law, and by examining the nature of Hardy's "geometrically constructed" plot, we will be able to reflect on the possible relation of these issues to the apparent ease with which, according to Hardy, the novel can be misread. A reading of *Jude* that attempts to account for this cluster of formal and thematic elements can, I think, provide a new perspective on Hardy's conception of the realistic novel.

A first difficulty in understanding the novel is thematic and stems from the portrayal in the text itself of numerous cases of misreading. From the beginning, for instance, Jude sees in Christminster and its university the image of an attainable ideal world. His desire for this ideal vision involves a rejection of reality. For his own sporadically controlled, partially understood world, he substitutes the image of a unified, stable, and understandable one. Beguiled by his desire for order, the young Jude thus turns initially to language study both as a means of entering university life and as a possible course of stability. The narrator tells us:

> Ever since his first ecstasy or vision of Christminster and its possibilities, Jude had meditated much and curiously on the probable sort of process that was involved in turning the expressions of one language into those of another. He concluded that a grammar of the required tongue would contain, primarily, a rule, prescription, or clue of the nature of a secret cipher which, once known, would enable him, by merely applying it, to change at will all words of his own speech into those of the foreign one. . . . Thus he assumed that the words of the required language were always to be found somewhere latent in the words of the given language by those who had the art to uncover them, such art being furnished by the books aforesaid.
>
> (part 1, chap. 4)

Jude feels betrayed, consequently, when in his attempt to learn Latin he finds that "there was no law of transmutation, as in his innocence he had supposed." Jude's desired "law of transmutation," the "secret cipher" to a system of translation, could exist only if a prior permanent code existed to allow a free substitution of signifiers for one autonomous signified. The metaphor of translation at this early point in the novel is doubly interesting. It both reveals Jude's desire for a serenely immobile text whose content might be transported without harm into the element of another language, and alludes to the relation Hardy establishes in the "Postscript" of 1912 between civil and natural law, making one the "enunciation" of the other. These will continue to be decisive issues throughout the novel. At this point, Jude has no doubt that the voice of nature can, indeed, be read and translated, for when he "address[es] the breeze caressingly,' it seems to respond: "Suddenly there came along this wind something towards him—a message . . . calling to him, 'We are happy here!'" (part 1, chap. 3). By imposing single terms on the disparate variety of experience, we come to know and control our environment. Early on, however, Jude intuits that language is not a fixed system through which meaning can be "transmuted" from one system to another. Yet this is precisely the insight that Jude refuses to apply to his other readings of the world around him.

As he proceeds into the countryside, where the markings that hint at the limitations already imposed on his life stand to be deciphered, Jude's readings continue: "The only marks on the uniformity of the scene were a rick of last year's produce . . . and the path . . . by which he had come. . . . [To] every clod and stone there really attached associations enough and to spare—echoes of songs . . . of spoken words, and of sturdy deeds" (part 1, chap. 2). History, echoing across the generations, seems to focus on Jude at the bottom of "this vast concave" field, but he does not yet understand its voice. The substance of this discourse latent in the countryside is the essential dimension of the tradition into which he has been born. These "marks" and "associations" in the landscape of Wessex are "signs" inscribed by the force motivating all events, which Hardy was in *The Dynasts* to name the "Immanent Will." Thus, long before his birth, long before the story of his family has been inscribed, this tradition has already traced the patterns of behavior within which are ordered the possible changes and exchanges that will occur in Jude's short life. Each crucial event in Jude's life seems to invite the reader to interpret Jude's actions as an attempted reading of the role ascribed to him in some determining book of fate.

Initially, the young orphan Jude seems to see the schoolmaster, Phillotson, as an embodiment of his controlling "dreams" (part 1, chap. 3), and as a symbolic substitute for the absent "real" father. Accordingly, when Phillotson leaves Marygreen, Jude replaces him with an ideal representation. Jude reads that ideal presence into the natural landscape of Wessex as Christminster, "that ecclesiastical romance in stone" (part 1, chap. 5):

> Through the solid barrier of cold cretaceous upland to the north-ward he was always beholding a gorgeous city—the fancied place he likened to the new Jerusalem. . . . And the city acquired a tangibility, a permanence, a hold on his life, mainly from the one nucleus of fact that the man for whose knowledge and purposes he had so much reverence was actually living there.
>
> (part 1, chap. 3)

In this ecstatic vision, Christminster, whose mark is "a halo or glow-fog," seems to send that "message" I mentioned earlier, but it is a message that must be translated from natural to human terms with all the inherent errors of language and its "figures." In a moment of revelation, George Eliot's narrator in *Adam Bede* comments that "Nature has her language, and she is not unveracious; but we don't know all the intricacies of her syntax just yet, and in a hasty reading we may happen to extract the very opposite of her real meaning." Now, as Jude attempts to learn the "syntax" of nature's "message," Christminster, through Phillotson, becomes the organizing center of his life: "It had been the yearning of his heart to find something to anchor on, to cling to—for some place which he could call admirable. Should he find that place in this city if he could get there?" The phrasing of his question in the rhetorical mode produces a grammatical structure that implies the existence of freedom of choice, when in fact, the pattern of choices has already been established for Jude by his own propensity for misreading. As he answers the questions posed in indirect discourse, beguiled by the transformation his mind has imposed on the scene through figurative language, Jude takes literally his own metaphors of the "new Jerusalem," "the city of light," and "the castle, manned by scholarship and religion."

Sue Bridehead is also presented in the metaphoric language that names Christminster. Jude has seen, for example, "the photograph of [her] pretty girlish face, in a broad hat, with radiating folds under the brim like the rays of a halo" (part 2, chap. 1). In fact, the metaphoric process by which Sue will later replace Christminster and Phillotson in Jude's dreams has been facilitated by the nature of Jude's language long before he is even conscious of Sue: earlier, he had become "so romantically attached to Christminster that, like a young lover alluding to his mistress, he felt bashful at mentioning its name" (part 1, chap. 3). The transfer from Phillotson, to Christminster, and finally to Sue as metaphors of that sustaining vision is thus a simple, determined step. Jude's false reading of Sue at a chapel in Christminster as being "ensphered by the same harmonies as those which floated into his ears" leads him to conclude that he has "at last found anchorage for his thoughts" (part 2, chap. 3). When Jude finally meets Sue, he approaches her cautiously and speaks to her as he has spoken of Christminster, "with the bashfulness of a lover" (part 2, chap. 4). At each step in the evolution of his story, his controlling dream is a fiction that he imposes on wayward circumstances.

From the beginning then, the object of desire is not "real" in any sense, but is a "phantasmal" (part 2, chap. 2) creation of Jude's own mind, as are the "ghosts" that haunt Christminster. For Jude, however, the ghosts of his desires disappearing into the "obscure alleys" of Christminster are as real as Arabella's "disappearance into space" (part 2, chap. 1). Constituting himself as a whole subject by an identification with another who repeatedly disappears, "A hungry soul in pursuit of a full soul" (part 3, chap. 10), Jude is accordingly threatened by the possibility of disappearing too: "Jude began to be impressed with the isolation of his own personality, as with a self-spectre . . . seeming thus almost his own ghost" (part 2, chap. 1). Phillotson, Christminster, Arabella, and most strikingly, Sue, thus become the figures of an ideal paradise, which is fundamentally inaccessible, insofar as it is one more metaphor in a structuring system of substitutions and exchanges of phantasmal dreams. The displacement of desire among the various characters points out the existence of a symbolic order, which creates the idea of autonomy when, in fact, the characters exist determined by their propensity for interpretive error.

As an exegetic scholar, "divining rather than beholding the spirit" of his texts (part 1, chap. 5), Jude can never resist the temptation to read deep meanings, the "assemblage of concurring and converging probabilities" of "truths," into a scene (part 2, chap. 1). Yet it is less "absolute certitude" that lies hidden beneath the manifest content of human experience in the novel than it is a mystified, but nonetheless threatening, organization of that content. When Jude thereafter looks into Sue's "untranslatable eyes" (part 2, chap. 2) and immediately begins to interpret her character, he is only repeating the established pattern of error. Despite the difference in the agency that produces it, Jude manifests again the desire for that earlier "law of transmutation." Here, Sue's eyes reveal a text to be translated; but, as with the Greek and Latin grammars, no master code exists to guarantee the authority of Jude's translation. The rules governing the metonymic transfer, the figure Latin rhetoric calls *transmutio,* belong to the same illusion of a metaphysics of presence in the word, and to the same hallucination of a language determined on the basis of a verbal representation. Just as language is constituted through repetition, so too does Jude's life acquire a narratable consistency. But the symbolic "inscription" of Jude's desires upon the surface of Wessex as he travels its roads from Christminster to Shaston, to Aldbrickham and back again, constitutes only the provisional creation of meaning through a process of deferment. As Jude's dreams are transmuted from Arabella to Christminster, and to Sue, the fantasy of stability creates an apparently meaningful and readable text. It is always only in retrospect, however, that Jude' perceptions of those illusions of totality and stability can be organized and lived as an aesthetically coherent *meaning.*

But it is more the inner tensions produced by the characters' shifting relations that shape the action than haphazard or indifferent circumstance. And it is not entirely coincidental that the act of reading surfaces again to indicate these changes in connection with the constant letters that reaffirm the importance of writings, signs, inscriptions, and marks in the lives of these characters. Altogether there are at least thirty-two letters indicated or implied in the novel, ranging from one-line suicide notes (*"Done because we are too menny"*) to full-sized "carefully considered epistle[s]" (part 6, chap. 4), directly or indirectly narrated, delivered or not delivered. The numerous instances of inscriptions and carvings reinforce the importance of the "letter" in the text as the emblem for the force of illusion.

The first of these letters between Jude and Sue had simply called for their initial meeting, but it was "one of those documents which, simple and commonplace in themselves, are seen retrospectively to have been pregnant with impassioned consequences" (part 2, chap. 4). By the time Sue is engaged to Phillotson, Jude is receiving sudden "passionate" letters (part 3, chap. 1) from her that seem to close the psychic distance between them in a way that they can never quite imitate in person. "'It is very odd—'" Jude says at one point. "'That you are often not so nice in your real presence as you are in your letters!'" "'Does it really seem so to you?'" asks Sue, who then replies, "'Well, that's strange; but I feel just the same about you, Jude'" (part 3, chap. 6). A letter is a medium that effectively separates the writer from the effects of the message, while the message received is often one created by the reader himself. Even in their coldest tones, Sue's letters, while banishing Jude, nevertheless constantly summon him to her by the very fact that they establish a link of communication between them. Similarly, Phillotson's letter relinquishing Sue paradoxically begins reestablishing his hold on her; for the "shadowy third" (part 4, chap. 5), like the substantial couple, is always primarily constituted by this act of communication.

Moreover, when Sue writes a letter, she simultaneously removes and retains her absence and distance. This simultaneity of absence and presence is primarily an outcome of written discourse and is indicative of Jude's more general mystification concerning the existence of a stabilizing meaning. Sue is an eminently desirable woman, but she also becomes a sign in Jude's mind for an absent source of meaning. Accordingly, the act of writing becomes a bolster for the illusion of presence and wholeness within a discourse that appears innocent and transparent. Sue's letter can never replace her, but, conversely, her "real presence" is never identical with the original self promised in the letter. The written word does not allow access to the thing in itself, but always creates a copy, a simulacrum of it that sometimes moves the reader of the word more strongly than can the actual presence of the represented thing. Thus, the curious result is that the graphic sign, rather than the actual presence, of the desired becomes the cause of emotive energy. For Jude, the desire for this originary "anchoring point" becomes an indispensable illusion situated in the syntax of a dream without origin.

The intersubjective complex that structures the novel *Jude the Obscure* offers us some version of the following schema:

1. dreams that fail—Jude, Phillotson, Sue

2. marriages that fail—Jude and Arabella; Sue and Phillotson; Jude
   and Sue; Arabella and Cartlett; both sets of parents; the legendary ancestor (mentioned in part 5, chapter 4)
3. returns to original failures—Jude and Arabella at Christminster;
   Sue and Phillotson at Marygreen.

We began, remember, with Jude and Arabella at Marygreen, and with Sue
and Phillotson at Christminster. The intervening movements in the plot that
lead to the present renewal of the characters' former relations thus trace the
pattern that characterizes the narrative structure. It is a *chiasmus,* the cross-
shaped substitution of properties: the original couples are reunited, but in
reverse locales. Hardy had referred to this structure more obliquely as the
"geometric construction" behind his novel. Elsewhere he calls it the "quad-
rille" that puts in motion the opposing qualities of the four main characters.
But it turns out that the very process of "construction" that the characters'
actions enact is really one more reversal of earlier misguided "constructions."
Would it not follow then that this new turn should restore the characters to
their "proper" places? That is, if Jude and Sue have been improperly associated at Christminster, might we not recover a measure of truth by simply
restoring her to Phillotson at Marygreen? Since this structure of reversal is
not only at work on the thematic level of the story, within the marital relationships among the characters, but also animates the greater structure of
the narrative, the plot itself, the deconstruction of its pattern has significant
implications for the novel's concept of a readable, constructive, integrating
process in general.

Jude's idea of a synthetic "anchoring point" of semantic stability originates as the effect of a prior requirement, namely, the requirement that the
elements of that synthesis can themselves be permanently fixed in relation to
stable qualities. Failing to integrate the ideal and the real with Sue, Jude is
no more likely to do so with Arabella. Sue's situation with Phillotson and
Jude is even more complex, for the two are versions of the same in different
registers. Further reversals, consequently, promise only continued instability.
And, I would say, it makes little difference in this novel whether one calls
the trope governing the structure of the narrative metaphor, metonymy,
chiasmus, or simply a "geometric construction," for from the first, the characters' roles have been inscribed in the determining contextual system defined
by the marriage laws.

In the Victorian novel marriage is preeminently the foundation of social
stability. As a quasi-contractual agreement, it sets up the participants as a
center for other integrating relationships. These relationships are not simply

necessary for society; they constitute it. And that larger social and historical life, the world of symbolic relationships, forms in dialectical turn the structure that orders individual behavior in Hardy's novels. In a moment of pure poetic insight Sue comments on the nature of those relations:

> "I have been thinking . . . that the social moulds civilization fits us into have no more relation to our actual shapes than the conventional shapes of the constellations have to the real star-patterns. I am called Mrs. Richard Phillotson, living a calm wedded life with my counterpart of that name. But I am not really Mrs. Richard Phillotson, but a woman tossed about, all alone, with aberrant passions, and unaccountable antipathies."
>
> (part 4, chap. 1)

With remarkable clarity Sue recognizes that the social woman is a representation, transposed and supplemented by desire, of her real self. But the relation between her natural and social selves is like the relation between "real star-patterns" and traditional interpretations of the "conventional" constellation shapes, like that between a referent and its linguistic sign—that is, *aesthetic* and hence *arbitrary.* The concept of the self is the product of an aberrant substitution of rhetorical properties. Sue here clearly understands that this rhetorical operation is at best a metaphorical, interpretive act—one that is necessarily open to a variety of figural misreadings.

We have seen that the law that regulates marriage ties in this novel superimposes the kingdom of *culture* on that of *nature.* Following its dictates, Jude artificially imposes a vision of organic totality (figured at different times by Phillotson, Christminster, Sue, etc.) onto nature and accords it a moral and epistemological privilege. In contrast, the narrator's ironic comments show Jude's substitutions and realignments within the marriage system and within the pattern of metaphors for his vision of an "anchoring point" to be purely formal, analogous only by contingency, and hence without privilege. When the value of those associations is questioned, when the notion of Sue as the representation of Jude's dreams is made problematic, the possibility of a simple relation between signified and signifier is also questioned.

That formerly unquestioned assumption is the original moment of illusion that the narrative demystifies. The narrator reveals to us that Jude's and Sue's notion of a privileged system of law is an hypothesis, or a fictional construct (a *doxa*), that makes the orderly conduct of human affairs possible. It is not a "true" and irrefutable axiom based on knowledge (an *episteme*). Their tendency, as revealed by the metaphorical rhetoric of their desires, is always to abide by the lawful order of "natural" logic and unity: " 'It is,' "

Sue says at one point, "'none of the natural tragedies of love that's love's usual tragedy in civilized life, but a tragedy artificially manufactured for people who in natural state would find relief in parting!" (part 4, chap. 2). But if the order of "natural" law is itself a hypothetical construct rather than a "natural" occurrence in the world, then there is no necessary reason to suppose that it can, in fact, provide "relief." And it is Sue once again, who, after the tragic deaths of their children, perceives that possibility when she says to Jude:

> "We said . . . that we would make a virtue of joy. I said it was Nature's intention, Nature's law and *raison d'être* that we should be joyful in what instincts she afforded us—instincts which civilization had taken upon itself to thwart. . . . And now Fate has given us this stab in the back for being such fools as to take Nature at her word!"
>
> (part 6, chap. 2)

Jude, who likes to think of himself "as an order-loving man" of an "unbiased nature" (part 4, chap. 2), can only stand by helplessly as he hears Sue destroy the basis of their "natural" marriage.

Hardy's novel situates itself explicitly within the context of the marriage laws that establish Victorian society. It portrays, as Hardy tells us, the attempted translation of the law of nature into civil terms. The characters, however, cannot legitimately perform this translation without confusing the names of two such divergent semantic fields as those covered by "natural law" and "civil law." Confusion arises because the terms designate contextual properties, patterns of integration and disintegration, and not absolute concepts. In Hardy's Wessex, the "law of nature" designates a state of relational integration that precedes in degree the stage of "civil law" since civil law only "enunciates" what is already present in nature to be read. The undoing of a system of relations codified in "civil law" will always reveal, consequently, a more fragmented stage that can be called "natural." This prior stage does not possess moral or epistemological priority over the system that is being undone. But Jude always does assign it priority.

Remembering that "his first aspiration—towards academical proficiency—had been checked by a woman, and that his second aspiration—toward apostleship—had also been checked by a woman," Jude asks himself ungallantly "'Is it . . . that the women are to blame; or is it the artificial system of things, under which the normal sex-impulses are turned into devilish domestic gins and springs to noose and hold back those who want to progress?'" (part 4, chap. 3). The weight of the second clause of the question makes it simply rhetorical: the women are of course not to blame. Although the "natural" pattern that Jude and Sue attempt to substitute for the accepted "civil" one is itself one system of relations among others, they see it as the sole and true order of things and not as an artifice like civil structure. But once the fragmentation of the apparently stable structure of civil law is initiated, endless other versions of "natural law" might be engendered in a repeating pattern of regression.

The decisive term characterizing Jude's and Sue's relationship, "natural law," thus presents itself to be read as a chiastic pattern also. Natural law deconstructs civil law; but natural law is then itself open to the process of its own analysis. Far from denoting a stable point of homogeneity, where they might enact the mythic integration of their "one person split in two," the "natural law" of Hardy's Wessex connotes the impossibility of integration and stability. Any of Hardy's texts that put such polarities as natural and civil law, desire and satisfaction, repetition and stability into play will have to set up the fiction of a synthetic process that will function both as the deconstructive instrument and as the outcome of that deconstruction. For Hardy, dualisms are never absolute. Deconstruction, however, is the process that both reveals the deluded basis of the desire for the synthesis of dualism, and also creates the elements necessary for a new and equally deluded desire for integration. *Jude the Obscure* thus both denies the validity of the metaphor that unites "natural" and "civil" law, and elaborates a new metaphor to fulfill the totalizing function of the original binary terms. This new metaphor of life as an organic and orderly process now allows the narrative to continue by providing a myth of a future moment when, as Phillotson's friend Gillingham says, Jude and Sue might make "their union legal . . . and all would be well, and decent, and in order" (part 6, chap. 4). This mythic moment, however, never comes.

It is crucial, then, that the basic conflicts of the novel occur within the "give and take" of marriage, for it situates the issue directly in the referential contexts of ethics and legality. Civil law, in fact, can be conceived as the emblem of referentiality *par excellence* since its purpose is to codify the rules for proper social intercourse. But to abide by the law, we must be able to read its text; ignorance is after all, in English common law, no excuse. Attempting to read it, Jude concludes that "we are acting by the letter; and 'the letter killeth'!" (part 6, chap. 8). Jude thus interprets the Pauline dictum, "The letter killeth but the spirit giveth life," as an injunction against a *literal* reading of the codes governing ethical action. Yet his *figural* reading leads to no spiritual truth either. On the contrary, Jude's illusions result from a figurative language taken literally, as with Sue he takes "Nature at her word."

For Jude and Sue, then, there is no text present anywhere that is yet to be transmuted, yet to be translated from natural to civil terms. There is no *natural* truth written anywhere that might be read without being somehow altered in the process. The text of associations Jude fabricates around him is already woven of interpretations and differences in which the meaning of dreams and the desire for illusions are unnaturally coupled. Everything in Wessex "begins" with repetition, with secondary images of a meaning that was never present but whose *signified* presence is reconstituted by the supplementary and belated word of Jude's desires.

I am saying, of course, that the narrative of *Jude the Obscure,* while telling the story of Jude's and Sue's unhappy marriages, also dispels the illusion of a readable truth; that the novel gains its narrative consistency by the repeated undoing of the metaphor of life as organic unity. But the story that tells why figurative denomination is an illusion is itself *readable* and *referential* to the negative truth that Jude never perceives, and the story thus relapses into the very figure it deconstructs. The structure of the narrative as chiasmus, the cross-shaped substitution of properties, also tells, therefore, another story in the form of allegory about the divergence between the literal and figural dimensions of language. That the text reverts to doing what it has claimed to be impossible is not a sign of Hardy's weakness as a novelist, for the error is not with the text, nor with the reader who attempts to understand it. Rather, I would say that with Jude we find that language itself, to the extent that it attempts to be truthful, necessarily misleads us about its own ability to take us outside its own structures in search of meaning.

The myth of a stabilizing natural or civil law, then, is actually the representation of our will to make society seem a unified and understandable organism. But Hardy's novel persists in showing society's laws as open to subversion by the actions of the individuals who make up society. In everyday life, there is an ever possible discontinuity between the word of the law, its spirit, and the practice, the letter, of the law. And the necessary failure of the law to enforce its monologic interpretations of the infinite variety of human behavior can lead to the subversion of the entire relational system. This explains why Jude, by his actions, constantly and unintentionally subverts the Word that he figures in Sue and in his dreams of a university career.

In applying the accepted social law to themselves, Jude and Sue constitute a version of the law, but in applying the general law to their particular situation, they instantaneously alter it. Rather than serving as a source of universal order from which social relations might be stabilized and unified within a social totality, the accepted social law exhibits its inability to constrain the heterogeneity of social relations. The law, then, is always shown to be grammatically structured, since it always engenders only a contingent, contextual meaning. Jude's revolutionary attempt to establish a ground for authentic meaning thus produces an anarchy of mutually exclusive readings of the one piece of language. "The letter killeth." This discontinuity between the "letter" and the "spirit" of the law, between a literal and a figural reading of its sign, is what constitutes Hardy's break with referentiality. Although the law indicates that "The letter killeth," Jude finds it impossible to decide what is the *letter* and what the *spirit* of the law. In each reading, whether within a "natural" or a "civil" system, the law is transposed, altered, and led to produce the conditions for its own undoing. Like Sue's ambiguous letters, the law is consequently only a promise (which cannot be kept) of a future stability and is never adequate to deal with the instability of the present moment.

The repetitions in the novel put at stake not only the relation between Jude's present actions and his family's history, but also the very readability of the initial text of that history. Everywhere about him, history calls out to be read, but Jude consistently fails to do so properly. Because he cannot read it, his actions are never simply a representation of that past, but are an interpretation that has gone awry. Since the novel is itself a kind of history, it too is open to all the errors of interpretation of which it speaks. Hardy's "Postscript," which calls attention to the decisive issues of reading and interpretation, must thus be seen in retrospect as an ironic repetition of the situation dramatized in *Jude* concerning the impossibility of authoritative readings, for it accuses the reader of partaking in Jude's error. We cannot read the novel as Jude reads the motto of his life, that is, with the expectation of encountering an ideally sanctioned stable truth.

But how *are* we to read it then? If the notion of representation is to be at all meaningful, we must presuppose the stability of subjects with stable names who are to be represented, and a rapport between the sign and the referent in the language of the representation. Yet both conditions are absent from this text (notoriously so in the allegorical figure of little Father Time). We can, of course, discern similarities among the characters' various actions. And as we read, attempting, in Hardy's words, "to give shape and coherence to this series of seemings," we too must rely on Jude's example in constructing an interpretive model. But we cannot accept his model of metaphoric synthesis as an absolute. Jude's model of metaphor (governing the patterns of idealization and substitution) is erroneous because it believes in its own referential meaning—it believes that the inwardly desired "anchoring point" can be concretely encountered in the external world as Phillotson, as Christminster, as Arabella, or as Sue. It assumes a world in which literal and figural properties can be isolated, exchanged, and substituted. For the reader and the narrator, metaphoric synthesis persists within the interpretive act, but not as the ground of ultimate reconciliations. Jude himself, however, remains caught in the error of metaphor. But it is an error without which reading could not take place.

We thus find that Hardy's narrative puts the assurance of the truth of the referent into question. But in making this situation thematic, it does allow a meaning, the text, to exist. We are not dealing simply with an *absence* of meaning, for if we were, then that very absence would itself constitute a referent. Instead, as an allegory of the breakdown of the referential system, *Jude the Obscure* continues to refer to its own chiastic operations. This *new* referentiality is one bounded strictly by the margins of textuality. In our courses on the nineteenth-century novel we find it convenient to use *Jude* as a "transitional" text; it is either the last of the Victorians or the first of the Moderns. Morton Zabel has written, for instance, that Hardy was "a realist developing toward allegory ... who brought the nineteenth century novel out of its slavery to fact." This seems to me fine, as far as it goes. But I would add that this allegorical pattern manifests itself in *Jude* primarily through the subversive power of the dialogic word, which refuses to be reduced to the single "anchoring point" of a transcendent and determining Will, Immanent or otherwise.

As Hardy came to see early on, the function of realistic fiction was to show that "*nothing* is as it appears." It is no wonder, then, that Hardy's last novel was misread. The suggestive and poetic force of *Jude* arises less from its positive attempt to represent appearance than from its rejection of any vision pretending to convey the totality and complexity of life. Accordingly, in *Jude* Hardy repudiates the notion that fiction can ever be Truth, that it can ever "reproduc[e] in its entirety the phantasmagoria of experience with infinite and atomic truth, without shadow, relevancy, or subordination." He dramatizes, instead, the recognition that in narrative "Nothing but the illusion of truth can permanently please, and when the old illusions begin to be penetrated, a more natural magic has to be supplied." To be realistic, the text must proceed as if its representing systems correspond to those in the world; it must create a new illusion of reference to replace the old of representation.

But this transmutation of illusions modifies the original considerably. Like Sue's "real presence," perpetually deviating from the ideal figure of Jude's dreams, the letter of the text, "*translat[ing]* the qualities that are already there" in the world, contains after all only the inadequate ciphers of the spirit of meaning, not the "thing" itself. The deconstruction of the metaphorical model of substitution and translation (operating in Jude's various desires for Christminster, Sue, natural law, etc.) is performed by the rhetorical structure of chiasmus, whose own figural logic both asserts and denies referential authority. From the reader's point of view, the results of each of the figural movements can then be termed "meanings," but only by forgetting that the resulting sociological, ethical, legal, or thematic categories are undone by the very process that creates them.

It may well be, therefore, that Hardy's final novel does not "mean"; but it does signify to a redoubtable degree. It signifies the laws of language over which neither Hardy nor his readers can exercise complete control. To read those laws is to undermine their intent. This is why Hardy, like Jude who adds to the textual allegory of Wessex and generates its history while marking its closure, is bound to allegorical narratives: he creates the fiction of an ideal reader while he constructs a narrative about the illusion of privileged readings. On this level of rhetorical self-consciousness, prose fiction is on the verge of becoming poetry.

SUSAN BEEGEL

# Bathsheba's Lovers: Male Sexuality *in* Far from the Madding Crowd

In 1875 an anonymous author for the *Saturday Review* faced the problem of briefly summarizing for his readers the plot of *Far from the Madding Crowd*. He described the story as follows: "'Bathsheba and her Lovers' the novel might have been called (except that its own title is very much better), and the story consists in contrasting the three lovers in their respective attitudes towards the heroine." Such reduction of a complex novel's plot is possible precisely because that plot is so obviously archetypal. How many of our myths and fairy tales are stories of an unusual, beautiful woman courted by three men? And how many of our culture's greatest literary masterpieces (*The Merchant of Venice* and *Portrait of a Lady* immediately come to mind) revolve around this always interesting romantic situation?

The critical problem of describing the novel's ending is far more complex. When, at the conclusion of *Far from the Madding Crowd*, Bathsheba weds Gabriel Oak, can we safely say that hero and heroine live happily ever after? Or do we regretfully admit that Bathsheba, despoiled by experience, makes a pragmatic, perhaps economic marriage; that she and Oak will live an undisturbed but uninteresting existence ever after? In other words, is this marriage the triumphant conclusion to a book that advocates a new, even Lawrentian, kind of love—one based on equality of the sexes and destined to survive the exigencies of the modern world? Or is *Far from the Madding Crowd* about the inferiority of passionate sexuality to utilitarian reason,

From *Sexuality and Victorian Literature,* edited by Don Richard Cox. © 1984 by the University of Tennessee Press.

making Bathsheba's marriage a kind of "settling for less" and a fitting conclusion to a tragedy of reduced expectations?

Critical tradition almost unanimously supports a tragic reading of the novel. Henry James was disappointed by Bathsheba's union with Gabriel, who was, in James's opinion, "much too good for her." J. Hillis Miller writes that the "happy" ending of *Far from the Madding Crowd* is in reality only "the lovers' acceptance of the gap between them. . . . Bathsheba Everdene and Gabriel Oak have outlived the time when they might have sought the bliss of full union with another person." Perry Meisel feels that Bathsheba "remains morally infected, even with the apparent reestablishment of peace and order by marriage at the end of the novel," and that the marriage resists "the deepest impulses" of this early work. Indeed, those critics who concede that *Far from the Madding Crowd* has a true "happy" ending take pains to point out that same ending's departure from the sexual pessimism expressed in the body of the novel and from the tragic endings of Hardy's mature work. Normally the anomalous ending of *Far from the Madding Crowd* is ascribed to Hardy's own marriage, approaching as he hastily concluded the novel and prompting an uncharacteristic optimism.

Of course critical controversy about the novel's ending is controversy about the nature of the novel itself. In the final paragraph of chapter 56, "After All," the narrator himself tells us what he thinks of Gabriel and Bathsheba's impending marriage:

> He accompanied her up the hill, explaining to her the details of his forthcoming tenure of the other farm. They spoke very little of their mutual feelings; pretty phrases and warm expressions being probably unnecessary between such tried friends. Theirs was that substantial affection which arises (if any arises at all) when the two who are thrown together begin first by knowing the rougher sides of each other's character, and not the best till further on, the romance growing up in the interstices of a mass of hard prosaic reality. This good-fellowship—*camaraderie*—usually occurring through similarity of pursuits, is unfortunately seldom superadded to love between the sexes, because men and women associate, not in their labours, but in their pleasures merely. Where, however, happy circumstance permits its development, the compounded feeling proves itself to be the only love which is strong as death—that love which many waters cannot quench, nor the floods drown, beside which the passion usually called by the name is evanescent as steam.

Many things about this passage have a disappointing ring for the person of Romantic sensibility. The impassioned speeches of *Wuthering Heights,* say, are missing here: the newly betrothed lovers discuss farming. We find a "mass of hard prosaic reality" at the very center of the passage; romance only grows up in its "interstices," like some sort of lichen growing in the crevices of a rock—not a very lovely or luxuriant plant, but, if you will excuse the pun, a hardy one. The narrator defines "good fellowship" and "*camaraderie*" as the qualities which give this rock-lichen love its strength, qualities perhaps less interesting than the passion Hardy says this love is stronger than.

Nor is the passage without Hardy's characteristic sexual pessimism. Pretty speeches are only "*probably* unnecessary" between lovers who are "tried friends." Gabriel and Bathsheba's "*camaraderie*" is "*seldom* super-added to love between the sexes," a "substantial affection" which, although it has arisen between them, usually does not arise at all. Yet it must be noted that the sexual pessimism of *Far from the Madding Crowd* is only pessimism. Hardy laments the rarity of the marriage he describes, but he has not yet embraced the nihilism that would deny its possibility.

I want to propose an alternative to the critical tradition which reads *Far from the Madding Crowd* as a tragedy of reduced expectations. Our readings of Hardy's later works have distorted our appreciation of *Far from the Madding Crowd*'s text. It is time to stop reading the novel as a failed tragedy, as a tragic novel botched by a "happy" ending like that imposed on *The Return of the Native* by publishers. Instead, we should sharpen our reading of the mature tragedy, the fulfillment of Hardy's early pessimism, by appreciating *Far from the Madding Crowd*'s early, though fragile, optimism. It is the novelist's fullest treatment of a rare, ideal love, written when Hardy, on the brink of his first marriage, still believed in both the existence of such love and the possibility of fulfilling it. Such a reading only strengthens the poignancy of the later novels. True cynicism proceeds from disillusionment, and we cannot fully appreciate the tragedy of doubt or disbelief without embracing the faith (or at least the faint hope) which preceded them.

In the passage quoted above, Hardy tells us that Gabriel and Bathsheba's love is not only stronger than passion, but stronger than death. This triumph over death is the stuff of comedy, not tragedy, and a comic reading of the novel depends on the truth of the narrator's claim. It is a substantial claim, and deserves careful consideration. Towards that end, we must return to the story an early critic called "Bathsheba and her Lovers," and give the three suitors and "their respective attitudes towards the heroine" the thorough comparison the novel's archetypal plot demands.

Bathsheba's most passionate lovers, Boldwood and Troy, are the purveyors of death in this novel. The intensity of Boldwood's jealousy more than once leaves Bathsheba frightened for her own life. Small wonder she is not interested in reading *Othello* when Liddy suggests it. The marriage Boldwood offers her is one of entombment, of suffocation. In fact, Boldwood proposes to Bathsheba by promising her that she will never have to step outdoors again. Bathsheba accepts his last proposal because she is hounded, because she feels guilty, and because her marriage to Troy has caused her to lose faith in the possibility of love. Such a marriage would be a living death for Bathsheba, and a true tragedy of reduced expectations.

It is after Bathsheba's acceptance that the incipient deadliness of Boldwood's passion bursts forth. He murders Troy and must be prevented from shooting himself. In Boldwood's case, passion and morbidity are clearly aligned. His idealized love for Bathsheba is a love which insists on exclusive possession of its object. He wants to lock her away from the rest of the world to be placed on a pedestal, ornamented, and worshipped. This is not love at all, but an insane amalgam of homicidal and suicidal impulses. Moreover, it is a reactionary passion. He is an old and old-fashioned landowner who seeks to turn a modern businesswoman back into a household goddess. There is a kind of bewildered, pathetic regressiveness about Boldwood, a desire to stop the earth from turning and the clocks from ticking. Boldwood is a character who cannot adapt to change and who is finally broken by it. His chief desire is to bring himself and his love into a deathlike condition of stasis.

Sergeant Troy's brand of death-dealing passion is superficially different from Boldwood's reactionary, frigid idolatry. Troy is hotly sexual, but his lust, like Boldwood's idealizing passion, is an agent of death. His affair with Fanny Robin leaves a dead mother and a stillborn child; his marriage to Bathsheba results in his own death. If Hardy uses Boldwood to expose the essential morbidity of the Victorian male's sentimental woman-worship, he uses Troy to expose the equivalent morbidity of that other-annihilating, self-consuming love exalted by Emily Brontë in her treatment of Cathy and Heathcliff. But Troy is no Heathcliff, although equally destructive. Troy lacks the dimension of a Byronic hero. While a rebel against conventional morality, Troy lacks Heathcliff's Romantic capacity for deep feeling and abiding love. Troy is a false front of words and red uniform, a cardboard cutout of a Byronic hero and therefore a criticism of the Romantic affinity for outlaw heroes and demon lovers.

Troy nevertheless possesses all the sexual magnetism of a Heathcliff. Bathsheba is hooked, both literally and figuratively, from the moment her skirt catches on the sergeant's spurs. She is trapped and, significantly enough, cannot escape without either tearing her skirt off or waiting until he pleases to release her. It is Bathsheba who initiates the novel's most explicit sexual encounter by begging Troy to perform the sword-exercise for her—not with a walking-stick, mind you, but with a real sword. The appointment is made in whispers, with many blushing protests, and Bathsheba arrives panting and trembling at the site of the rendez-vous, the hollow amid the ferns. Keeping in mind those useful concepts of phallic symbol and feminine space, let us have a close look at the sword-play in the fernpit.

Troy exhibits the different sorts of cuts, and Bathsheba is much impressed. "How murderous and bloodthirsty!" she exclaims. The foreplay over with, Troy then proposes a more exciting game.

> "They are rather deathy. Now I'll be more interesting, and let you see some loose play—giving all the cuts and points, infantry and cavalry, quicker than lightning, and as promiscuously—with just enough rule to regulate instinct and yet not to fetter it. You are my antagonist, with this difference from real warfare, that I shall miss you every time by one hair's breadth, or perhaps two. Mind you don't flinch, whatever you do."
>
> . . . He flourished the sword by way of introduction number two and the next thing of which she was conscious was that the point and blade of the sword were darting with a gleam towards her left side, just above her hip; then of their reappearance on her right side, emerging as it were from between her ribs, having apparently passed through her body. The third item of consciousness was that of seeing the same sword, perfectly clean and free from blood held vertically in Troy's hand (in the position technically called "recover swords.") All was as quick as electricity.
>
> "Oh!" she cried out in affright, pressing her hand to her side. "Have you run me through?—no, you have not! Whatever have you done?"

At this juncture, Bathsheba becomes frightened, and Troy only gains permission to proceed by lying, telling her that the sword is not really sharp. We then proceed to the scene's climax, in the sexual as well as literary sense, for if "motion and light destroy the materiality of bodies," so does orgasm:

> In an instant the atmosphere was transformed to Bathsheba's eyes. Beams of light caught from the low sun's rays, above, around, in front of her, well-nigh shut out earth and heaven—all

emitted in the marvelous evolutions of Troy's reflecting blade, which seemed everywhere at once, and yet nowhere specially. These circling gleams were accompanied by a keen rush that was almost a whistling—also springing from all sides of her at once. In short, she was enclosed in a firmament of light, and of sharp hisses, resembling a sky-full of meteors close at hand.

This chapter is obviously a brilliantly written paradigm of sexual intercourse. No wonder Bathsheba feels as if "she had sinned a great sin" when Troy finally kisses her and departs. But what does the sword-exercise tell us about the nature of sexual passion? In Troy's own words, it is "rather deathy." The iridescent, world-obscuring blur of the sword in the air and the fresh luxuriance of the fern-pit are undeniably sensual and attractive. But the scene's real excitement depends on the sword's capacity to deal death. The lovers are arrayed as antagonists in a mortal combat. Bathsheba flirts with death by standing still for Troy—at first unknowingly, and then willingly, as he lops off a lock of her hair and splits a caterpillar on her breast. Twice Bathsheba believes he has murdered her by penetrating her with the blade; and Troy exerts all his skill to bring her as near to death as possible without actually killing her.

It is the sword-exercise which wins Bathsheba's love, but her love is also "rather deathy." It is self-destructive, a desertion of will. Hardy writes, "Bathsheba loved Troy in the way that only self-reliant women love when they abandon their self-reliance. When a strong woman recklessly throws away her strength she is worse than a weak woman who never had any strength to throw away. One source of her inadequacy is the novelty of the situation. She has never had practice in making the best of such a condition. Weakness is doubly weak by being new." Bathsheba's love for Troy is a love which embraces helplessness; his feeling for her one which exults in the powerlessness of its victim. Although Bathsheba is weakened by her love, her strength is not entirely dissipated, for she remains the head of the household, whom the unemployed Troy must pester for pocket money. He finds the situation unendurable, and it seems to typify the sexual power struggle of their marriage. Throughout the book, Troy both fears and resents Bathsheba's proud independence of character.

The essential morbidity of their relationship is dramatized when the corpses of Fanny Robin and her child are laid out in Bathsheba's parlor. Bathsheba recognizes Fanny as Troy's lover, and is immediately consumed with jealousy for the dead woman. Bathsheba believes her rival has eclipsed her in Troy's eyes through the simple expedient of dying, and she is right.

When Troy comes in, he kisses Fanny with all the affection he is capable of, spurning Bathsheba's pleas to kiss her too. Troy's passion smacks of necrophilia, for his ideal woman is a dead woman. He announces this fact to Bathsheba: "'Ah! don't taunt me, madam. This woman is more to me, dead as she is, than ever you were, or are, or can be. . . .' He turned to Fanny then. 'But never mind, darling,' he said; 'in the sight of Heaven you are my very, very wife!'" Bathsheba contemplates suicide twice in this scene: once, as a means of successfully competing with Fanny for Troy's love; the second time as a means of escaping the degradation of continuing in his presence. Bathsheba and Fanny have exchanged places. The servant girl, by dying, has become Troy's accepted, legitimate wife; the wife remains behind as the soiled and ruined lover.

Bathsheba flies from Troy and hides herself in that same fern-pit where the sword exercise took place, but the season has changed and the brake of fern "is now withering fast." Contact with Troy has turned the novel's feminine space, and Bathsheba's perception of her own sexuality, into a "loathsome, malignant thing."

There was an opening towards the east, and the glow from the as yet unrisen sun attracted her eyes thither. From her feet, and between the beautiful yellowing ferns with their feathery arms, the ground sloped downwards to a hollow, in which was a species of swamp, dotted with fungi. A morning mist hung over it now— a fulsome yet magnificent silvery veil, full of light from the sun, yet semi-opaque—the hedge behind it being in some measure hidden by its hazy luminousness. Up the sides of this depression grew sheaves of the common rush, and here and there a peculiar species of flag, the blades of which glistened in the emerging sun, like scythes. But the general aspect of the swamp was malignant. From its moist and poisonous coat seemed to be exhaled the essences of evil things in the earth, and in the waters under the earth. The fungi grew in all manner of positions from rotting leaves and tree stumps, some exhibiting to her listless gaze their clammy tops, others their oozing gills. Some were marked with great splotches, red as arterial blood, others were saffron yellow, and others tall and attenuated, with stems like macaroni. Some were leathery and of richest browns. The hollow seemed a nursery of pestilences small and great, in the immediate neighborhood of comfort and health, and Bathsheba arose with a tremor at the thought of having passed the night on the brink of so dismal a place.

The site of the novel's most explicit sexual encounter has been despoiled. Troy's once dazzling scarlet and brass are, as many have pointed out, echoed in the blood and saffron of the fungi. His sword, exchanged for a less romantic instrument perenially allied with death's harvest, is recalled by the scythe-like blades of flag. The morning mist that silvers and beautifies the scene asks us to remember the *aurora militaris* produced by Troy's blade but reveals its deceptive and impermanent beauty. Morning mist, like passion, the evanescent steam of the novel's conclusion, must rise and evaporate before the sun, unveiling the face of reality.

As a reading of the second fern-pit sequence shows, Fanny's death has destroyed the sexual metaphor that originally surrounded Troy and made him glamorous. A dark tower surmounted by a hideous gurgoyle now replaces the gleaming blade, and the chapter titled "The Gurgoyle: Its Doings" is a metaphor for sexual intercourse far more sinister than the sword-exercise. I want to look closely at some passages in this chapter, but before I do, let me mention that "gurgoyle" does not precisely mean a mythical beast carved in stone. The word is derived from Old French "*gargouille*," meaning "throat," and literally means a "hideous spout," which may take either human or animal form. All of which, combined with a tower taller than it is wide and a certain tendency on Hardy's part to overuse the word "erect," is my justification for giving this chapter a sexual reading. The gurgoyle:

> The tower of Weatherbury Church was a square erection of fourteenth-century date, having two stone gurgoyles on each of the four faces of its parapet. Of these eight carved protuberances only two at this time continued to serve the purpose of their erection—that of spouting the water from the lead roof within.
>
>      . . . only that at the south-eastern corner concerns the story. It was too human to be called like a dragon, too impish to be like a man, too animal to be like a fiend, and not enough like a bird to be like a griffin. This horrible stone entity was fashioned as if covered with a wrinkled hide; it had short, erect ears, eyes starting from their sockets, and its fingers and hands were seizing the corners of its mouth, which they thus seemed seemed to pull open to give free passage to the water it vomited. The lower row of teeth was quite washed away, though the upper still remained. Here and thus, jutting a couple of feet from the wall against which its feet rested as a support, the creature had for four hundred years laughed at the surrounding landscape, voicelessly in dry weather, and in wet with a gurgling and snorting sound.

Troy slept on in the porch, and the rain increased outside. Presently the gurgoyle spat. In due time a small stream began to trickle through the seventy feet of aerial space between its mouth and the ground, which the water-drops smote like duckshot in their accelerated velocity. The stream thickened in substance, and increased in power, gradually spouting further and yet further from the side of the tower. When the rain fell in a steady and ceaseless torrent the rain dashed downward in volumes.

We follow its course to the ground at this point of time. The end of the liquid parabola has come forward from the wall, has advanced over the plinth mouldings, over a heap of stones, over the middle border, into the midst of Fanny Robin's grave.

The gurgoyle chapter represents male sexuality as a malignant, destructive outpouring, and its female receptacle as a grave. Troy's nearest approach to love is the sentiment which compels him to plant Fanny's grave with spring flowers. This sentimentality is too weak to withstand a pestilential torrent of passion, and Troy has been too weak to refrain from ruining Fanny.

The persistent torrent from the gurgoyle's jaws directed all its vengeance into the grave. The rich tawny mould was stirred into motion, and boiled like chocolate. The water accumulated and washed deeper down, and the roar of the pool thus formed spread into the night as the head and chief among other noises of the kind created by the deluging rain. The flowers so carefully planted by Fanny's repentant lover began to move and writhe in their bed. The winter-violets turned slowly upside down, and became a mere mat of mud. Soon the snowdrop and other bulbs danced in the boiling mass like ingredients in a cauldron. Plants of the tufted species were loosened, rose to the surface, and floated off.

The fragile flowers of sentiment are easily overturned, and their roots are ugly ones. Troy's feeling for Fanny, perhaps because of the ugliness of its origins, is also easily uprooted, and he retreats from her despoiled grave.

Hardy spoke of Gabriel and Bathsheba's love as "a love . . . strong as death—that love which many waters cannot quench, nor the floods drown." We've reviewed the loves of Boldwood and Troy for Bathsheba Everdene, and find that the emotions these men call love are variously idolatry, lust, and sentiment. There is no question of whether such loves are weaker or stronger than death: Boldwood and Troy are agents of death; their passions destroy them and others as well. In Troy's case, his love for Fanny is quickly quenched by a flood, and the origin of that flood is his own morbid sexuality.

I turn to Gabriel with a sense of relief. Compared with the passions of Boldwood and Troy, the idea of "*camaraderie*" and "good fellowship" between the sexes seems enormously refreshing. If we are still disappointed, perhaps it is because we associate "*camaraderie*" and "good fellowship" with Platonic love, and Platonic love with asexuality. A complete relationship between a man and a woman must include healthy sexuality, and when this is lacking we are disappointed. For Bathsheba, scarred by her encounters with Boldwood and Troy, to settle for a Platonic, indifferently sexual union, would be a tragedy of reduced expectations indeed.

Our reading of the novel, then, and particularly our reading of its conclusion, depends on Gabriel Oak's sexuality. Whether the book's conclusion is triumphant or anticlimactic hinges on Gabriel's adequacy as a lover. It is because I see in Gabriel a potent, life-affirming sexuality that I read *Far from the Madding Crowd* as a *Paradise Regain'd* rather than a *Paradise Lost*.

Gabriel, like Troy, comes equipped with phallic instruments. Whereas Troy's are the sword and gurgoyle, Gabriel's are the sheep shears, trochar, marking iron, ricking rod, and flute. (I apologize for ignoring Boldwood in this respect, but since, as Troy sadistically points out, the gentleman-farmer never attains possession of Bathsheba, his sexuality is less important to our study than that of his more powerful rivals. Hardy himself devotes most of his energy to developing parallels between Gabriel and Troy in which Boldwood does not participate. However, if we were to assign phallic instruments to Boldwood, I suppose they would be the cane and the rifle, signifying the crippled, murderous nature of his love.) Let's look at a passage in which Gabriel shears a sheep:

> Bathsheba, after throwing a glance here, a caution there, and lecturing one of the younger operators who had allowed his last finished sheep to go off among the flock without re-stamping it with her initials, came again to Gabriel, as he put down the luncheon to drag a frightened ewe to his shear-station, flinging it over upon its back with a dextrous twist of the arm. He lopped off the tresses about its head, and opened up the neck and collar, his mistress quietly looking on.
>
> "She blushes at the insult," murmured Bathsheba, watching the pink flush which arose and overspread the neck and shoulders of the ewe where they were left bare by the clicking shears—a flush which was enviable, for its delicacy, by many queens of

coteries, and would have been creditable, for its promptness, to any woman in the world.

Poor Gabriel's soul was fed with a luxury of content by having her over him, her eyes critically regarding his skilful shears, which apparently were going to gather up a piece of flesh at every close, and yet never did so. Like Guildenstern, Oak was happy in that he was not over happy. He had no wish to converse with her: that his bright lady and himself formed one group, exclusively their own, and containing no others in the world, was enough.

So the chatter was all on her side. There is a loquacity that tells nothing, which was Bathsheba's; and there is a silence which says much: that was Gabriel's. Full of this dim and temperate bliss he went on to fling the ewe over upon her other side, covering her head with his knee, gradually running the shears line after line round her dewlap, thence about her flank and back, and finishing over the tail.

"Well done, and done quickly!" said Bathsheba, looking at her watch as the last snip resounded.

"How long, miss?" said Gabriel, wiping his brow.

"Three and twenty minutes and a half since you took the first lock from its forehead. It is the first time that I have ever seen it done in less than half an hour."

The clean, sleek creature arose from its fleece—how perfectly like Aphrodite rising from the foam should have been seen to be realized—looking startled and shy at the loss of its garment, which lay on the floor in one soft cloud, united throughout, the portion visible being the inner surface only, which, never before exposed, was white as snow, and without flaw or blemish of the minutest kind.

Again the sexual metaphor is clear. Gabriel flings the ewe over on her back and opens her neck and collar as if she were a woman and he were undressing her. The sheep even blushes. But more important are the parallels between the sheep-shearing and the sword-exercise. Both are sexual displays intended to impress Bathsheba with the performer's prowess. Gabriel is plainly showing off; with Bathsheba's eyes "critically regarding his skilful shears," he clips the ewe faster than his mistress has ever seen it done before. The object of sheep-shearing and sword-exercise is also the same—to shave a body as closely and as quickly as possible without cutting. Gabriel even lops off the ewe's tresses, to correspond with Troy's cutting a curl from

Bathsheba's head. Both men are clearly masters of their respective instruments.

There the similarity between the two incidents ends. Unlike the sword-exercise, the sheep-shearing is neither deathy nor ultimately despoiling. Instead, the images are of birth, renewal, and cleansing. The newly shorn sheep rising from its fleece is described as Aphrodite, the newborn and naked goddess of love, rising from the sea. The fleece is snow-white, Gabriel having cut until he reached the inner, pure wool, and leaving the soiled side against the floor. The wool reverses the motion of the flowers on Fanny's grave. Whereas Troy overturns things to reveal their dirty undersides, Gabriel overturns them to reveal their inner purity.

The idea of describing a shorn sheep, a ridiculous object if ever there was one, as Aphrodite, is certainly at least mildly amusing. Gabriel generates much of the comedy in this book, while Troy generates only tragedy. Gabriel is a bringer of life and liveliness (one thinks of him standing in the tavern door with newborn lambs slung over his shoulders), while Bathsheba's other suitors are purveyors of death. Often Gabriel's phallic instruments are instruments of salvation, objects which change death into life. I think particularly of the trochar, the tool for sticking bloated sheep. Shortly after Bathsheba has dismissed Gabriel for criticizing her flirtation with Boldwood, her sheep break through a fence and "blast" themselves on young clover. There is comic force to the passage in which her men inform her that she must send for Gabriel Oak to save her flock:

> "There's only one way of saving them," said Tall.
>
> "What way? Tell me quick!"
>
> "They must be pierced in the side with a thing made on purpose."
>
> "Can you do it? Can I?"
>
> "No, ma'am. We can't, nor you neither. It must be done in a particular spot. If ye go to the right or the left but an inch you stab the ewe and kill her. Not even a shepherd can do it, as a rule."
>
> "Then they must die," she said in a resigned tone.
>
> "Only one man in the neighborhood knows the way," said Joseph, now just come up. "He could cure 'em all if he were here."
>
> "Who is he? Let's get him!"
>
> "Shepherd Oak," said Matthew. "Ah, he's a clever man in talents!"

"Ah, that he is so!" said Joseph Poorgrass.

"True—he's the man," said Laban Tall.

"How dare you name that man in my presence!" she said excitedly. "I told you never to allude to him, nor shall you if you stay with me. Ah!" she added, brightening, "Farmer Boldwood knows."

"O no, ma'am," said Matthew. "Two of his store ewes got into some vetches t'other day, and were just like these. He sent a man on horseback here posthaste for Gable, and Gable went and saved 'em. Farmer Boldwood hev got the thing they do it with. 'Tis a holler pipe, with a sharp pricker inside. Isn't it Joseph?"

Bathsheba's blind questions and false starts pile up until they lend melodramatic force to the recognition that Gabriel Oak alone can do the job. Not only is Gabriel the only man who can save the sheep, but also the only man who can wield the dangerous trochar without killing the sheep with the instrument itself. If the sheep-shearing business in the barn does not convince us that Gabriel possesses a strong, life-affirming sexuality, then the trochar passage must. Gabriel comes equipped with his own trochar (he doesn't have to borrow Farmer Boldwood's after all) and performs the operation out of love for Bathsheba. His act of salvation is successful; he saves most of Bathsheba's flock, restoring the half-dead sheep to life with the trochar.

Gabriel's phallic instruments, the sheep shears and trochar, are literally tools. Boldwood and Troy are characterized by implements of destruction (rifles and swords) and ornamentation (walking sticks and gurgoyles). Gabriel's instruments of salvation are the tools of his trade. His sexuality is inseparable from his work. This is scarcely surprising, since *Far from the Madding Crowd* elevates work to the status of religion. The farmer's work in this novel is a procreative process—he or she joins with others to cause the flocks to multiply and the earth to bear fruit.

Hardy describes the shearing-barn as resembling a church. The description is one of the novel's most moving passages; Hardy makes the barn a symbol of an eternal purpose not subject to the fluctuating, transient demands of church and state. The barn is, in fact, superior to a church, and its description an interesting contrast with the description of the gurgoyle-topped Weatherbury church.

> One could say about this barn, what could hardly be said of either the church or the castle, akin to it in age and style, that the

purpose which had dictated its original erection was the same
with that to which it was still applied. Unlike and superior to
either of these two typical remnants of medievalism, the old barn
embodied practices which had suffered no mutilation at the hands
of time. Here at least the spirit of the ancient builders was at one
with the spirit of the modern beholder. Standing before this
abraded pile, the eye regarded its present usage, the mind dwelt
upon its past history, with a satisfied sense of functional continuity throughout—a feeling almost of gratitude, and quite of
pride, at the permanence of the idea which had heaped it up. The
fact that four centuries had neither proved it to be founded on a
mistake, nor given rise to any reaction that had battered it down,
invested this simple grey effort of old minds with a repose, if not
a grandeur, which too curious reflection was apt to disturb in its
military and ecclesiastical compeers. For once medievalism and
modernism had a common standpoint. The lanceolate windows,
the time-eaten archstones and chamfers, the orientation of the
axis, the misty chestnut work of the rafters, referred to no exploded fortifying art or worn-out religious creed. The defence
and salvation of the body by daily bread is still a study, a religion,
and a desire.

To-day the large side doors were thrown open towards the sun
to admit a bountiful light to the immediate spot of the shearers'
operations, which was the wood threshing-floor in the centre,
formed of thick oak, black with age and polished by the beating
of flails for many generations, till it had grown as slippery and
as rich in hue as the state-room floors of an Elizabethan mansion.
Here the shearers knelt, the sun slanting in upon their bleached
shirts, tanned arms, and the polished shears they flourished, caus-
ing these to bristle with a thousand rays strong enough to blind
a weak-eyed man. Beneath them a captive sheep lay panting,
quickening its pants as misgiving merged in terror, till it quivered
like the hot landscape outside.

One of the shearers kneeling to his work in this barn-church is Gabriel,
and the Aphrodite passage follows almost immediately. Shepherd Oak appears as the high priest of both love and work. Certainly he understands the
intimate connection between the two, and finds a species of fulfillment in
working for his beloved. The moment when Gabriel turns the lambs he has
rescued into living love-tokens is only one example: "Oak took from his

illimitable pockets a marking iron, dipped it into the pot, and imprinted on the buttocks of the infant sheep the initials of her he delighted to muse on— 'B.E.,' which signified to all the region round that henceforth the lambs belonged to Farmer Bathsheba Everdene, and to no one else."

The relationships between love, death, sex, work, and religion are dramatized in a serious and complicated way in the chapter titled "The Storm." The thunderstorm which threatens Bathsheba's ricks is apocalyptic in its dimensions. There are seven flashes of lightning, each one numbered and accompanied by images of death and demonism. One flash crosses the sky like a flapping of phosphorescent wings, another gleams in the heavens like a mailed army, another breaks with the spring of a serpent and the shout of a fiend. Naturally the seventh flash, like the opening of the seventh seal, is the final and climactic one:

> Heaven opened then, indeed. The flash was almost too novel for its inexpressibly dangerous nature to be at once realized, and they could only comprehend the magnificence of its beauty. It sprang from east, west, north, and south, and was a perfect dance of death. The forms of skeletons appeared in the air, shaped with blue fire for bones—dancing, leaping, striding, racing around, and mingling together in unparalleled confusion. With these were intertwined undulating snakes of green, and behind these was a broad mass of lesser light. Simultaneously there came from every part of the tumbling sky what may be called a shout; since, though no shout ever came near it, it was more of the nature of a shout than of anything else earthly.

This apocalyptic storm is an impressive example of that "blind force which drives all things" in Hardy's world. As J. Hillis Miller has pointed out, "sexual passion is the chief way in which Hardy's characters participate in the impulsions of this force." The dangerous flashing of Troy's sword is only a miniaturization of this grand electric "*aurora militaris*" of malignant nature.

Gabriel has recognized the unpredictable deadliness of nature ever since his overzealous dog drove his flock into the chalk-pit. It is Gabriel who reads the signs of the approaching rain of death, and Gabriel who opposes himself to the fury of the universe. He risks his life against the storm because there is "important and urgent labour" to be done. The ricks must be covered, or the harvest will be lost. Gabriel's labor is two-fold. First, it is a labor of love: he has sworn to help to his last effort the woman he loves. Second, it is labor in the procreative sense. Gabriel is a kind of midwife to nature. He brings the lambs safely into the world, and here he is concerned with the bringing forth of the harvest. Again, Gabriel appears as a savior. He is not interested in the monetary value of the ricks, but endeavors to save them because they are Bathsheba's and because they are food for man and beast, nourishment and employment for his little community. Gabriel emerges in the storm chapter as a defender of love and life, fragile things in a death-dealing universe.

The instrument Gabriel opposes against the storm is another phallic tool, "his ricking-rod, or poniard, as it was indifferently called—a long iron lance, polished by handling." The rod is stuck among the sheaves in the stack to support them against the wind. Ungrounded, Gabriel's rod jeopardizes his life by attracting lightning. In this condition, it conducts deadly electricity from the sky—the kind of sinister sexual energy that characterizes Troy. Gabriel, however, wishes to proceed with his work in safety. He grounds the ricking rod with a chain, turning it into an "extemporized lightning-conductor," and this foresight ultimately saves both his life and Bathsheba's: "In the meantime one of the grisly forms had alighted upon the point of Gabriel's rod, to run invisibly down it, down the chain, and into the earth. Gabriel was almost blinded, and he could feel Bathsheba's warm arm tremble in his hand—a sensation novel and thrilling enough; but love, life, everything human, seemed small and trifling in such close juxtaposition with an infuriated universe." Gabriel clasps Bathsheba to preserve her from the lightning. Gabriel is grounded by the ricking-rod, and Bathsheba is grounded by Gabriel's embrace. Their union is not without a sexual dimension—Gabriel is acutely aware of Bathsheba's trembling, and this moment constitutes their only physical contact in the novel—but grounded by love and reason, Gabriel's sexual energy brings life in defiance of the infuriated universe. The grounded ricking rod is an emblem of an heroic sexuality opposed to Troy's unfettered passion. The rod directs destructive natural energies to serve the demands of life and love, to work "the defence and salvation of the body."

The storm causes Bathsheba to turn to Gabriel for the first time. She confesses to him her shame at having married Troy, whose drunken irresponsibility has so nearly destroyed her farm and the community's livelihood. She confesses, too, the circumstances of coercion surrounding her marriage, her appreciation for Oak's devotion, and her fear lest he be injured in the storm. Some recognition of Oak's worth has taken place in Bathsheba, perhaps in that blinding moment on the haystack. Love brings her to her shepherd-lover with confidence and concern, causes her "to speak to him more warmly [tonight] than she ever had done whilst unmarried and free to speak as warmly as she chose."

If we recall the passage describing Gabriel and Bathsheba's marriage, we'll recall that the "good fellowship" between the sexes Hardy believed essential to a love stronger than death arises only when the sexes associate in their labors as well as in their pleasures. Naturally any work of procreation requires the participation of both sexes. Bathsheba frequently works with Gabriel (none of her other suitors will work with her or even for her): she leaves the house to help Gabriel protect the ricks against the storm; she sings while he plays the flute; and, most significantly, she works with him to repair Fanny Robin's grave. Gabriel refills the hollowed grave, a feminine space previously emptied by the novel's second big storm, and Bathsheba restores the space to loveliness by replanting the uprooted flowers. Gabriel and Bathsheba's combined and harmonious labors oppose themselves to the gurgoyle's deathy sexuality. Like an ungrounded ricking rod, the gurgoyle has been a conduit for destructive natural energies. When the couple's work together is ended, however, the gurgoyle's stream has been permanently rerouted.

Since Gabriel's attendant phallic symbols are tools, and since the sexes are expected to work together in Hardy's revisionary sort of love, Bathsheba sometimes gets to handle the symbols right along with Gabriel—although like most men he is a bit grouchy and superior when a woman gets hold of his tools. Perhaps *Far from the Madding Crowd*'s most extraordinary love passage is the one in which the two grind shears together.

> Oak stood somewhat as Eros is represented when in the act of sharpening his arrows: his figure slightly bent, the weight of his body thrown over on the shears, and his head balanced sideways, with a critical compression and contraction of the eyelids to crown the attitude.
>
> His mistress came up . . . then she said—
>
> ". . . I'll turn the winch of the grindstone. I want to speak to you, Gabriel."
>
> . . . Bathsheba turned the winch, and Gabriel applied the shears.
>
> The peculiar motion involved in turning a wheel has a wonderful tendency to benumb the mind. It is a sort of attenuated variety of Ixion's punishment, and contributes a dismal chapter to the history of gaols. The brain gets muddled, the head grows heavy, and the body's centre of gravity seems to s⸱     ⸱egrees in a leaden lump somewhere between the eyeᴜ. crown. Bathsheba felt the unpleasant symptoms after two oɪ . dozen turns.
>
> "Will you turn, Gabriel, and let me hold the shears?" she said. "My head is in a whirl, and I can't talk."

Gabriel turned. Bathsheba then began, with some awkward-
ness, allowing her thoughts to stray occasionally from her story
to attend to the shears, which required a little nicety in sharp-
ening.

". . . You don't hold the shears right, miss—I knew you
wouldn't know the way—hold like this."

He relinquished the winch, and enclosing her two hands completely in his own (taking each as we sometimes take a child's
hand in teaching him to write), grasped the shears with her. "Incline the edge so," he said.

Hands and shears were inclined to suit the words, and held
thus for a peculiarly long time by the instructor as he spoke.

"That will do," exclaimed Bathsheba. "Loose my hands. I
won't have them held! Turn the winch."

Bathsheba's other, death-purveying suitors are idle men, and share no
work with her. Boldwood is a gentleman-farmer. His hirelings do his work
for him, and eventually he must hire Gabriel Oak to manage his land. Boldwood resents Bathsheba's working as bailiff on her own farm—he proposes
to make her an idle lady. One of her reasons for rejecting his first proposal
is the pleasure she still takes in farming. Similarly, Troy begins as a soldier
who has never fought. His courtship of Bathsheba is deceitful—he pretends
to be a man who enjoys farm labour. Troy hives the bees, plays at haymaking,
and tells Bathsheba that he loves to work for her. In short, to win Bathsheba,
Troy pretends to be like Gabriel. But Troy is a man of words rather than
action, his interest in work is purely verbal. After the wedding, Troy settles
down to live in idleness off Bathsheba's earnings, and his pursuit of pleasure
in the form of gambling nearly destroys the farm.

Both Boldwood and Troy fail the test of the apocalyptic storm. Boldwood fails through a kind of despairing apathy. He is aware of the approaching thunderstorm, but he does not lift a hand to save his ricks, and
will not even order his men to work. Boldwood's behavior in the storm
illustrates his fundamental self-destructiveness. Troy fails through an other-
destructive negligence. He persists in making Bathsheba's workers drunk at
the harvest-home supper, and presides over their revels like a demon in his
red coat. The debauchery takes place in the shearing barn, and Troy's
drunken desecration of work's temple almost seems to bring on the storm
in the first place. In any event, Troy makes the storm doubly dangerous to
Gabriel and Bathsheba by depriving them of their assistants.

Troy is not the man, and Boldwood is not the man, but Gabriel *is* the

man. Bathsheba proceeds through a series of mistaken identities which culminates in the recognition of a hero. The brief passage in which she questions
her men and learns that only Gabriel can save her sheep is a paradigm for
the plot of *Far from the Madding Crowd*, or "Bathsheba and her Lovers."
"Can you do it? Can I do it? Can Farmer Boldwood do it? No, only one
man can do it—Shepherd Oak." This kind of series of mistaken identities is
commonly used in our culture to dramatize the entrance of a hero. And
although Oak is rewarded fairy-tale fashion with the hand of the princess
and a kingdom (Boldwood's farm) to rule, Hardy undoubtedly derived the
pattern from the archetypal Biblical story in which the Lord tries many men,
and finds all wanting but one. Given Hardy's affinity for the Old Testament
stories about David, one thinks particularly of Samuel's consecutive rejection
of each of Jesse's seven sons, until the eighth is sent for and revealed as God's
choice for the future king of Israel:

> And Samuel said unto Jesse, Are here all *thy* children? And he
> said, there remaineth yet the youngest, and behold, he keepeth
> the sheep. And Samuel said unto Jesse, Send and fetch him: for
> we will not sit down until he come hither.
>
> And he sent, and brought him in. Now he *was* ruddy, *and*
> withal of a beautiful countenance, and goodly to look to. And
> the Lord said arise, anoint him: for this *is* he.
>
> (1 Sam. 16:11–12)

Gabriel is a true hero, and his marriage to Bathsheba a truly happy
ending to the novel. *Far from the Madding Crowd* is no tragedy of reduced
expectations, but a comic triumph of good over evil, and life over death.
Let's return once more to the paragraph with which we began:

> He accompanied her up the hill, explaining to her the details of
> his forthcoming tenure of the other farm. They spoke very little
> of their mutual feelings; pretty phrases and warm expressions
> being probably unnecessary between such tried friends. Theirs
> was that substantial affection which arises (if any arises at all)
> when the two who are thrown together begin first by knowing
> the rougher sides of each other's character, and not the best till
> further on, the romance growing up in the interstices of a mass
> of hard prosaic reality. This good-fellowship—*camaraderie*—usu
> ally occurring through similarity of pursuits, is unfortunately
> seldom superadded to love between the sexes, because men and
> women associate, not in their labours, but in their pleasures

merely. Where, however, happy circumstance permits its development, the compounded feeling proves itself to be the only love
which is strong as death—that love which many waters cannot
quench, nor the floods drown, beside which the passion usually
called by the name is evanescent as steam.

If the lovers talk about farming, it is because work is the language of
love in this novel. All other language is unreliable: Troy lies; Boldwood
speaks in clichés. The good fellowship between the sexes which grows out
of shared work is not asexual at all, because work in this novel is a common
labor of procreation—of bringing food from the earth, of standing between
man and death. Beside it all other passions are deadly and sterile. Hardy tells
us that this kind of love grows in the crevices of hard prosaic reality. The
lichen metaphor works well here, for the lichen is not a plant at all, but a
symbiotic relationship between fungi and algae. It is a community of organisms mutually dependent on one another for the defense and salvation of the
body. It is stronger than death. It does not wither or change with the seasons.
It is not easily uprooted. If we still find it unlovely, we can compare it to the
withering fern-pit and the uprooted flowers on Fanny's grave. And if we still
doubt the beauty of such a love, we can consider its restorative powers.
Gabriel's love rejuvenates Bathsheba; it is "as though a rose should shut and
be a bud again." It is a love which converts instruments of death (trumpet
and cannon) to instruments of community rejoicing. And that restorative
power is the result of passion fettered by reason, and is the miracle of Gabriel's rod.

# Chronology

1840    Thomas Hardy is born on June 2 in Higher Bockhampton, a community in the parish of Stinsford, Dorset. He is the son of Thomas Hardy, a stone mason, and Jemima Hand Hardy.

1848    Begins his education at a school in Lower Bockhampton.

1849    Hardy is moved to a school in Dorchester.

1855    Begins teaching at the Stinsford Church Sunday School.

1856    Hardy is accepted at the office of architect John Hicks as pupil. Also in this year Hardy meets Horace Moule and William Barnes.

ca. 1860    Hardy writes his first poem, called "Domicilium."

1862    After settling in London, Hardy goes to work for architect and church restorer Arthur Blomfield. He reads widely, studies paintings at the National Gallery, and becomes an agnostic.

1863    The Royal Institute of British Architects awards Hardy an essay prize.

1865    *Chambers' Journal* publishes "How I Built Myself a House." Hardy attends French classes at King's College, Cambridge.

1867    Hardy returns to Dorset and resumes working for John Hicks. At this time, he also begins work on his first novel, *The Poor Man and the Lady*.

1868    *The Poor Man and the Lady* is rejected by Macmillan; Hardy resubmits the manuscript to Chapman & Hall.

1869    Hardy meets George Meredith. Begins his second novel, *Desperate Remedies*.

1870    Hardy travels to Cornwall, where he meets Emma Lavinia Gifford, his future wife. Publisher William Tinsley agrees to produce *Desperate Remedies* at the author's expense.

1871    *Desperate Remedies* is published. Also in this year Hardy writes *Under the Greenwood Tree* and begins *A Pair of Blue Eyes*.

1872    *Under the Greenwood Tree* is published. *A Pair of Blue Eyes* appears in serial form.

1873    Hardy's friend Horace Moule commits suicide. Hardy is invited by Leslie Stephen to contribute to *Cornhill*; Hardy then begins the serialized version of *Far from the Madding Crowd*. *A Pair of Blue Eyes* is published.

1874    *Far from the Madding Crowd* is published. Hardy marries Emma Lavinia Gifford; they travel to France after the wedding, and upon return settle in Surbiton.

1876    *The Hand of Ethelberta* appears. Hardy and his wife travel to Holland and Germany, and then move to a home at Sturminster Newton, in Dorset.

1878    *The Return of the Native* is published. Hardy moves once again, to London, where he is elected to the Savile Club.

1879    Hardy pursues research for *The Trumpet-Major* in the British Museum.

1880    *The Trumpet-Major* is published. Hardy meets the Poet Laureate, Alfred, Lord Tennyson. The writing of *A Laodicean* is slowed by a serious illness.

1881    *A Laodicean* is published.

1882    *Two on a Tower* is published.

1883    Hardy moves to Dorchester where he begins building his home, Max Gate. "The Dorsetshire Labourer" appears in *Longman's Magazine*.

1884    Hardy begins composition of *The Mayor of Casterbridge*.

1885  Moves into Max Gate. He starts writing *The Woodlanders*.

1886  *The Mayor of Casterbridge* is published.

1887  *The Woodlanders* is published. Hardy visits Italy.

1888  *The Wessex Tales,* a collection of short stories, is published. Composition of *Tess of the D'Urbervilles* begins.

1889  Several publishers reject the first installments of *Tess*.

1890  Hardy finishes *Tess*.

1891  Both *Tess of the D'Urbervilles* and *A Group of Noble Dames* are published.

1892  Hardy's father dies. The first version of *The Well-Beloved* is serialized. Relations with his wife begin to deteriorate, and worsen over the next two years, particularly during the composition of *Jude the Obscure*.

1893  Hardy travels to Dublin and Oxford, where he visits Florence Henniker, with whom he writes a short story, and, it is believed, falls in love.

1894  *Life's Little Ironies,* a collection of poems, is published.

1895  *Jude the Obscure* is published and receives primarily outraged reviews. As a result Hardy decides to discontinue novel-writing and henceforward produces only poetry. Also in this year Hardy works on the Uniform Edition of his novels.

1897  *The Well-Beloved* is published.

1898  Publishes *The Wessex Poems.*

1901  Publishes *Poems of the Past and the Present.*

1904  *The Dynasts,* part 1, is published. Hardy's mother dies.

1905  Hardy receives an honorary LL.D. from Aberdeen.

1906  *The Dynasts,* part 2, is published.

1908  *The Dynasts,* part 3, is published.

1909  Publishes *Time's Laughingstocks.* Hardy becomes the governor of the Dorchester Grammar School.

1910    Hardy is awarded the O.M. (Order of Merit).

1912    Hardy's wife Emma Lavinia dies on November 27.

1913    *A Changed Man* is published. Hardy receives an honorary
        D.Litt. degree from Cambridge; he is also made an honorary
        Fellow of Magdalen College, Cambridge.

1914    Hardy marries Florence Emily Dugdale. The collection of
        poems called *Satires of Circumstance* is published. As World
        War I begins Hardy joins a group of writers dedicated to the
        support of the Allied cause.

1915    Hardy's sister Mary dies.

1917    *Moments of Vision*, a collection of poetry, is published.

1919    Hardy's first *Collected Poems* is published.

1920    Oxford University awards Hardy an honorary D.Litt.

1921    Publishes *Late Lyrics and Earlier*. Becomes honorary Fellow at
        Queen's College, Oxford.

1923    *The Famous Tragedy of the Queen of Cornwall* is published.
        Hardy receives a visit from the Prince of Wales at Max Gate.

1925    *Human Shows* is published.

1928    Hardy dies on January 11; his ashes are buried at Westminster
        Abbey, and his heart is placed at his first wife's grave in the
        Stinsford churchyard. *Winter Words* published posthumously.
        Florence Emily Hardy publishes *The Early Life of Thomas
        Hardy,* believed to have been written largely by Hardy himself.

1930    *Collected Poems* published posthumously. Florence Emily
        Hardy publishes *The Later Years of Thomas Hardy.*

# Contributors

HAROLD BLOOM, Sterling Professor of the Humanities at Yale University, is the author of *The Anxiety of Influence, Poetry and Repression,* and many other volumes of literary criticism. His forthcoming study, *Freud: Transference and Authority,* attempts a full-scale reading of all of Freud's major writings. A MacArthur Prize Fellow, he is general editor of five series of literary criticism published by Chelsea House.

ROY MORRELL is the author of *Thomas Hardy: The Will and the Way.*

J. HILLIS MILLER is Frederick W. Hilles Professor of English and Comparative Literature at Yale University. His books of criticism include *Poetry of Reality: Six Twentieth-Century Writers, Fiction and Repetition: Seven English Novels,* and *The Linguistic Moment: From Wordsworth to Stevens.*

JEAN R. BROOKS is the author of *Thomas Hardy: The Poetic Structure.*

IAN GREGOR is Professor of Modern English Literature at the University of Kent. He is the author of several books and has edited a collection of critical essays on the Brontës.

DENNIS TAYLOR is Professor of English at Boston College. His publications include *Hardy's Poetry, 1860–1928.*

JAN B. GORDON is Professor of English at Doshiha University in Kyoto, Japan. He has published many articles on the poetry and criticism of the last century.

ROSS C. MURFIN, Professor of English at the University of Miami, is the author of essays and books on Hardy, Lawrence, and other nineteenth- and twentieth-century writers.

MARGARET MAHAR taught at Yale University and has written on Hardy and other novelists.

231

ELAINE SHOWALTER is Professor of English at Princeton University. She is the author of numerous essays, and her books include *A Literature of Their Own: British Women Novelists from Brontë to Lessing*.

RAMÓN SALDÍVAR teaches at the University of Texas at Austin. His publications include *Figural Language in the Novel: The Flowers of Speech from Cervantes to Joyce*.

SUSAN BEEGEL is Adjunct Professor of American Civilization at the University of Massachusetts, Boston. She has published on Hemingway, Fitzgerald, and Dante Gabriel Rossetti.

# Bibliography

Abercrombie, Lascelles. *Thomas Hardy: A Critical Study*. London: Martin Secker, 1912.

Alcorn, John. *The Nature Novel from Hardy to Lawrence*. New York: Columbia University Press, 1977.

Allen, Walter. *The English Novel*. London: Phoenix House, 1954.

Arkans, Norman. "Hardy's 'Religious Twilight.'" *Texas Studies in Literature and Language* 21 (1979): 413–32.

———. "Vision and Experience in Hardy's Dream Poems." *Modern Language Quarterly* 41 (1980): 54–72.

Auden, W. H. "A Literary Transference." *The Southern Review* 6 (1940–41): 78–86.

Bayley, John. *An Essay on Hardy*. Cambridge: Cambridge University Press, 1978.

Beach, Joseph Warren. *The Technique of Thomas Hardy*. Chicago: The University of Chicago Press, 1922.

Bloom, Harold, ed. *Modern Critical Interpretations: Thomas Hardy's* Jude the Obscure. New Haven: Chelsea House, forthcoming.

———, ed. *Modern Critical Interpretations: Thomas Hardy's* Mayor of Casterbridge. New Haven: Chelsea House, forthcoming.

———, ed. *Modern Critical Interpretations: Thomas Hardy's* Return of the Native. New Haven: Chelsea House, forthcoming.

———, ed. *Modern Critical Interpretations: Thomas Hardy's* Tess of the D'Urbervilles. New Haven: Chelsea House, forthcoming.

Blunden, Edmund. *Thomas Hardy*. London: Macmillan, 1942.

Boumelha, Penny. *Thomas Hardy and Women: Sexual Ideology and Narrative Form*. Brighton, Sussex: The Harvester Press, 1982.

Brooks, Jean R. *Thomas Hardy: The Poetic Structure*. Ithaca: Cornell University Press, 1971.

Brown, Douglas. *Thomas Hardy*. 1954. Reprint. Westport, Conn.: Greenwood Press, 1980.

Buckler, William E. "The Dark Space Illuminated: A Reading of Hardy's 'Poems of 1912–13.'" *Victorian Poetry* 17, nos. 1–2 (1979): 98–107.

Carpenter, Richard. *Thomas Hardy*. New York: Twayne Publishers, 1964.

Casagrande, Peter J. *Unity in Hardy's Novels*. Lawrence: Regents Press of Kansas, 1982.

————. "The Shifted Centre of Altruism in *The Woodlanders:* Thomas Hardy's Third 'Return of a Native.'" *ELH* 38, no. 1 (1971): 104–25.

Cecil, David. *Hardy the Novelist*. New York: Bobbs-Merrill, 1946.

Chew, Samuel C. *Thomas Hardy: Poet and Novelist*. 2d revision. New York: Russell & Russell, 1964.

Childers, Mary. "Thomas Hardy, The Man Who 'Liked' Women." *Criticism* 23, no. 4 (1981): 317–34.

Cox, R. G. *Thomas Hardy: The Critical Heritage*. London: Routledge & Kegan Paul, 1970.

Daiches, David. *Some Late Victorian Attitudes*. New York: Norton, 1969.

Davie, Donald. *Thomas Hardy and British Poetry*. New York: Oxford University Press, 1972.

De Laura, David J. "'The Ache of Modernism' in Hardy's Later Novels." *ELH* 34, no. 3 (1967): 380–99.

Dobree, Bonamy. "*The Dynasts.*" *The Southern Review* 6 (1940–41): 109–24.

Drabble, Margaret, ed. *The Genius of Thomas Hardy*. New York: Alfred A. Knopf, 1976.

Edwards, Duane. "Chance in Hardy's Fiction." *Midwest Quarterly* 11 (1970): 427–41.

————. "*The Mayor of Casterbridge* as Aeschylean Tragedy," *Studies in the Novel* 4 (1972): 608–18.

Eggenschwiler, David. "Eustacia Vye, Queen of Night and Court Pretender," *Nineteenth-Century Fiction* 25 (1971): 444–54.

Elliott, Albert Pettigrew. *Fatalism in the Works of Thomas Hardy*. Philadelphia: University of Pennsylvania Press, 1935.

Ellis, Havelock. *From Marlowe to Shaw: The Studies, 1876–1936, in English Literature of Havelock Ellis,* edited by John Gawsworth. London: Williams & Norgate, 1950.

Emmett, V. J., Jr. "Marriage in Hardy's Later Novels." *Midwest Quarterly* 10 (1969): 331–48.

Firor, Ruth A. *Folkways in Thomas Hardy*. Philadelphia: University of Pennsylvania Press, 1931.

Gerber, Helmut E., and W. Eugene Davis, eds. *Thomas Hardy: An Annotated Bibliography of Writings about Him*. De Kalb: Northern Illinois University Press, 1973.

Gregor, Ian. *The Great Web: The Form of Hardy's Major Fiction*. London: Faber & Faber, 1974.

————. "What Kind of Fiction Did Hardy Write?" *Essays in Criticism* 16 (1966): 290–308.

Guerard, Albert J. *Thomas Hardy: The Novels and Stories*. Cambridge: Harvard University Press, 1949.

————, ed. *Hardy: A Collection of Critical Essays*. Englewood Cliffs, N.J.: Prentice-Hall, 1963.

Hardy, Barbara. *Forms of Feeling in Victorian Fiction*. London: Peter Owen, 1985.

Hardy, Evelyn. *Thomas Hardy: A Critical Biography*. London: Hogarth Press, 1954.

Hardy, Florence Emily. *The Life of Thomas Hardy, 1840–1928*. London: Macmillan, 1962. Reprint. Hamden, Conn.: Shoe String Press, 1970.

Hornback, Bert A. *The Metaphor of Chance: Vision and Technique in the Works of Thomas Hardy.* Athens: Ohio University Press, 1971.

Howe, Irving. *Thomas Hardy.* New York: Macmillan, 1967.

Jacobus, Mary. "Hardy's Magian Retrospect." *Essays in Criticism* 32, no. 3 (1982): 258–79.

Johnson, Bruce. *True Correspondence: A Phenomenology of Thomas Hardy's Novels.* Tallahassee: University Presses of Florida, 1983.

Johnson, Lionel. *The Art of Thomas Hardy.* New York: Russell & Russell, 1965.

Jones, Lawrence O. "Imitation and Expression in Thomas Hardy's Theory of Fiction." *Studies in the Novel* 7, no. 4 (1975): 507–25.

Kendrick, Walter M. "The Sensationalism of Thomas Hardy." *Texas Studies in Literature and Language* 22 (1980): 484–503.

Kramer, Dale. *Thomas Hardy: The Forms of Tragedy.* Detroit: Wayne State University Press, 1975.

LaValley, Albert J. *Twentieth Century Interpretations of* Tess of the D'Urbervilles: *A Collection of Critical Essays.* Englewood Cliffs, N.J.: Prentice-Hall, 1969.

Lawrence, D. H. *Phoenix: The Posthumous Papers of D. H. Lawrence.* New York: Viking Press, 1972.

Leavis, F. R. "Hardy the Poet." *The Southern Review* 6 (1940–41): 87–98.

Leavis, Q. D. "Thomas Hardy and Criticism." *Scrutiny* 11 (1943): 230–37.

Levine, George. *The Realistic Imagination.* Chicago: The University of Chicago Press, 1981.

Lucas, John. *The Literature of Change: Studies in the Nineteenth Century Provincial Novel.* 2d ed. Sussex: The Harvester Press, 1980.

Marsden, Kenneth. *The Poems of Thomas Hardy: A Critical Introduction.* New York: Oxford University Press, 1969.

May, Charles E. "Thomas Hardy and the Poetry of the Absurd." *Texas Studies in Literature and Language* 12 (1970): 63–73.

———. "Hardy's 'Darkling Thrush': The 'Nightingale' Grown Old." *Victorian Poetry* 11, no. 1 (1973): 62–65.

Meisel, Perry. *Thomas Hardy: The Return of the Repressed.* New Haven: Yale University Press, 1972.

Miller, J. Hillis. *Thomas Hardy: Distance and Desire.* Cambridge: Harvard University Press, 1970.

———. "*The Well-Beloved:* The Compulsion to Stop Repeating." In *Fiction and Repetition: Seven English Novels.* Cambridge: Harvard University Press, 1982.

Millgate, Michael. *Thomas Hardy: A Biography.* New York: Random House, 1982.

———. *Thomas Hardy: His Career as a Novelist.* New York: Random House, 1971.

Millgate, Michael, and Richard Little Purdy, eds. *The Collected Letters of Thomas Hardy.* 3 volumes to date. Oxford: Oxford University Press, 1978–.

Morrell, Roy. "Thomas Hardy and Probability." In *On the Novel: A Present for Walter Allen on His Sixtieth Birthday from His Friends and Colleagues,* edited by B. S. Bededikz, 75–92. London: J. M. Dent and Sons, 1971.

———. *Thomas Hardy: The Will and the Way.* Kuala Lumpur: University of Malaya Press, 1968.

Muir, Edwin. "Novels of Thomas Hardy." In *Essays on Literature and Society.* London: Hogarth Press, 1949.

Murfin, Ross C. *Swinburne, Hardy, Lawrence, and the Burden of Belief.* Chicago: The University of Chicago Press, 1978.

Osborne, L. Mackenzie. "The 'Chronological Frontier' in Thomas Hardy's Novels." *Studies in the Novel* 4 (1972): 543–55.

Page, Norman, ed. *Thomas Hardy: The Writer and His Background.* London: Bell & Hyman, 1980.

Paulin, Tom. *Thomas Hardy: The Poetry of Perception.* London: Macmillan, 1975.

Pinion, F. B., ed. *Thomas Hardy and the Modern World: Papers Presented at the 1973 Summer School.* Dorchester, Dorset: The Thomas Hardy Society, 1974.

———. *A Hardy Companion: A Guide to the Works of Thomas Hardy and Their Background.* New York: St. Martin's Press, 1968.

Porter, Katherine Anne. "On a Criticism of Thomas Hardy." In *The Days Before*, 23–35. New York: Harcourt, Brace, 1952.

Richards, Max. "Hardy's Poetry: Voice and Vision." *The Critical Review* 21 (1979): 24–35.

Salter, K. W. "Lawrence, Hardy and 'The Great Tradition.'" *English* 22, no. 113 (1973): 60–65.

Sherman, G. W. *The Pessimism of Thomas Hardy.* Rutherford, N.J.: Fairleigh Dickinson University Press, 1976.

Spivey, Ted R. "Thomas Hardy's Tragic Hero." *Nineteenth-Century Fiction* 9 (1954): 179–91.

Starzyk, Lawrence J. "The Coming Universal Wish Not to Live in Hardy's 'Modern' Novels." *Nineteenth-Century Fiction* 26 (1972): 419–35.

Stewart, J. I. M. *Eight Modern Writers.* Oxford: Clarendon Press, 1963.

———. "The Integrity of Hardy." *Essays and Studies* (English Association), n.s. 1 (1948): 1–27.

———. *Thomas Hardy: A Critical Biography.* New York: Dodd, Mead, 1971.

Tate, Allen. "Hardy's Philosophic Metaphors." *The Southern Review* 6 (1940–41): 99–108.

*Thomas Hardy Annual*, 1983–.

*The Thomas Hardy Society Review*, 1975–.

*The Thomas Hardy Yearbook*, 1970–.

Thurley, Geoffrey. *The Psychology of Hardy's Novels.* Queensland: University of Queensland Press, 1975.

Vigar, Penelope. *The Novels of Thomas Hardy: Illusion and Reality.* London: Athlone Press, 1974.

Wing, George. *Thomas Hardy.* New York: Grove, 1963.

Wittenberg, Judith Bryant. "Early Hardy Novels and the Fictional Eye." *Novel, A Forum on Fiction* 16, no. 2 (1983): 151–64.

Woolf, Virginia. "Novels of Thomas Hardy." In *The Second Common Reader*, 266–80. New York: Harcourt, Brace, 1932.

———. "Half of Thomas Hardy." In *The Captain's Death Bed and Other Essays*, 62–68. New York: Harcourt, Brace, 1950.

Zabel, Morton Dauwen. "Hardy in Defense of His Art: The Aesthetic of Incongruity." *The Southern Review* 6 (1940–41): 125–49.

Zietlow, Paul. *Moments of Vision: The Poetry of Thomas Hardy.* Cambridge: Harvard University Press, 1974.

# Acknowledgments

"The Dynasts" by Roy Morrell from *Thomas Hardy: The Will and the Way* by Roy Morrell, © 1965 by the University of Malaya Press. Reprinted by permission.

"The Refusal of Involvement" by J. Hillis Miller from *Thomas Hardy: Distance and Desire* by J. Hillis Miller, © 1970 by the President and Fellows of Harvard College. Reprinted by permission of the Belknap Press of Harvard University Press.

"*The Return of the Native*: A Novel of Environment" by Jean R. Brooks from *Thomas Hardy: The Poetic Structure*, © 1971 by Jean R. Brooks. Reprinted by permission of the publisher.

"The Great Web: *The Woodlanders*" (Originally entitled "The Great Web: *The Woodlanders* (1887)") by Ian Gregor, from *The Great Web: The Form of Hardy's Major Fiction* © 1974 by Ian Gregor. Reprinted by permission of the author and Faber & Faber Ltd.

"The Patterns in Hardy's Poetry" by Dennis Taylor from *ELH* 42, no. 2 (Summer 1975), © 1975 by The Johns Hopkins University Press. Reprinted by permission of the Johns Hopkins University Press.

"Origins, History, and the Reconstitution of Family: Tess's Journey" by Jan B. Gordon from *ELH* 43, no. 3 (1976), © 1976 by The Johns Hopkins University Press. Reprinted by permission of the Johns Hopkins University Press.

"New Words: Swinburne and the Poetry of Thomas Hardy" (Originally entitled "Swinburne and the Poetry of Thomas Hardy") by Ross C. Murfin from *Swinburne, Hardy, Lawrence, and the Burden of Belief* by Ross C. Murfin, © 1978 by the University of Chicago. Reprinted by permission of the University of Chicago Press.

"Hardy's Poetry of Renunciation" by Margaret Mahar from *ELH* 45, no. 2 (Summer 1978), © 1978 by The Johns Hopkins University Press. Reprinted by permission of the Johns Hopkins University Press.

"The Unmanning of the Mayor of Casterbridge" by Elaine Showalter from *Critical Approaches to the Fiction of Thomas Hardy* edited by Dale Kramer, © 1979 by

Elaine Showalter. Reprinted by permission of the author and the Macmillan Press Ltd.

"*Jude the Obscure*: Reading and the Spirit of the Law" by Ramón Saldívar from *ELH* 50, no. 3 (Fall 1983), © 1983 by The Johns Hopkins University Press. Reprinted by permission of the Johns Hopkins University Press.

"Bathsheba's Lovers: Male Sexuality in *Far from the Madding Crowd*" by Susan Beegel from *Sexuality and Victorian Literature*, edited by Don Richard Cox. (also *Tennessee Studies in Literature*, volume 27), © 1984 by the University of Tennessee Press, Knoxville. Reprinted by permission.

# Index

177770

03/11/87
THOMAS HARDY
(6) 1987 823.8 T457
5605   03 181056  01 9   (IC=0)

## DATE DUE